THE ECONOMICS OF AFRICAN COUNTRIES

THE ECONOMICS
OF AFRICAN COUNTRIES

by EDITH H. WHETHAM

Sometime Gilbey lecturer in the history and economics of agriculture, University of Cambridge, and fellow of Newnham College, Cambridge.
Sometime visiting professor in agricultural economics, Ahmadu Bello University, Northern Nigeria

and JEAN I. CURRIE

Sometime lecturer in economics, Ahmadu Bello University, Northern Nigeria

CAMBRIDGE
at the University Press 1969

Published by the Syndics of the Cambridge University Press
Bentley House, 200 Euston Road, London N.W.1
American Branch: 32 East 57th Street, New York, N.Y.10022

© Cambridge University Press 1969

Library of Congress Catalogue Card Number: 69–12931

Standard Book Number:
Clothbound 521 07070 8
Paperback   521 09534 4

Printed in Great Britain
at the University Printing House, Cambridge
(Brooke Crutchley, University Printer)

Contents

[v]

Tables and graphs

TABLES

GRAPHS

Preface

This book is designed for a first-year course in economic theory for students whose interest lies mainly in the development of African countries. For such students, the text books commonly used in British and American universities may be both confusing and misleading; their examples have little relevance to African conditions and they give inadequate attention to the problems of subsistence farming and its emergence into a money economy, the varieties of land tenure, the working of monetary policy when only a fraction of the population uses banks, the development of industry with imported techniques, and the dependence of African economies upon international trade. Such matters should occupy a considerable part of an introductory course for African students, as the future developers of their countries.

After an introductory section explaining the concepts and methods of economic analysis, Part 2 of this book takes up the theory of production to explain the constraints which limit the output from the types of agriculture commonly found in tropical Africa. This 'theory of the farm' is then enlarged to include the theory of the firm (and farm) in commercial production, when the use both of capital and of paid labour involves the balance between costs and prices. In Part 3, the elementary theory of supply and demand is applied to show the workings of the local markets, and the problems of the international markets for agricultural products.

Part 4 develops the basic principles of micro-economics already expounded to discuss at an elementary level the problems of macro-economics—the banking systems found in Africa, the control of the supply of money, the general level of wages, prices and incomes, public finance, international trade and the balance of payments. Part 5 introduces the concept of economic growth, in order to show would-be developers the forces at work in the process of increasing output and alleviating poverty.

Such a work of synthesis and exposition draws on the accumulated experience of many economists, rather than on the detailed researches of individuals; the tables and factual materials are used more to illustrate points of theory than to convey information. The references have therefore been confined as far as possible to books and journals likely to be available in African libraries. The *Readings in the Applied Economics of Africa*, edited by the present authors and published by the Cambridge University Press in 1967, are mentioned in the footnotes as *Readings*, followed by the volume number. Graphs have been used sparingly and with full explanations of their construction, since many students have little experience of them in schools.

Warmest thanks are expressed to Miss Phyllis Deane, of the Faculty of Economics and Politics, University of Cambridge, and Fellow of Newnham College, and to Mrs Holmans, formerly of the University of Canterbury in Kent, for their criticisms of earlier drafts of this book. We owe the index to the kindness of Mrs Anderson.

E. H. W.
J. I. C.

NOTE. Economic terms explained in the glossary are italicized at the first mention in the text

PART 1

Concepts and methods

1. Introduction

Economics, or the theory of economics, can be defined as the study of men earning their living, as workers on farms or in trade or in industries; as suppliers of services such as education, nursing, local and national governments; and as buyers of goods and services, whether for resale in a different form or in a different place, or for their own consumption. Economics thus studies some aspects of society and like other branches of learning, has its separate parts. The economics of agriculture, for instance, is the study of agriculture as a business—of farmers producing food and raw materials either for their own consumption, or for sale against money in order to buy other things. The economics of agriculture includes therefore the study of farm management, and of agricultural prices and markets, which link together the production of food and its consumption. The economics of business is the study of the working of industries and of trade, while public finance is the study of the effects of taxation and the expenditure of governments upon the economic structure (or economy) of their countries.

Why should we study economics? Men have unlimited wants; they have limited resources to satisfy those wants, and millions of families in Africa can barely satisfy the basic wants of adequate food, water and shelter. If they are to be lifted out of their existing poverty, existing resources must be used more efficiently and new resources created, so that human beings can enjoy better lives, with better health and education. Using resources more efficiently requires the work of scientists, engineers, managers of firms and progressive farmers, as well as the administrators and planners who organise governments. Scientists breed new types of cotton, for instance, which, with the right treatment, can give higher yields than existing varieties. Farmers must then fit the new practices into their rotation of crops and the regular work upon other crops. Economists can help by studying the different choices open to farmers who grow cotton and comparing the results obtained in different circumstances. In advising upon agricultural policy, the economists in the government need to know something about the costs of growing cotton in different areas, the probable yields under varying rainfall, and they will want forecasts of the probable prices of cotton for the next few years, so that they can judge how far the production of cotton should be encouraged, and in what region. And the economists and the sociologists must also study methods of working on farms, and the varieties of land tenure, which may make it difficult for farmers to adopt the techniques recommended by the scientists.

In trying to understand the complex economies of African countries, economists start from assumptions about human behaviour. The first assumption is that people spend their energies, and their incomes, so as to obtain the maximum satisfaction of their wants. These wants vary between countries, between groups of people in one country, and between periods of time, because of differences in climate, religion, education, custom, income or experience of foreign travel. Economists must accept 'wants' as their basic data, since their main task is the study of how these wants can be more fully satisfied—how the annual output of goods and services can be altered or increased to give greater satisfaction. Economists therefore study 'demand' as people choose through markets and shops the goods and services to satisfy their wants, and as farmers take decisions in growing food for their families.

The second basic assumption is that most people want a larger income, in order to acquire more goods and services. Of two alternative actions, they will generally choose that one which seems most likely to bring in the larger income, either now or at some future date. People will therefore produce and offer for sale the goods or services likely to be most profitable, and it is this assumption which governs the process of supply, whether of commodities or of services.

In subsistence farming, demand and supply both occur within the same economic unit, of family and village; wants are satisfied by the direct production of goods and services with a small amount of direct exchange between neighbours and relatives. Yet only a limited range of goods and services can be produced by any one family or village, while the use of money makes exchange easy over a wider area. Almost every family in Africa now sells some crop or service in order to acquire money, with which to pay taxes or to buy from other people goods which it cannot provide for itself. But the majority of African families still grow most of the food they consume, and they have therefore a limited diet and may even be short of food for a few weeks at the end of the dry season, or for a few months in a year of drought.

A third basic assumption of economics is the existence of governments, which effectively maintain law and order, which issue some form of acceptable money in their respective territories, and which follow some kind of economic policy. The division of powers between federal, regional and local governments varies, but here we assume for simplification that 'government' is a single entity, carrying out a known and agreed policy.

Such a policy may allow the economic structure to be moulded by supply and demand working through free markets; or it may try to assist changes thought desirable and hinder those thought undesirable. Some sectors of the national output may be organised directly by government; or all supply and demand may be regulated by government departments. In this study of African countries, it is assumed that their economies are 'mixed'—that they work mainly through free markets, but under some general policy and with some producing units under government control.

Economies therefore consist of a huge number of businesses, farms and firms. The vast majority of these businesses in African countries consist of a single family, engaged in a mixture of agriculture and trade or handicraft, growing some food for its own consumption, processing a little for sale, and selling crops or livestock or labour, as seems most profitable. Many of the shops, transport businesses and small factories are also family concerns, perhaps employing one or two relatives, or a few hired men. Some businesses are run by companies or partnerships, in which a number of people combine their resources of finance, technical knowledge and managerial skill to conduct a business with a common policy. Finally, there is the government department or public corporation, which provides some service for the public benefit, either sold on the market or paid for out of taxation—hospitals, education, libraries, roads, electricity, broadcasting, railways, docks and the like. All these units situated within the boundaries of a country constitute its 'economic structure' or economy, which is bound together by markets, a common money, and the authority of a government.

To these basic assumptions, economists add others, depending on the kind of problems which they study. *Static analysis* (the analysis of a stationary or unchanging structure) assumes that only one thing is changed in an economy—the price of cocoa, the output of cotton, the level of taxes, the agreed rate of wages in one factory; economists analyse the effect of this one change on the other parts of the economy. The analysis is then checked, so far as is possible, against the statistical evidence on the results of such changes, to ascertain whether the analysis explains the subsequent changes, and whether the size of these changes agrees with the result expected from the calculations.

Static analysis is applied in two ways. *Micro-economics* (from the Greek word micros meaning small) studies the decisions of the individual family, farm or firm, buying and selling within the national economy; *macro-economics* (from the Greek word macros, meaning large) studies the decisions which affect a large section of an economy—the general level of prices, wages or incomes; the distribution of incomes between different groups of people; the expansion of exports; the rate of investment, and so on. The distinction between micro- and macro-economics is largely one of convention and common sense, rather than of logic.

Dynamic analysis studies the process of change in an economy, changes which lead, not to equilibrium between the component parts, but to continuing change in the aggregate size and in the relative importance of its different parts. As applied to the modern world, dynamic analysis may be called the theory of economic growth or of economic development; as applied to previous centuries, it may be called economic history. It includes both micro- and macro-economics, but in recent years dynamic analysis has tended to concentrate upon macro-economics—population and its rate of growth and its distribution between different occupations; changes in the size and composition of the national output and national income; the expansion of foreign trade; the relationship between the growth of capital and the growth of output.

Many of the difficulties of economists arise from the lack of basic information about most countries. Some governments do not know with any accuracy even the number of people in their territory, nor their birth and death rates. There are great difficulties in estimating the output of millions of tiny plots of land, each containing a mixture of crops, and often a succession of crops within one season; it is impossible to get records of business from the millions of traders in African markets. Economists have therefore to work with inadequate statistics, and many of their conclusions are consequently tentative and cautious.

Further, economists cannot conduct experiments to test their theories about the effects of certain changes, as an agricultural scientist conducts field trials to test the effect of fertilisers upon the yield of cotton in different soils. Consequently, different theories exist about the cause or effect of certain actions, about the influences judged important and those that can be ignored, in any particular set of circumstances. What appear to be conflicting theories are often found, upon closer analysis, to refer to changes operating in different types of economies, or to reactions of groups of people with different institutions and customs. In spite of these difficulties, a substantial body of economic knowledge has been accumulated over recent decades, which enables us to understand something of the working of economies at different stages of development.

In chapter 2, we look at the main characteristics of some African economies, as revealed by their statistics of national output and incomes. In the next chapters, the basic principles of static analysis are applied to show how such economies function, at the levels both of micro-economics and of macro-economics. Finally, some elementary concepts of dynamic analysis are used to explain the changes which have been observed in recent years, and to indicate the problems with which people and governments are now grappling in countries undergoing economic development.

2. The national output and the national income

INTRODUCTION

In analysing the working of any economy, we need to have some ideas of the quantities and values involved, both of the economy as a whole, and also of its important parts. We want to know what the country produces in a given period of time, such as one year—the *national output* (or product) of its people working with the available resources. Secondly, we may want to know how this output is used— the pattern of *national consumption*, as shown by the *national expenditure* on goods and services both for immediate consumption and for investment in capital equipment. Thirdly, we may want to know how this consumption or expenditure is earned—the distribution of the *national income*, for instance, between wage-earners and farmers, between individuals, firms and governments, or between different regions. To show how an economy is changing over time, we shall need to have such information for several years; if we wish to compare one economy with another, we shall need such estimates as income or output per head of the relevant populations, with some idea of the exchange rate between the two kinds of currency. All estimates of national outputs and national incomes must necessarily be made in money, since we can only add together the output, or consumption, of a thousand head of cattle, a million yards of cloth and ten million units of electricity in terms of their value in money.

CALCULATING THE NATIONAL INCOME

For any one country, the national output, the national consumption, the national expenditure and the national income all refer to the same total, but looked at from different angles. In any one year, a flow of goods and services is being produced for final use and for export, and this flow is being used in different ways. There is also a flow of money, earned in producing those goods and services, which is being spent either on consumption or on capital goods for investment. We thus have two continuous flows, a flow of goods and services, and a flow of money:

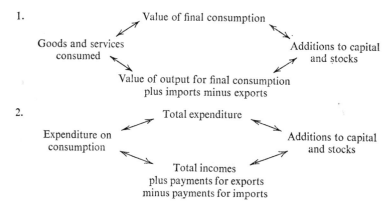

1.
Value of final consumption

Goods and services consumed

Additions to capital and stocks

Value of output for final consumption plus imports minus exports

2.
Total expenditure

Expenditure on consumption

Additions to capital and stocks

Total incomes plus payments for exports minus payments for imports

Whichever way we calculate this object, which we may call the annual national income, the result should be the same, though the processes of calculation will provide different answers about its composition.

Obviously, there are enormous difficulties in the way of estimating these quantities for African countries. For a general discussion of these difficulties, and of various methods of tackling them, readers are referred to the references given below.[1] Here we may note a few major problems. There is firstly the problem of the *intermediate goods*, the things sold not for final consumption but for further processing, as cotton is sold for manufacture into shirts. If we included the value both of the cotton and of the shirts, we should be counting the cotton twice in the value of goods for final consumption. The cotton represents part of the output of agriculture; to obtain the value of the output of the textile industry, we must deduct from the total of its sales all its purchases from other industries, including agriculture; we then arrive at the *value added* by the textile industry, which represents the value of its *net output*. Later, we shall look at this flow of intermediate goods between different sectors of the economy, but it must be carefully excluded from estimates of the national income.

[1] P. Okigbo, 'Nigerian National Accounts 1950–7', in *Readings*, vol. II; *Economic Bulletin for Africa*, vol. VII, no. 1 (Jan. 1966), chap. 4.

A second problem is that some prices contain either a tax (cigarettes or imported goods), or a subsidy, as education is often provided for fees which do not fully meet the costs of the service provided. It is sometimes convenient to use the market prices in valuing the output of these goods and services, but more often the taxes and subsidies are both omitted, giving the output valued at *factor cost*, valued at the incomes received by the *factors of production*, or resources, engaged in providing that output, the suppliers of labour, land, capital and enterprise.

Thirdly, there is the problem of valuing the large quantity of goods and services which are provided by farm families for themselves, without going through a market, the so-called *subsistence sector*. In industrialised countries, there is a convention that activities which take place within the home are excluded from calculations of the national income, but this convention leads to absurd results if applied to some African countries where most families grow most of the food they eat. In order to compare the national incomes of different countries, econometricians (the economists who measure quantities) must therefore apply some kind of price to the estimated output of these families, which itself can only be an informed guess. Some econometricians have used retail prices, as representing what farmers might have to pay if they bought their food; others have used farm-gate prices, as representing what farmers would have received if they had sold their crops and livestock. A third method is to value subsistence output at farm-gate prices, but to value the corresponding consumption at market prices, the difference between the two aggregates being imputed to the value of output of transport and distribution.[1] Objections can be raised against all these methods; but calculations of the national income should at least show what method has been used, so that comparisons are not made between aggregates compiled differently.

Fourthly, there is the problem of defining the boundary of the economy for which a national income is calculated. Who are the people whose economic activities should be included? When workers migrate from Nigeria to the Sudan, and from Ruanda into Uganda, are their incomes regarded as part of the national incomes of their countries of origin, or of the countries of employment? The same

[1] Economic Commission for Africa, *Report of the working group on the treatment of non-monetary (subsistence) transactions within the framework of national accounts* (Addis Ababa, 1960).

problem arises when British and French companies operate factories in Africa with imported staff and capital, and when American companies operate factories in Britain and in Europe. Thus between 1950 and 1951, the estimates of national income in what was then Northern Rhodesia rose by more than half, simply because the mining companies transferred in that year their legal place of registration from London, the source of their finance, to the country of operation and the national income figures were based upon incomes of resident persons and firms.[1] Here again, what is important is that the basis of calculation should be clearly stated, so that subsequent users of the figures are made aware of the assumptions behind them. All calculations of national incomes in all countries contain, not accurate figures, but estimates of different degrees of reliability; but the dangers of making wrong comparisons are lessened if the various assumptions are clearly stated and understood. And the particular assumptions made on any occasion depend, of course, on the purpose for which particular calculations were made, on the kind of questions which were asked of the econometricians.

PRESENTING THE NATIONAL ACCOUNTS

The tables on pp. 12–13 show recent estimates of the national income of Uganda which are presented each year with the Budget. Table 1 begins with the *gross domestic product* at factor cost at current prices. 'Gross' implies that no allowance has been made for the resources used in maintaining capital equipment in working order. All capital equipment—houses, other buildings, machinery, railway lines, roads—requires repair and renewal from time to time if it is to continue working, and the resources so used are not available for producing output for consumption. The word gross, then, warns us that not all the output included in this table was in fact available for consumption, since a small part of it was required for the maintenance of capital. Domestic product implies that only output produced in Uganda is here accounted for and that the output and incomes of Ugandans working in other countries are excluded.

The Ugandan accounts distinguish between the output of agriculture which is sold and the output which is consumed by the

[1] Information from Miss P. Deane, Faculty of Economics and Politics, University of Cambridge.

TABLE 1. *Gross domestic product of Uganda at factor cost (£ million)*

By industry of origin at current prices					
	1962	1963	1964	1965	1966
Monetary economy				estimate	forecast
Agriculture	44·0	57·5	60·5	56·8	56·1
Processing of cotton, coffee, sugar	3·6	5·7	5·7	5·7	5·4
Forestry, fishing, hunting	2·5	2·4	2·4	2·5	2·5
Mining, quarrying	2·6	2·8	5·3	7·3	7·3
Manufacture of food products	1·3	1·3	1·7	1·9	2·1
Miscellaneous manufactures	4·9	5·5	6·2	8·6	10·0
Electricity	2·5	2·7	2·9	3·3	3·7
Construction	3·9	3·5	3·5	4·6	4·9
Commerce	14·5	18·4	19·6	22·4	23·2
Transport, communications	5·8	6·2	6·2	6·4	6·6
Government	4·9	4·6	6·0	6·7	6·9
Local government	2·4	2·4	2·9	2·9	2·9
Miscellaneous services	11·5	12·1	14·0	17·5	18·7
Rents	3·6	3·8	3·9	4·3	4·5
Total monetary economy	107·9	128·6	140·8	150·8	154·9
Non-monetary economy[a]					
Agriculture	42·6	40·7	47·3	63·8	65·4
Forestry and fishing	6·1	6·6	7·1	9·5	9·8
Grand total	156·7	175·9	195·1	224·1	230·0

By industry of origin at 1960 prices					
	1962	1963	1964	1965	1966
Monetary economy				estimate	forecast
Agriculture	44·5	53·7	57·4	58·6	57·6
Processing of cotton, coffee, sugar	4·5	6·4	6·8	6·9	6·7
Forestry, fishing, hunting	2·4	2·3	2·3	2·3	2·4
Mining, quarrying	2·8	2·9	3·2	3·1	3·1
Manufacture of food products	1·1	1·1	1·3	1·3	1·4
Miscellaneous manufactures	4·6	4·6	4·7	5·5	6·5
Electricity	2·1	2·3	2·3	2·7	3·0
Construction	3·7	3·3	3·1	4·0	4·3
Commerce	15·1	17·8	18·8	20·5	21·3
Transport, communications	5·9	6·4	6·7	7·1	7·4
Government	4·3	3·8	4·5	4·3	4·4
Local government	2·0	1·8	2·1	1·7	1·7
Miscellaneous services	10·6	10·9	11·7	14·1	15·1
Rents	3·4	3·5	3·5	3·8	4·0
Total monetary economy	106·8	120·7	128·7	135·9	138·9

TABLE 1 (*cont.*)

By industry of origin at 1960 prices (*cont.*)

	1962	1963	1964	1965	1966
Non-monetary economy[a]					
Agriculture	38·2	38·7	40·1	40·9	42·0
Forestry and fishing	5·2	5·3	5·5	5·6	5·8
Grand total	150·2	164·7	174·2	182·5	186·7

By type of income at current prices

	1962	1963	1964	1965 estimate	1966 forecast
Monetary economy					
Paid employment:					
Public services	16·9	16·7	19·9	21·6	22·7
Private industry	22·2	22·8	24·6	29·9	31·4
Operating surpluses:					
Public services	2·2	2·3	2·3	2·2	2·3
African enterprises:					
(*a*) agricultural	37·9	50·5	53·2	50·0	49·3
(*b*) other	10·2	10·4	10·8	11·9	12·3
Other enterprises	14·8	22·2	26·0	30·9	32·4
Rents:					
Public services	2·1	2·2	2·3	2·6	2·7
Private industry	1·5	1·5	1·6	1·8	1·8
Total monetary economy	107·9	128·6	140·8	150·8	154·9
Non-monetary economy[a]	48·7	47·3	54·3	73·3	75·2
Grand total	156·7	175·9	195·1	224·1	230·0

SOURCE. Uganda Government *Background to the Budget* (1966–1967).

[a] Estimated output valued at producer prices (Uganda Government, *Background to the Budget*, 1955, p. 7).

families that grow it, the non-monetary economy. Taking these two together, it will be seen that the output of agriculture, forestry and fishing amounted to £115 millions in 1964, out of a total gross domestic product estimated at £195 millions; some 60 per cent of the national output originated from agriculture.

These estimates of total value reflect both the quantities of output and the average prices at which that output was sold. If we wish to know how the quantities were changing, we must value the output of successive years at constant prices, as in the second part of

TABLE 2. *Gross domestic product of Nigeria, 1957 by types of expenditure at current prices (£ million)*

Consumers' expenditure	815·5
Government expenditure on goods and services	47·6
Gross fixed investment in Nigeria	113·0
Increase in marketing boards' stocks	9·1
Plus exports of goods and services	129·1
Final expenditure	1,114·3
Less imports of goods and services	−175·6
Gross domestic product	938·7
Plus net income from abroad	4·2
Gross national product	942·9

table 1. We then see that the rise in total values of output of nearly 25 per cent between 1962 and 1964 was caused by a rise both in quantities and in prices.

The first two parts of these tables give estimates of the national output by industry of origin. The third part shows estimates of the flow of incomes earned in producing that output. It will be remembered that the net output of each industry was defined as the value of its output minus all its purchases from other industries; net output therefore equals the total of payments made to the factors of production—labour, land, capital and enterprise. Here again is shown the dominance of agriculture in the national life of Uganda, for more than half of the total income arises from agriculture, either from sales of produce or from the imputed value of subsistence production, while paid employment accounts for about one-quarter of the total.

Another form of national accounts may present information about the final use of the national output, as shown by Dr Okigbo[1] for Nigeria in table 2, which also shows how incomes were spent.

As might be expected, consumers' expenditure accounts for almost 90 per cent of the final output, while the governments spent only 4 per cent. Of the gross domestic product, about £130 millions were exported in 1957, while imports were valued at £176 millions, and gross investment was estimated at £122 millions.

[1] P. Okigbo, 'Nigerian National Accounts 1950–7', in *Readings*, II, 5.

TABLE 3. *Inter-Sectoral Accounts of Ghana, 1960*

| | | | | | | | | | | | | | | | £G million Gross capital formation | | |
Outputs / Inputs	1 Agriculture	2 Forestry	3 Cocoa	4 Mining and quarrying	5 Manufacturing	6 Electricity	7 Construction	8 Fuel	9 Public utilities	10 Services	1–10 Total	Exports	Private consumption	Public consumption	Fixed	Increase in stocks	Grand total
1. Agriculture	≈	≈	.	.	0.3	.	.	.	.	3.7	4.0	1.8	81.9	0.2	.	.	87.9
2. Forestry	.	≈	≈	0.1	5.6	.	.	.	.	.	5.7	8.4	6.9	.	.	0.1	21.1
3. Cocoa	.	.	≈	≈	2.1	.	.	.	.	.	2.1	36.0	.	.	.	8.1	46.2
4. Mining and quarrying	.	.	.	≈	.	.	0.6	.	.	.	0.6	26.9	.	.	.	-0.3	27.2
5. Manufacturing	.	0.1	0.7	0.4	≈	≈	4.1	.	0.2	1.1	6.6	7.1	9.4	0.5	0.4	2.4	26.4
6. Electricity	.	.	.	0.4	0.2	≈	0.1	.	0.1	0.3	1.1	.	0.9	0.4	.	.	2.4
7. Construction	.	.	.	.	.	.	≈	.	.	.	.	.	.	4.7	61.2	.	65.9
8. Fuel	.	0.3	.	1.1	0.5	0.9	1.9	≈	0.9	5.5	11.1	.	3.2	0.3	.	.	14.6
9. Public utilities	.	.	.	0.1	0.3	.	0.2	0.3	≈	1.0	1.9	4.0	3.9	0.8	0.3	0.2	11.1
10. Services	.	0.1	0.7	0.5	2.0	.	3.6	0.1	1.2	≈	7.5	11.7	147.3	10.7	4.1	0.7	182.0
1–10 Total	≈	.	0.7	2.6	11.0	0.9	10.5	0.4	2.4	11.6	40.6	95.9	253.5	17.6	66.0	11.2	484.8
Imports[a]	0.3	0.3	.	2.0	6.0	0.4	12.1	6.8	0.9	12.9	41.7	1.2	68.6	4.6	32.1	11.2	148.2
Indirect taxation	.	.	.	0.2	1.2	.	0.7	3.9	.	0.3	6.3	25.5	17.3	0.9	0.9	.	50.0
subsidies	.	.	-0.4	.	.	.	.	.	.	.	-0.4	.	-0.4	.	.	.	-0.8
Gross value added	87.6	20.3	45.9	22.4	8.2	1.1	42.6	3.5	7.8	157.2	396.6	.	.	23.9	.	.	420.5
Grand Total	87.9	21.1	46.2	27.2	26.4	2.4	65.9	14.6	11.1	182.0	484.8	122.6	339.0	46.1	99.0	11.2	1,102.7

[a] Goods and non-factor services.

NOTE. The horizontal rows show, from left to right, the distribution by value of the output of each industry, or *sector*. Thus the greater part of the output of agriculture in Ghana went directly into consumption, but about £8 m. of output, mainly timber and cocoa, was sold to industry for further processing. The vertical columns show the inputs taken from other sectors to produce each output. Thus the column headed agriculture shows that farmers buy little from other sectors, their inputs being mainly labour; their purchases of seeds or cattle from each other are not shown in this table which measures only purchases between different sectors. The aggregate flows of intermediate goods are thus larger than is shown here, since many factories buy partially processed things from other firms in the same sector.

Finally, there are the outputs of each industry sold for processing by other industries, the flow of intermediate goods. Estimates of these quantities have not been generally published for African countries, but table 3 was compiled by Professor Szereszewski[1] for Ghana for the year 1960.

INTERNATIONAL COMPARISONS OF NATIONAL INCOMES

One of the common uses of estimates of national incomes is the comparison of the wealth or poverty of different countries. Such comparisons are dangerous for various reasons. Firstly, tables of national incomes for different countries are often compiled on different assumptions, in spite of the attempts at standardisation promoted by the United Nations and the Economic Commission for Africa. Secondly, some countries have no reliable estimates for production, for population, or for the distribution of incomes between social classes. Thirdly, comparisons of output per head have little meaning unless much of the output consists of the same types of goods in each country; Eskimos in northern Canada and farmers in tropical Africa produce and consume quite different things, and it would be difficult to decide which group was richer than the other. Nevertheless, international comparisons can be useful in showing the structure of rather similar economies at different stages of wealth, and thus indicating the direction of expected change. Consider for instance the comparisons shown in table 4.[2]

In the poorer countries, most people must spend most of their time and income in obtaining food, so that there is little demand for industrial products. Secondly, with the low output per man from existing methods of cultivation, a high proportion of each population must be engaged in growing food, in order that all families, whether in the towns or on the farms, may have enough to eat. A low output per man engaged in agriculture, forestry and fishing (the *primary occupations*), is thus a main cause of poverty; a group of people

---

[1] R. Szereszewski, 'Sectoral Structure of the Economy, 1960', in W. Birmingham, *et al.*, *A Study of Contemporary Ghana*, (London, 1966), p. 64. See also, N. G. Carter, *An Input-Output Analysis of the Nigerian Economy 1959–60*, Working Paper, School of Industrial Management, Massachusetts Institute of Technology (Cambridge, U.S.A., 1963).

[2] Adapted from Food and Agriculture Organisation, *State of Food and Agriculture* (Rome, 1963), p. 132.

TABLE 4. *Growth of domestic markets for foods (43 countries, 1950–1955)*

No. of countries	Average personal expenditure per head per year U.S.A. ($)		Per cent of male working force engaged in agriculture	No. of families fed by each farm family
	Total	On food		
7	1,261	134	12	8·3
7	916	128	22	4·5
9	542	101	37	2·7
11	305	83	58	1·7
7	167	58	61	1·6
2	70	43	69	1·4

become richer as fewer of them are required to produce the basic requirements of food and raw materials, and more of them can move into *secondary occupations*, the industries and services producing other types of consumer goods, and also capital goods for increasing future production. In the poorer countries shown in table 4, one farm family can produce the food for only one or two other families who might be engaged in secondary occupations; with the tools and knowledge available in the richer countries, each farm family can produce enough to supply five or ten other families with a varied and satisfying diet, as well as providing raw materials such as cotton and wool.

The division between primary and secondary occupations is often blurred in African countries, where many farm families spend part of their time in marketing their surplus crops, in processing foods for sale locally, or in making small articles from leather, wood, metal or textiles—the handicrafts. Another distinction between rich and poor countries is the much greater degree of specialisation in work which develops partly as a cause and partly as a result of rising output per man. The richer countries produce a huge variety of goods and services, offering a huge variety of employments, so that farmers become milk producers or vegetable growers, buying most of their own foods; economists become specialists in public finance, or in agricultural economics, or in econometrics. In the poorer countries, farmers will grow most of their own foods as well as engaging in trade and handicrafts, while economists may be called upon to teach or to advise in many branches of the profession.

A third important distinction between rich and poor countries is the difference in the amount of *capital* available to assist production. For most purposes, capital may be defined as man-made tools of production, and capital is most easily seen in the form of large machines in a factory, or in a huge dam which supplies power and water to a wide area of a country. Yet cocoa trees and breeding cows are also forms of capital, important in farming, and houses which do not add to production but shelter human beings must also be included as another form of capital. However we define this thing called capital, it exists in far greater quantity in rich countries than in poor countries, partly because people with high incomes can afford to devote more resources to making tools to assist production than is possible for people with very low incomes, who have such little surplus over their basic needs. Poverty is thus both the result of the lack of capital, which restricts output per man; and it is also a cause of the lack of capital. Moreover, the knowledge how to use capital and labour in profitable combinations depends on education, which again can only be afforded by communities with some surplus of income and of energy left above the struggle for mere survival.

The ultimate purpose of economic development is to provide people with more goods and services, and to do this in the way most consistent with an increase in happiness, which (unfortunately for the economists) cannot be measured. Increasing the supply of goods available for consumption implies the creation, at some stage, of large quantities of capital which will help to raise the output per head but which will absorb resources withdrawn from immediate consumption. Moreover, the increased supply of goods and services for final consumption must somehow be related to what people will wish to buy, since nothing is gained by producing commodities which are not used. In the process of economic development, there will be marked changes in the kind and the quantity of things which people want, in the methods of producing them, in the patterns of employment. In the analysis of prices and markets, we shall see how employment, production and consumption are connected with each other, and with the flows of income between people, firms and governments.

We begin this study therefore by looking at the constraints which limit output in African countries. We begin with the process of making decisions in subsistence farming, partly because of its importance in many areas of Africa, partly because the constraints which restrict production are there seen most clearly. Then we consider the planning of production when farmers consider market prices, both of the output they sell and of the resources which they buy. This analysis of production is then extended to include the process of making decisions about the output of firms and industries and of the public services. In Part 3, the theory of prices and markets shows how production, prices and consumption are related in a static economy.

PART 2

The economics of production

3. The economics of subsistence farming

INPUT AND OUTPUT

The production of goods and services involves the combination of resources, or *factors of production*, into units called firms, or farms. These resources can be classified under five headings—*labour*, the work of human beings; *natural resources*, such as land, water, trees or minerals; capital, whether the hand tools used on farms or the complex of machinery found in an oil refinery; *enterprise*, the ability to organise resources in the expectation of future output, taking the risk that the output may be more or less than was planned; and *management*, the taking of decisions about the daily working of these firms or farms. Those who provide both enterprise and management are sometimes called *entrepreneurs*, a term which includes farmers, traders and business men generally. When these resources are combined into a firm or farm, we can call them *inputs*, to distinguish them from the outputs which are available either for consumption or for sale.

We begin the study of economics by looking at subsistence farming, for two reasons; the majority of families in Africa still plan their output primarily for their own subsistence, and their experience demonstrates the principles which lie behind commercial production. The basic fact is known to all farmers—that a large village cannot be fed from five acres of land, by adding more and more workers to this fixed area. After a point, the addition of more men (the varying input) to a fixed area of land will bring a diminishing output per man. Again, the output of a factory of fixed size cannot be increased indefinitely by taking on more and more men; after a point, the addition of more men to a fixed quantity of capital results in a diminishing output per man. Obviously, if a farm or factory is undermanned to begin with, adding more men may at first yield a rising output per man, but after a point, depending on the size of the fixed input, the addition of more units of the variable input will eventually cause a diminishing output per unit of the variable input, as shown in table 5.

TABLE 5. *Inputs and outputs*

1 Units of variable input	2 Total output	3 Marginal output	4 Average output 2÷1
1	3		3
2	8	5	4
3	15	7	5
4	23	8	5·75
5	30	7	6
6	35	5	5·83
7	39	4	5·54
8	42	3	5·25
9	43	1	4·78
10	43	0	4·33

NOTE. Col. 1 shows the units of input employed with a fixed quantity of some other input; we may call the variable input men and the fixed input land or capital. With one man, the total output is 3 units. The addition of a second man raises the total output to 8 units; the average output of the two men is therefore 4 units (8÷2). Col. 3 shows the additional output obtained by employing one more unit of input at each stage. Employing the second man adds 8−3 = 5 units of output; employing the third man adds 15−8 = 7 units of output, and so on. Such a relationship between input (col. 1) and output (col. 2) may be called a *production function*.

The imaginary figures given in table 5 illustrate a common trend in the relation of output to variable inputs, when some other input is fixed in quantity. Total output at first increases rapidly with more units of the variable input; the rate of increase then slows down; and finally, output does not increase at all. This trend is shown in col. 3, giving the *marginal output*, defined as the addition to output caused by employing one more unit of the variable input with a fixed quantity of some other input. If the output has to be shared equally between all the inputs of the variable factor, as we may suppose happens within one family working on one farm, then col. 4 shows how much each man can expect as his share, calculated by dividing the total output at each stage by the number of units of the variable input. The information given in table 5 can also be shown as in graph 1.

Looking both at table 5 and at graph 1, consider the case of a farmer who employs four relatives on a fixed area of land, and who might employ a fifth, and who pays them by an equal share of the output of the farm. From previous experience, the farmer no doubt has a fairly clear idea of how much extra output he will obtain in an average season from employing a fifth man; this extra man is likely

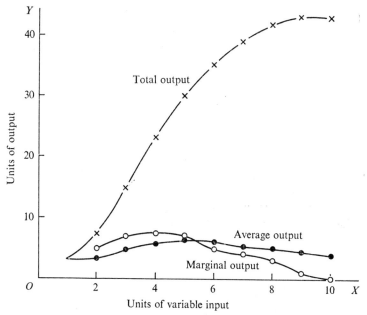

Graph 1. Inputs and outputs. (NOTE. Two lines called *axes* (singular, axis) are drawn at right angles (90 degrees) to each other. On the vertical, or *Y axis*, are measured units of output; on the horizontal, or *X axis*, are measured units of the variable input, as given in col. 1 of table 5. The curve of total output is plotted by taking the points where the lines drawn vertically upward from the units given in col. 1 cross the lines drawn horizontally from the corresponding units of total output given in col. 2. The curve which joins all these points shows how the total output, here the *dependent variable*, changes with changes in the units of the variable input. The curves of marginal and average output are derived by a similar method from cols. 3 and 4 of table 5. The graph thus gives a picture of the way in which the three dependent variables, total output, marginal output and average output, change with changes in the variable inputs.)

to add less to the output than the fourth man, but he will add more to the output than he takes by way of an average share of the output. Everyone will therefore be better off if the fifth man is employed on the farm. But a sixth or seventh man will add less to the total output than an average share; the relatives already employed will be worse off if these extra relatives must be given work on the farm, unless, indeed, these extra workers can be paid only what they add to the output.

The addition of one more unit of a variable input to a fixed combination of other inputs may therefore add varying amounts to the total output, depending on the number of the varying inputs already employed. There may be *increasing returns* to each unit of the variable input, when the marginal output is rising; there may be *constant returns* to each unit of the variable input, when the marginal output is constant; or there may be *diminishing returns* to each unit of the variable input, when the marginal output is falling.

The existence of diminishing returns is the basis for the decisions made by African farmers about the quantity of land to be cultivated by their families. A farmer with two or three adult workers, and with the right to occupy as much land as he wishes, knows by experience from what quantity of land he can, on the average of seasons, obtain the greatest quantity of output. When his sons grow up to become full workers, or if a younger brother comes to live with him, the farmer will cultivate an appropriate amount of extra land; he knows that if the extra workers share in the cultivation of the same area of land as before, there will be diminishing returns. But if two or three acres of land can be added to the family farm for every extra man, possibly helped by his wife and small children, then the farmer can obtain constant returns at the highest level to inputs which are used in constant proportions. He will thus avoid the diminishing returns which might result if the extra workers merely cultivated more thoroughly the fixed area of land.

Consider now what may happen in districts where land is scarce in relation to the demand for it, so that farmers with growing families cannot acquire extra land. An example may be taken from a study made by Miss Haswell[1] of the inputs of labour and the outputs of groundnuts in a Gambian village, where the families who could not obtain more land applied more hours of work to their small plots. Her findings are shown in table 6, and the reader is advised to draw a graph of these figures, on the lines of graph 1.

Here again we have a demonstration firstly of increasing returns, when the marginal output is rising, and the marginal cost, in terms of hours per 100 lb of nuts, is falling; then of constant returns, when the marginal output is constant; and finally of diminishing

[1] M. R. Haswell, *The Changing Pattern of Economic Activity in a Gambian Village* (London, H.M.S.O., 1963), p. 109.

TABLE 6. *Inputs and outputs in groundnut production, Genieri, Gambia, 1949*

1	2	3	4	5
		Marginal output	Average output	Marginal cost
Hours worked per acre	Total output	per hour	per hour	(hours per 100 lb of nuts)
		lb undecorticated groundnuts		
130	250		1·92	
150	280	1·5	1·87	67
170	310	1·5	1·82	67
190	340	1·5	1·79	67
210	370	1·5	1·76	67
230	425	2·8	1·85	57
250	465	2·0	1·86	50
270	505	2·0	1·87	50
290	545	2·0	1·88	50
310	580	1·8	1·87	56
330	610	1·5	1·85	67
350	640	1·5	1·83	67
370	665	1·3	1·80	77

NOTE. In col. 1, the units are 20 hours. To obtain the marginal output, as in col. 3, the difference between successive outputs in col. 2 must be divided by 20, e.g. $(280-250) \div 20$. Col. 5 answers the question, how many hours must be worked to obtain an extra output of 100 lb of nuts; it is obtained by dividing the differences between successive figures in col. 1 by those in col. 2 and multiplying by 100, e.g. $(170-150) \div (310-280) \times 100 = 67$.

returns, when the marginal output is falling, and the marginal cost is rising. The average output per hour also shows us why some large families on small plots of land are relatively poor, in terms of groundnuts; they apply many hours of work in order to increase their total output, but the average return per worker, or per 100 hours of work, may be lower than that obtained by the families with more land.

If we asked any of these families how many hours they worked to obtain one hundred pounds of groundnuts, we might get the kind of answers set out in col. 5, showing the *marginal cost* of groundnuts, in terms of the hours worked. The marginal cost can be defined as the addition to total costs caused by producing one more unit, here taken as 100 lb of undecorticated nuts; it is therefore the opposite of marginal output, which gives us the answer to the question, what is the extra output to one more unit of input? In subsistence farming, the workers probably think of the extra output obtained by applying an extra effort or an extra man—that is, in terms of marginal output per unit of input; but in commercial farming, as in other forms of commercial production, business men think more often of marginal costs—of the addition to total costs likely to be caused by producing one more unit of output. The reader must be careful to distinguish between these two concepts— *marginal output* per *unit of input,* and the *marginal cost* per *unit of output,* whether expressed in terms of effort or of money.

SOIL FERTILITY AND EQUAL MARGINAL RETURNS

In farming, the relationship between inputs of labour and the output of crops is complicated by the varying degrees of fertility found within quite small areas; and the appropriate use of labour between plots of differing fertility, suitable for different crops and requiring different methods of working, is part of the local knowledge of farm families. Certain plots with good water supplies and deep soils are known to yield a higher output for the same quantity of work than less fertile plots; they can therefore be worked with more intensity—more inputs applied to them—before the onset of diminishing returns. Such a variation between two plots is illustrated in graph 2, which gives for plot *A* the same information that was given in graph 1 (though on a smaller scale) and adds information for a more fertile plot, plot *B.*

If a farmer has two such plots and only a few workers, he will obviously concentrate his inputs upon the most fertile land, which gives the highest output for his inputs. But if he has seven or eight workers, then some of them should be moved to Plot *A,* since the marginal output for an extra worker upon plot *B* will be less than that obtained by one or two workers upon plot *A.* In order to obtain the greatest output from a given quantity of resources subject to diminishing returns in two or more uses, the input should be applied so that *equal marginal returns* are obtained from all the alternative uses, so that output cannot be increased by moving one unit of input between the different uses. Fertile land will therefore be worked intensively until diminishing returns reduce the marginal output to that obtained from applying labour to the less fertile plots.

If we look again at table 6, we can deduce that the families which applied labour intensively to their plots for a comparatively low output of groundnuts were unable to find a more profitable alternative use for their labour, either by working for their richer neighbours, or by acquiring more land, or by engaging in some other occupation. Inputs were not applied to the land of this village so as to secure equal marginal returns, and thus to maximise output for equal

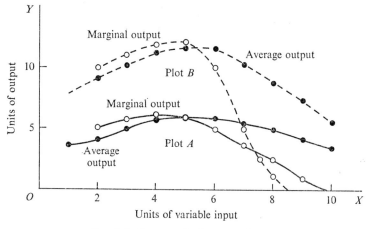

Graph 2. Comparative inputs and outputs

division among all workers. Family rights to the occupation of particular plots of land, the unequal size of families, and difficulties in finding more profitable occupations kept some workers cultivating plots for a relatively low output.

WEEDS AND WORK

Diminishing returns are normally found wherever increasing inputs of one resource are applied to a fixed combination of other resources, without technical innovations. But we must look more closely at the problems of African agriculture to understand why diminishing returns operate within it to restrict output per man to levels which, by the standards of the industrialised countries, are low, and which imply poverty for so many millions of farm families.

The traditional tools have been the short-handled hoe and the long-handled knife, or axe. Prevented from using animals by tsetse fly or by lack of fodder in the dry season, the traditional patterns of cultivation rely upon the application of human labour to land;

apart from the application of manure to plots near villages or large towns, there are few inputs other than labour. The main determinants of crop yields under human control are firstly the time of planting, secondly the control of weeds during the growing season, and thirdly the duration of continuous cropping on each plot. Planting of crops cannot begin until the soil is sufficiently moist to be broken up and hoed into mounds or ridges; these conserve moisture and also keep the plants above the temporary water-logging of the rainy season. Good farming requires a labour force adequate to perform this heavy work speedily after the first rains, so that planting may follow without delay, but little is gained by planting so early that the crops have inadequate moisture at the time of maximum growth. Similarly, crops must be kept hoed to suppress the growth of weeds, until the crops themselves can out-grow them, but the gain in crop yields from intensified hoeing rapidly diminishes. When land is freely available farmers will cultivate as much as they can plant and keep reasonably free from weeds in the growing season, in order to obtain the maximum output from the input of labour.

The time of planting is determined by the onset of the rains, in areas both of single-peak and of double-peak rainfall. There is thus a heavy concentration of labour needs in the early weeks of the rainy seasons, when land must be ridged, planted with the early crops, and kept weeded during the planting of the later crops. This peak in the pattern of labour inputs over each season is, of course, common in all types of cultivation of annual crops, but it is intensified in those areas of Africa where there is a single rainy season each year. The demand for workers at the times of planting and weeding usually absorbs all the labour available in rural areas and, indeed, often creates a considerable demand for immigrants. The increase in output from the traditional types of African agriculture is thus limited, firstly by the onset of diminishing returns to the intensive cultivation of small areas; secondly, by the amount of labour available in the busiest part of the season; and thirdly, by the small area which each man can plant and weed when he is using only hand tools.

In these conditions, shifting cultivation is the economic method of using labour with plentiful land. On fertile land, which might naturally be covered by high forest under a double-peak rainfall, the period required under bush fallow to restore the fertility of the soil may not exceed the period under crop, possibly three or four years. In savannah areas of low rainfall and thin soils, the resting period may much exceed the cropping period before the soil has regained the nutrients lost by the harvesting of crops. The critical ratio of land in use to land under fallow may therefore range from 1 : 1 upwards, till the poorest lands may need eight or ten years under fallow for every year under crop.[1]

Under shifting cultivation, no labour is required to restore to the soil the minerals taken from it by the cropping. The work of periodically clearing the regrowth of bush after a fallow can usually be done during the dry season, when there is little pressure of work; burning the cut material checks the growth of annual weeds from the seeds lying on the top of the soil, and also gives a favourable surface for the growth of the planted crops.

This shifting cultivation breaks down when the density of population, both human and animal, requires the renewed cultivation of land before its fertility has been restored by a natural fallow—when the ratio of land in use to land in fallow exceeds the critical level for each particular type of soil and climate. For then each period of cultivation gives lower average yields than the preceding period for the same inputs of work, so that communities must either reduce their consumption as population increases, or migrate, or develop new types of cultivation which enable them to crop land continuously without loss of fertility. Migration has been perhaps the most common method of avoiding diminishing returns and falling crop yields, whether migration of whole communities, of families, or of individuals seeking land or employment in other areas. Migration of villages and families in search of new land still occurs from over-crowded areas in Africa to those still sparsely populated, but it obviously becomes less easy as the population grows in almost every district, and each community comes nearer to that critical ratio between land in use and land in fallow which indicates the breakdown of the system of shifting cultivation.

In a number of places, the period under cultivation has been extended by the use of animal and human wastes as manures. In most African villages, some form of manure is applied to the compound plots, which therefore support more intensive cultivation

---

[1] W. Allan, *The African Husbandman* (Edinburgh, 1965), chaps. II and III; P. H. Nye and D. J. Greenwood, *The Soil under Shifting Cultivation*, Commonwealth Bureau of Soils Technical Communications no. 51 (Commonwealth Agricultural Bureaux, 1960).

than the more distant plots to which little attention is given. In the densely populated region round Kano, in Northern Nigeria, manure is taken four or five miles by donkeys for use on cultivated land.[1] Crop farmers sometimes pay in farm output for migratory herdsmen to graze their animals over plots after harvest, so that the soil can benefit from the manure. In this case, the cultivated land benefits from minerals obtained from the grazing areas; there is a transference rather than a restoration of fertility, and grazing lands themselves often suffer from too intensive stocking, erosion and falling fertility. But all these methods of manuring land involve inputs of labour or the cost of payment, and they will therefore only be adopted if there are no cheaper methods of maintaining crop yields.

We must leave to the next chapter the discussion of the improved methods which may permit continuous cultivation based on the integration of crops, livestock and fertilisers, since these involve costs and incomes in terms of money. Here, it may be noted that the allocation of labour between different tasks—bush clearance or the cartage of manure, weeding one plot or ridging another, harvesting or carrying crops to market—is a matter of continuous choice, where farmers are continuously applying the principle of equal marginal returns to inputs which are likely to yield diminishing returns in each use. Moreover, these decisions which collectively make up the art of farm management cannot follow a set pattern, because of the changing circumstances of soil, rainfall, onset of disease and the like; farmers take their decisions on the basis of experience and of observation of existing conditions, which influence the probable return expected from the various alternative uses of today's labour.

PRODUCTION, OUTPUT AND SUPPLY

A major feature of agriculture is the uncertainty of crop production, and the variation in yields from year to year. In the semi-arid regions of Africa dependent on a single-peak rainfall, the duration and intensity of the rainy season is probably the principal cause of variation in crop yields; but there are also risks of crop pests and diseases, while illness in farm families may restrict the digging, planting or harvesting.

---

[1] M. J. Mortimore and J. Wilson, *Land and People in the Kano Close-Settled Zone*, Ahmadu Bello University, Nigeria, Department of Geography Occasional Paper no. 1 (1965).

The traditional farm practices of any area can usually be interpreted as a balance between maximum production from the available resources, and a risk of loss in a bad season. Farmers plant a variety of crops, partly because different crops are affected differently by variations in rainfall; a plot with a mixture of crops growing on it is likely to yield something, while a large area of a single crop may occasionally yield nothing. The crops are shifted from plot to plot in successive years, in order to avoid a multiplication of the pests and diseases peculiar to each plant. A low-yielding crop may be grown if it can be harvested early, and thus reduce the length of the 'hungry gap' at the end of each season, before the next season's main crop is ready for consumption. Land may be planted with cassava as a reserve against famine; in good years, much of it may not be harvested, but the inputs of labour may be highly valued in a bad season.

For annual crops, it is important to distinguish between production, output and supply. There are no reliable statistics of the annual production of food crops in most African countries, that is, of the weight of crops harvested. Farmers have a rough idea of the production of individual plots, as measured by the number of baskets, of the local size, which can be expected in an average year from the harvest. From this production, farmers must reserve seed for the next year's sowing, and the amount required by the farm families for consumption until the next harvest. Moreover, there will certainly be some wastage in grain or yams stored for several months, and a correspondingly larger amount should be allowed, before the remainder is sold. The output can be defined as the amount available for exchange or sale outside the family, and this quantity may be even more variable than the production, since farm families retain roughly the same quantity, year by year, for their own consumption. For instance, the sale of maize by African farmers from a certain area of Northern Rhodesia, now Zambia, varied between 1957, a good harvest, and 1958, a very bad harvest, as shown below:—[1]

	1957	1958
Thousand bags of 200 lb	832	55

In the second year, output from these farms fell to 7 per cent of the sales in the previous season; by contrast, output from the European farms, which did not use their own maize to any extent, fell by

[1] Allan, *African Husbandman*, p. 43.

slightly more than half, which probably represents the actual fall in yields between the two seasons. Those who grow food crops specifically for sale thus show a smaller range of variability in their output than the farms which habitually use a high proportion of their own production.

Finally, food crops are normally harvested at one season of each year, but are eaten over a period of several months. The supply of these crops can be defined as the amount actually offered for sale in any given period of time; the supply is thus a flow out of a stock whose size is fixed until the next harvest is reached. The flow out of the stock may itself vary greatly, according to the farmers' expectations of prices, their storage, or their need for cash and for food. The difficulties which arise from this variability in the output and in the supply of crops are further considered in Part 3.

The connection between output and supply is more complicated in the case of livestock for the meat trade. Here, the supply of meat comes from the older bulls, together with the barren cows and casualties; within short periods, the supply reaching the market can vary considerably, according to the prospects for market prices, the supply of feed for the animals, and the need of the livestock owners for money. The supply is drawn from the stock of breeding cows and their young calves, and the annual production of young calves is determined by accidents of birth, disease and drought.

LAND AND PEOPLE

The basic resources required for the production of food are the labour of human beings, land and water. Rights to use land and water for the production of food and other materials—firewood, minerals—can be acquired in very different ways. Even between adjacent villages, there may be differing customs for inheriting rights to use land, for acquiring such rights by marriage or by payments, for mutual assistance in harvesting or house-building or bush clearing. Students from different parts of Africa will find interest and education in comparing such local customs, in discussing their origins, and their influence in promoting or hindering the efficient use of natural resources.

The variety of local customs relating to land, collectively known as *land tenure*, reflects in part the different types of farming in areas with different soils, climate or altitude. But it also reflects three dominant features of African agriculture, the importance of subsistence farming in the economy of most villages; the existence of land in excess of immediate needs which permits the general practice of shifting cultivation; and the rights of each household in a village to the use of land and water within a definite territory, excluding from such use families who do not 'belong' to that community.

The rights of an individual to use land and water may, at one extreme, imply only the right to graze cattle, along with herds owned by other people of the same group, over a vast range of semi-arid territory. At the other extreme, an individual may have permanent rights to cultivate one particular plot, from which he can legally exclude all other rights, and which he can sell or bequeath without restriction. Below, four types of land tenure in Africa are described—grazing rights among the pastoral people of East Africa; rights to cropping land among the Tiv in Nigeria and among the Bantu peoples in south and south-central Africa, and the rights to cocoa farms in Ashanti, Ghana.

It appears to be true of African pastoralists, or most of them, that they recognise no specific grazing rights of any sort. All the land of the tribe is, in theory at least, open grazing for the animals of all members of the tribe. In practice there is a fairly clear association between groups and grazing areas. The [Masai] tribe is divided into sections (*loshun*), said to represent successive waves of migration, and each section is associated with a vaguely defined area. The clans which compose the sections also tend to move within limited areas, but these associations are regarded merely as matters of convenience and not as implying any exclusive right. The livestock of one section or clan may, and do, graze in areas associated with others, and in years of drought cattle from badly stricken sectors are admitted to the areas of the more fortunate... This concept of grazing land and surface water as free goods of the tribe is found also, according to Gulliver, among the Karamojong, Dodoth, Jie, and Donyiro of Uganda and the Turkana of Kenya. Nevertheless, 'owners' of herds— the head of a nuclear family among the Turkana and a group of full brothers among the Jie—tend to move their animals in an established annual grazing cycle over country with which they are familiar, and they are likely to resent encroachment by other groups in times of dearth... Among the Tonga of Northern Rhodesia [Zambia], on the other hand, an agricultural people who have been conscious of increasing shortage of garden and pasture land for a good many years, grazing is restricted to a division or *cisi*—a segment of the tribal land now replaced by the modern chieftaincy. As a general rule any member of the *cisi* has the right to graze whatever number of cattle or other stock he pleases anywhere within the *cisi*, but no cattle of one *cisi* may graze within the boundaries of another...Restriction, or localisation, of grazing rights has reached a more advanced stage among the Chagga of Kilimanjaro who are acutely short of land...Private rights to grazing are being asserted and these mingle and conflict with public rights in a medley of confusion.[1]

The Tiv see geography in the same image as they see social organisation. The idea of genealogy and descent provides not only the basis for lineage grouping, but also of territorial grouping. The minimal lineage, made up of men descended from a single ancestor, plus their wives and unmarried daughters, is located spatially beside another of precisely the same sort, descended from the brother of the ancestor of the first...The 'map' in terms of which the Tiv see their land is a genealogical map, and its association with specific pieces of ground is only of brief duration—a man or woman has precise rights to a farm during the time it is in cultivation, but once the farm returns to fallow, the rights lapse...Every year when new fields are selected, a man who needs more land expands in the direction of the neighbour most distantly related to him, then disputes the precise boundary of his new farm if necessary. Judges, either those recognised by the Administration or some other, then settle the disputes and the situation remains more or less static until the next year, when similar adjustments must again be made.[2]

[In South Africa and south-central Africa] the chief was regarded as the owner of his land as trustee for his people. Anyone coming on to the land had to pay allegiance to the chief and he in turn was under an obligation to provide all his subjects with a sufficiency of arable and building land, and to protect them in free access to wild products, public fishing waters and pasturage...In practice, in all the southern Bantu tribes, and among the Barotse, Ngoni, Yao and other central African peoples, chiefs did not give the land directly to the subjects who would use it. Land was generally allocated to sub-chiefs who in turn allotted shares to village headmen; but sometimes the allotment was directly to headmen. The number of steps in this hierarchy of land rights depended on the political hierarchy. At the village level, the headman allotted lands of sub-sections or heads of families, and they distributed land for use to their dependents. Each of the persons granted land in this way was secure in his rights and could not be expropriated without fault. He could transmit his rights to his heirs, but could not transfer them to anyone else without permission of his seniors. If rights were vacated, they rested with the next senior in the hierarchy.[3]

[In Ashanti] cocoa farms are very rarely 'lineage' property in the same sense as food gardens for subsistence. In the case of these farms the

---

[1] Allan, *African Husbandman*, pp. 294–6.
[2] P. Bohanan, 'Land', 'Tenure' and 'Land Tenure', in *African Agrarian Systems*, ed. D. Biebuyck (Oxford, 1963), pp. 105–6.
[3] Allan, *African Husbandman*, pp. 360–1.

emphasis is on individual ownership of the farm by the man who established it, and the rules applicable to personally acquired wealth come into play; but, as Fortes points out, cocoa farms may become lineage land by the operation of the customary laws of inheritance. But he noted contrary tendencies. Inheritance of cocoa farms was becoming restricted to closest kin in the matrilineal succession and there was a strong desire to leave property to children instead of nephews and nieces...If a man wants to sell or mortgage his cocoa farm he usually has a complete legal liberty to do so. In all this we may see a confusion and a difficulty created by the introduction of permanent cash crops, a confusion between the hierarchial rights vested in groups or individuals, or in this case the holder of the Stool, and the rights of the individual to the control of the land he has improved by planting a permanent crop.[1]

To the Masai in East Africa and the cattle Fulani in West Africa, land and water are free gifts of nature to which certain groups of people, by long use, have acquired rights, and can exclude others from using them in certain areas. Land has no cost to its users, it is available without effort or payment, and the users do not normally consider the effect of their own actions upon its future condition. Families will increase the number of cattle they keep upon the traditional grazing lands, without considering the effects of excessive grazing by all the herds, since their own herds are only a small part of the total. In the same way, farmers under shifting cultivation have no inducement to consider the effects of their cropping upon the long-term fertility of the village lands. As long as land is freely available to residents, and new plots can be obtained as old ones become exhausted, there is no gain from spending labour or money on applying manures; for each family, shifting cultivation provides the highest return for the inputs of labour. As the population increases, so the output increases by cultivating more land in the same pattern; if the territory becomes overcrowded, so that each cycle of production leads to a falling level of output, no family has any inducement to set about manuring, or applying fertilisers, or restricting the use of the grazing. For people will not usually devote labour and money to such tasks, unless they will reap the benefit by the continued use of the particular piece of land which they have improved, just as they wish to control for a long period of years the land on which they have planted cocoa or coffee trees. Once such improvements have been made, there will be a growing emphasis upon personal and family rights to particular pieces of land.

[1] Allan, *African Husbandman*, pp. 363–4.

Ideas about land tenure are changing rapidly in Africa, partly because in some areas land has become scarce in relation to the demand for it; partly because tree crops require the occupation of the same plot for many years; partly because farmers who apply fertilisers or manure want to obtain the benefit of their investment. In many areas also there is the influence of the European concept of *freehold*, whereby a man can buy, or sell, the right to the sole use of a piece of land, excluding the rights of others. Progressive farmers who have adopted modern practices in farming now generally favour the development of the freehold type of land tenure; but the majority of cattle owners and cultivators cling to the traditional customs of land tenure, partly because they wish to preserve the social structure and religious beliefs of their community, and these are often closely connected with land tenure.

The economist is concerned with two aspects of land tenure—whether local customs encourage occupiers to make the most profitable use of the existing resources, given the current knowledge about farming; and secondly, whether existing customs encourage measures to improve the fertility of the land, or are gradually diminishing it. Thus small scattered plots of irregular shape may make it impossible to introduce animal-drawn ploughs and cultivating implements, or to employ a tractor. On the other hand, if families can cultivate land anywhere within a certain area, it will be easy for them gradually to assemble plots together into sizeable fields, which can then be bunded or ridged against erosion, and cultivated by animal ploughs. Again, family customs of dividing every plot equally between sons, upon the death of the father, may make impossible any improved type of farming upon the scattered fragments. Indefinite boundaries and vague rights of occupation or inheritance lead to many disputes over land, which in turn restrict the efficient use made of it, and cost the disputing families a lot of time and money. Fewer occasions for such disputes was noted as one of the chief advantages obtained from the consolidation and enclosure of plots in parts of Kenya in recent years.[1]

Further, the use of land for crops which can be sold for money has created a market for land in many areas, between those who control more land than they can use, and those who have surplus labour and inadequate land. Thus in Ghana in the early years of this

[1] G. J. W. Pedraza, 'Land Consolidation in the Kikuyu Area of Kenya', in *Readings*, vol. I.

century, farmers on the crowded ridge to the east of the River Densu began to establish cocoa plantations on the empty western bank; the communities controlling that land offered either to sell the land 'freehold', or to lease it in return for a third share in the crops at every harvest, or to provide an area free of charge for the return of half the land planted with trees. The cocoa farmers generally preferred to buy the land on instalments which were paid to the chiefs of the villages concerned.[1] In the western region of Nigeria, 'about two-thirds of an acre was transferred for 4s in cash and a bottle of gin around the turn of the century, and for about 70s in 1938; it now costs about £5' (1954).[2] Such transactions in land are now becoming common all over Africa, though many communities limit them to members of the same village, and disapprove of land being transferred to strangers from some other district.

APPENDIX: THE PRODUCTION POSSIBILITY BOUNDARY AND CHOICE OF CROPS

We noted on p. 30 that with unlimited land available, the limit to the area cultivated is set by the amount of labour available at the period requiring most inputs of work. This constraint upon output can be illustrated by geometry (see table 7 and graph 3).

Assume that a farm family can cultivate as much land as it likes, and that it consists of two adults, each working 25 days a month, and one child, equivalent to nearly half an adult; the inputs of labour available therefore equal 60 hours per month (50 plus 10). The family grows two crops, each singly on separate plots, and these are called grain and beans. On the average of years, we assume that these crops require the following inputs of man-days per month per acre in order to give an average yield of 500 lb of grain per acre and 800 lb per acre of beans. Col. 1 shows the months counted from the one when the rains begin at the end of the dry season, and work becomes possible on the fields. Cols. 5 and 6 show the maximum production which is possible if all the labour is devoted each month to one of the two crops. Thus in month 2, both grain and beans require 15 man-hours of labour, and therefore the maximum output of each crop is found by $(60 \div 15 \times 500)$ lb for grain, and by $(60 \div 15 \times 800)$ for beans. The information contained in this table can now be transferred to graph 3.

Here, the output of grain is measured on the vertical (or Y) axis, and the output of beans on the horizontal (or X axis), both in 1,000 lb. Taking

[1] P. Hill, *Migrant Cocoa Farmers*, (London, 1963), p. 35.
[2] D. Galletti *et al.*, *Nigerian Cocoa Farmers* (London, 1956), p. 121.

TABLE 7. *Constraints on production*

1	2	3	4	5	6
				Maximum production of	
Month of rainy season	Man-days available	Man-days required per acre		each crop (lbs)	
		Grain	Beans	Grain	Beans
1	60	12	0	2,500	—
2	60	15	15	2,000	3,200
3	60	10	20	3,000	2,400
4	60	10	12	3,000	4,000
5	60	15	10	2,000	4,800
6	60	10	15	3,000	3,200
	Yield from 1 acre			500	800
		2 acres		1,000	1,600
		etc.			

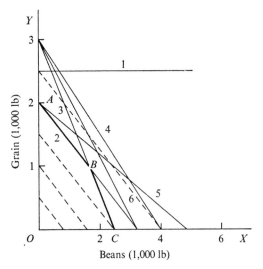

Graph 3. Production possibility boundary

for example the possible inputs of labour for the second month, the maximum possible output of grain, if only grain is grown, is 2,000 lb, and that of beans is 3,200 lb; the line joining these points, on the two axes, shows all combinations of output of these two crops which are possible with the labour inputs for that month, 60 man-days. If all six lines are drawn, one for each month, it can be seen at once that the present constraints upon production are set by the labour inputs required for the second and third months. If more grain is grown, then the high labour inputs in the second month restrict the area cultivated, the line *AB*; if the family grows mostly beans, then it is the labour requirements of the third month which restrict output, the line *BC*. The line *ABC* shows the combinations of output which can be grown within these constraints and is therefore termed the *production possibility boundary*, or the *production possibility envelope*.

The importance of this concept may be shown if we consider how this family could increase its output. Since the existing level of production is limited by the amount of weeding required in the second and third months of the rains, there is no use in suggesting improvements in breaking up land, which is normally done in the first month, or of harvesting in the last two months. But an improved method of weeding crops, or of planting beans, which reduced the man-hours required for these tasks, would then push the production possibility boundary outward from the point *O*, and increase the area which could be cultivated. Or the family might use fertilisers to raise yields per acre, since there is still spare labour in the time of harvesting. After such improvements, the new constraint upon production might then be the labour required for harvesting in the fifth month, and that constraint would then need to be tackled, either by labour-saving devices or by hiring labour for that task. Or output might then be limited because the family could not acquire extra land for further cultivation; the dotted lines in the graph show the production possibility boundary, under the existing conditions, for 1 acre, 2 acres etc. (the dotted lines joining the average output for each crop for each of these areas). Before the existing constraints upon production can be removed, they must be understood, but understanding them implies detailed knowledge of existing farm practices, which is often still lacking in Africa.

The production possibility boundary shows what combinations of the output of the two crops are possible, given the production functions (the relationship between inputs and outputs) set out in the table; but it does not tell us which of the possible combinations farmers may choose. The table and graph give a choice between two crops, one supplying mainly carbohydrates, which could be derived from grain or yams or cassava, and one, beans, with a higher content of protein. It is commonly reckoned that a working adult needs at least 250 kg (or roughly 500 lb) of edible grain per year,[1] together with a certain quantity of edible protein and other foods. Let us assume that this family of two adults and one child will plan to grow at least 1000 lb of grain a year; once it has obtained that quantity, it values another pound of grain equally with a pound of beans. In graph 4, the production possibility boundary, *ABC*, is taken from the previous graph, together with the lines showing the areas. The line *DEF* is drawn to represent the *exchange ratio* between grain and beans

[1] C. Clark and M. Haswell, *Economics of Subsistence Agriculture* (London, 1964), chap. 1.

for this family. This leaves the grain axis at *A*, at 1,000 lb, since the family will devote all its resources to this output at first; from *A* the line is drawn to divide the right-angle *ADG* equally, since the family values additional lbs of grain and beans equally. This line crosses the production possibility boundary at *E*, showing that the preferred output for this family, working with these production functions, is about 1,500 lb of grain and about 800 lb of beans, obtained from cultivating about 4 acres of land. The student is advised to draw other exchange ratio lines and note the effect on the preferred output.

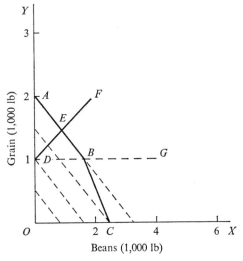

Graph 4. Choice of crops

At this point, the reader may feel that the economist only complicates the simple facts of farming; farmers do not use production possibility boundaries or exchange ratios in planning their daily work. It is true that farmers do not use this kind of language, but the decisions they take—how much land to cultivate, what crops give the best output for labour, where to use today's labour—do depend on such relationships as the equal marginal returns to inputs, diminishing returns to the application of labour to more intensive weeding, the relative value given to different crops. Economists need to appreciate just how complex the traditional patterns of farming are, how skilfully, in most cases, the African farmers manage their resources to obtain the greatest satisfaction of their wants; and how difficult it often is to devise improvements which, within the constraints of the available resources and techniques, will certainly improve the standard of life of the farm families.

4. Commercial farming

FOOD CROPS AND CASH CROPS

The extent of subsistence farming still to be found in Africa varies greatly. As a proportion of the total value of all agricultural output, production by farm families for their own use varied from 20 per cent in the specialised cocoa-growing regions of Ghana to 80 per cent among African farmers in Malawi.[1] In some areas, many families still grow only crops for their own consumption, while one or more of the men migrate to other areas to obtain employment for wages; migration is here an alternative to the growing of crops for sale, to earn the money which every family now needs, in order to pay taxes or to buy the things which they cannot make themselves.

The present stage of farming in Africa shows a number of differences from the pattern of farming in industrialised countries, from which come so many advisers to African governments. Firstly, as mentioned above, most farm families still grow the traditional food crops for their own consumption; methods of working and the division of labour within the family are closely linked with these traditional crops. Cash crops, such as cotton, cocoa or vegetables are often grown, not as part of the food farm, but as a separate enterprise. Secondly, scattered plots, shifting cultivation and hand labour are still the general rule, with little in the way of inputs except labour; consolidated farms using manures or fertilisers or implements are exceptional. Thirdly, many African farms are not a single unit organised by one man who takes both the decisions and the money income; the wife, or wives, and the grown sons may all work to some extent on the land belonging to the head of the family, but they often cultivate land of their own as well, retaining the output for their personal use, whether in the form of food for personal consumption, or as crops for sale. Fourthly, the customs relating to the occupation and inheritance of land differ greatly between different parts of Africa, but seldom include the concept of freehold as known in Europe and America, or the free market in land. These

[1] K. C. Abercrombie, *Subsistence Production and Economic Development*, Monthly Bulletin of Agricultural Economics and Statistics (F.A.O., May, 1965).

differences make comparisons with agriculture in Europe or America somewhat dangerous; improving the conditions of African farming depends more upon understanding the constraints which at present limit the choices available to African farmers than upon the import of foreign practices and machinery.

When some cash crops are grown for sale, in addition to the food crops grown for consumption by the family, the planning of production widens from the balance between inputs of effort and the quantity of output to include the balance between costs of the inputs and the value of the output. A farmer may grow cash crops by hiring men for some of the work, in which case there is a direct cost in money to be set against the money received from the sale of the crops. If he employs his family or works on the cash crops himself, he can make an estimate of the value of that work in terms either of what he would have to pay to hire other workers, or of the market value of the expected output. Crops grown for family consumption then acquire an *opportunity cost*, the cost of going without the income which could have been earned in growing cash crops by the land and labour devoted to food crops. The calculation of opportunity cost becomes more complicated if the family must reduce its production of food crops in order to grow cash crops, because the land or labour at its command is limited. In this case, a family may compare the cost of buying food out of the income earned by growing a cash crop, against the quantity of food which could have been grown by the resources devoted to the cash crop. A farmer urged to grow more cotton, for instance, would be wise to consider whether the extra income earned by the sale of the cotton will leave a margin over the cost of buying more food, possibly at the end of the season when prices are high in local markets; the opportunity cost of growing more cotton and a smaller area of food crops might easily be greater than the extra income earned from the cotton. Opportunity costs thus link together the cash crops and food crops which make up the production on African farms.

Expenditure upon inputs takes three forms. There are firstly the costs incurred for individual crops—the cost of buying the seed, of harvesting and of transport to market, perhaps the labour hired to weed the crop, if it is grown by itself. These are called by economists *variable* (or *direct*) *costs*, since they vary with the scale of the output of each crop. Secondly, farmers often grow several crops together or in succession, clearing and burning land for several years of cultivation, and weeding the first crop while they plant the second. Here we have *joint costs*, which cannot be allocated to any specified crop, but which vary with the scale of output and with the balance of the different crops in the total plan. Finally, the farmer may have a pair of work-oxen and some implements which he uses for ploughing and for cultivating. The oxen have to be fed, and perhaps bought in the first place; their harness and the implements must be repaired and replaced as necessary. These are *fixed* (or *overhead*) *costs*, which must be met as long as the farmer cultivates the land in this way, but such costs do not vary with the type or extent of the crops grown. We have therefore three kinds of costs—variable costs incurred specifically for each output; joint costs which are incurred in producing more than one type of output but which vary with the scale and composition of that output; and fixed costs, which must be paid so long as the farmer continues in his existing pattern. In addition, there are opportunity costs for the resources used in crops grown for direct consumption.

INCREASING COSTS AND MARGINAL REVENUE

In this discussion about costs, we are looking for the constraints upon production, so that we can help to remove them, one by one, and thus increase the output of goods and services. In subsistence agriculture, we noted that the constraint upon production might be set, firstly, by diminishing returns to inputs of labour engaged in cultivating small areas by hand tools; secondly, by the small area which each family can cultivate by such methods; and thirdly, by the amount of labour which is available in the busiest seasons. Let us take these points in turn and see how they appear in the form of costs.

In table 5 on p. 24, we looked at the varying returns which may occur to successive units of a variable input applied to a fixed quantity of some other input. And in table 6 we applied the expression marginal cost to the relationship between the inputs of the variable resource and the resulting units of output. Let us now assume that each of these units of input costs 10 units of local currency, and work the same figures as those given in table 5 in terms of money costs, as shown in table 8.

Up to 3 units of input, there are increasing returns per unit of input, and there are falling costs per unit of output; after that point,

TABLE 8. *Marginal cost and price*

1 Units of variable input	2 Total output	3 Marginal output	4 Average output	5 Total variable cost	6 Average variable cost per unit of output	7 Marginal cost per unit of output
1	3		3	10	3·33	
		5				2·00
2	8		4	20	2·5	
		7				1·42
3	15		5	30	2·0	
		8				1·25
4	23		5·75	40	1·75	
		7				1·42
5	30		6	50	1·66	
		5				2·00
6	35		5·83	60	1·71	
		4				2·50
7	39		5·54	70	1·80	
		3				3·33
8	42		5·25	80	1·90	
		1				10·00
9	43		4·78	90	2·09	
		0				—
10	43		4·33	100	2·33	

NOTE. Cols. 1, 2, 3, 4 are the same as those in table 5. Col. 5 is the cost of the inputs shown in col. 1, at 10 units of currency each. Col. 6 is obtained by dividing col. 5 by col. 2, to give cost per unit of output; col. 7 is obtained by dividing the increase in cost shown in col. 5 by the increase in output shown in col. 3, to give the cost of the marginal unit of output. Thus with 2 units of input, the marginal cost is $(20-10) \div 5 = 2$.

there are diminishing returns per unit of input, and rising costs per unit of output. The reader is warned that it is easy to confuse increasing returns and rising costs, or diminishing returns and falling costs. But the expression increasing returns describes the behaviour of output per unit of input; it implies that the cost of each extra unit of output is falling since there are increasing units of output to each unit of input. Similarly, the expression diminishing returns per unit of input implies that the cost of each unit of output is rising. The phrase constant returns per unit of input implies, however, that we also have *constant costs* per unit of output, which is roughly what is shown in table 8 for 4 or 5 units of input.

From this table, let us return to the farmers, some of whom can only obtain a limited area of land, while others can cultivate as much land as they like, and let us suppose that all farmers employ hired men, costing 10 units of currency for each day or week of work. The farmers with a limited area of land will find that as they employ more workers, diminishing returns per unit of input bring rising costs per basket of beans or maize. They clearly will not employ a man unless the expected output from his work can be sold for at least the cost of his wages, but it will pay them to employ men as long as the receipts leave any margin over variable costs. Let us assume that, in the conditions of table 8, each unit of output can be

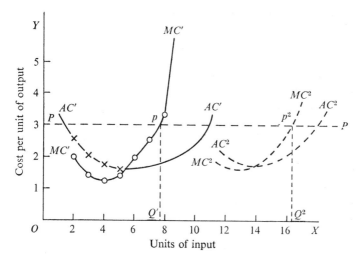

Graph 5. Marginal cost and price. (NOTE. The curve MC' shows the marginal cost per unit of output, where units of input are marked along the horizontal axis, and cost, or price, per unit of output is marked on the vertical axis; the curve AC' shows the corresponding average cost. The line PP shows the price (3 units) per unit of output, which is here cut by MC' at point p. The vertical taken from point p to the horizontal axis OX shows that for inputs in excess of 7, marginal cost will be greater than price.)

sold for 3 units of local currency. Then it can be seen that it would not pay farmers to employ more than 7 units of input, or to produce more than about 40 units of output; above this limit, marginal cost—the cost of additional units of output—is greater than the expected price of 3, and there would be a loss, not a profit, on the extra units sold. In conditions of diminishing returns and of increasing costs, output is limited by the rising marginal cost of producing more units of output. This constraint is shown in graph 5, giving part of the same information as in table 8, with a price of 3 units of local currency per unit of output.

How could this constraint upon output be removed? One answer is by a fall in costs, which would enable farmers to apply more inputs before the marginal cost equalled the price of the output. This implies new curves of average and marginal costs, to the right of our original curves, as is shown by the dotted lines on graph 5. Such a fall in costs could be brought about either by a rise in *productivity*—defined as the output per unit of input—or by a fall in the price of the input. A second answer would be a rise in the price of the output, so that farmers could employ more units of input. Either of these events would enable output to be increased without marginal cost exceeding price, but at the new level of cost or of price, output would still be limited, after a period of adjustment, by the balance of marginal cost against price.

Let us now consider those farmers who can cultivate as much land as they choose, by employing other people for a wage. Here there is no obvious fixed resource, since both land and labour can be adjusted and combined in the most profitable unit; why therefore should there be any limit on output?

This question brings us back from the simplified example of the tables and the graphs to the real world in which people plan production, grow crops and take them to market. In the first place, land is not of the same fertility and quantity, nor is it the same distance from market. For commercial production, farmers will naturally cultivate first the more fertile land which gives a high yield before diminishing returns and rising costs restrict output; they will also cultivate first the land nearest the market, so as to have low costs of transport. As production increases, so the new farmers must cultivate less fertile land, or land farther from the market, thus raising costs as output increases. Further, we assumed that farmers could engage as many men as they found profitable for a constant wage, and that they could sell their output for a constant price. Neither of these assumptions is likely to be true, if all farmers in one area expand production at the same time; competition among farmers for resources and for markets might both raise wages and lower prices for their output, so that costs would rise and prices fall, as output expanded.

Finally, we must recognise that each farmer is himself a 'fixed input' for his own business, since he supplies that necessary resource called enterprise, which here includes both the art of management and the taking of risks. It is the farmer who has to begin commercial production, who has to obtain the land for it, to hire workers, to find credit to pay their wages before harvest, to decide what combination of crops is likely to be most profitable, to organise the work of each man, including himself, to suit the changing conditions of soil and climate and plant growth.

Successful management is perhaps more difficult in farming than in most industries, for a variety of reasons. Go round the fields of any African village, and you will find farmers growing different mixtures of crops, different rotations of crops, in what is apparently the same environment. Yet small differences in soil and slope often exist which alter the most profitable combination of crops; farmers have differing needs for food crops, or control different quantities of labour and of credit, and they adjust their patterns of cropping to make best use of their resources.

Secondly, changes in weather and in the condition of crops and of livestock involve farmers in constant changes in the details of their work, both during the course of one season, and between seasons. They cannot plan a steady sequence of crops and of work, and apply it without further thought. Observation is an important part of the work of farmers, since small changes in the appearance of animals, of crops or of soils may indicate that a change in plan is needed, to ward off disease, to take advantage of favourable conditions, to remedy some crop failure.

Thirdly, as a farmer increases the scale of his business, so he normally increases the area which he must supervise, and the number of people he must organise. If plots are scattered over the village fields, detailed supervision becomes more difficult, the quality of the work falls, output per man may fall while costs per unit of output rise. The farmer perhaps spends more time in marketing, and has therefore less time to give to the close observation of his farm upon which efficiency so much depends.

These are some of the reasons why costs per unit of output are likely to rise in farms as they get bigger; these difficulties may be intensified if enlarging a farm means acquiring separate fields scattered over a wider territory. Yet in all communities, there are good and bad managers, both in subsistence production and in commercial farming. In what are almost similar circumstances, a good manager may obtain two or three times as much output and more income than a poor manager, partly because of greater energy, partly because of better observation and knowledge, partly because of better organisation of other people, partly because of more skilled judgement in the taking of risks.

RISK AND UNCERTAINTY

All production implies the taking of some risk, since the cost or the effort has to be incurred in advance of the final output, which may turn out to be more or less than was expected. There are, firstly, those risks arising from events which happen from time to time but to an unpredictable degree and at an unpredictable time—rains arriving early or late, too much rain or not enough rain for normal plant growth, interruptions to local transport by floods, and so on. If there were adequate statistics of such events for past years, so that the chances of their occurrence could be calculated, farmers might be able to insure against them, as farmers in other countries can now insure against the loss of crops by hail, or of stored crops by fire. By such insurance, an unpredictable risk, which may ruin a farmer when it occurs, can be converted into an annual cost, represented by a small premium paid every year, against the certainty of compensation if and when the risk happens.

Secondly, there is the uncertainty about each year's income caused by minor variations in the output of the main crops. Here again, farmers often grow several crops in order to ensure against the partial failure of any one of them; they often try to occupy land in different places or of different quality, precisely in order to diminish the risks of disease or storm. Thirdly, there is the uncertainty about each year's income caused by variations in prices, either for the things which farmers sell, or for the inputs which they buy. Good information about market prospects and skilful bargaining can no doubt minimise the effects of unfavourable prices and enable farmers to get the most out of favourable prices, but generally farmers have to take the risk of good prices along with the risk of bad prices, within each season for which their crops are already planted.

It is sometimes not realised that many of the current practices of farmers are aimed at minimising such risks and uncertainties. Farmers growing cotton, for instance, often plant food crops first and the cotton later in each season, so that yields of cotton are lower than they would be if the cotton was planted first, but the food crops are not so likely to be affected by a short rainy season. In effect, farmers forgo the extra income from the higher yields of cotton in all years in order to reduce the cost of having to buy food in years of poor crops and of high prices for them; they accept what may be a lower average income in money over several years in order not to have to incur high costs after a bad harvest.

Fourthly, there are the exceptional risks which increase with the duration of the project and with the degree of specialisation. Hiring a man for a week to pick cotton involves the expenditure of the agreed sum against an estimate of the man's probable output and the price to be received for it, perhaps in the next week; here the uncertainty is small. A decision to hire men to clear land for cultivation over four or five years depends on a calculation of the expected balance between receipts and costs over that period, in which there may be changes in costs and in prices, and uncontrollable variations in output. But a variety of crops can be grown, and the choice of what to sow can be made annually in the light of current information, so that the risks of a large loss may be small. But most of the costs of buying land and hiring labour to plant cocoa or coffee trees must be incurred five or six years before returns begin, and the investment cannot be converted to any other use. Here the risk from uncertainty is high, and the delay in obtaining receipts is long.

Finally, we may note that the ability to incur costs now in the hope of future receipts implies the command over resources in excess of those needed for current consumption. Farmers must either control surplus labour, or they must have ready money to hire such labour, or they must be able to borrow in order to incur such costs. The poorer the family, the less likely it will have resources above the immediate needs of the moment for investment in the hope of distant gain, and the less likely that it will risk present goods for an uncertain improvement in the future. Many improvements suggested in the techniques of farming involve considerable costs, and advisers do not always realise what sacrifices families may have to make of current consumption, and what risks they may have to take, in order to carry out some simple improvement.

CAPITAL AS A RESOURCE

We have hitherto assumed that the African farmers work their land with only one other resource, that of labour, but the planning of investment brings in another resource, that of capital. There are many definitions of this word, which was used by business men before economists began to analyse the processes of economic life. Here we may define capital as (1) man-made tools used in the production of goods and services—*fixed capital*; (2) stocks of goods—*circulating* or *working capital*; (3) money or other financial *assets*. (In this definition of capital we may include, as a special case, natural objects such as breeding livestock and trees planted for the subsequent use of their products.)

There are four points to be noticed here about this resource called capital which can take many forms. First, capital exists because of a previous decision to increase future output, rather than to consume resources. The cows are kept for breeding, the oxen for ploughing, instead of consuming beef, or selling them for cash; a farmer devotes labour to clearing land and planting cocoa trees when he might be taking crops to market. Capital implies either saving out of current income, or not using resources in consumption.

Secondly, the existence of capital implies some measure of specialisation; tools are not equally suitable for all types of production. Trees are again the obvious example of a highly specialised form of capital which can only yield one form of output; a plough can be used in the cultivation of many crops, but it cannot pick cotton. In the industrialised world, some forms of capital, such as factory buildings, can often serve for a variety of purposes, while a plant for producing cement or steel is highly specialised; if the original investment proves unprofitable, it cannot easily be converted to some other form of output. The creation of durable tools thus involves risks that their output may become unprofitable before their costs have been repaid.

Thirdly, capital can greatly increase output and lower the cost of production, but its right use involves careful choice between the variety of tools which might be suitable for the purpose in hand; chosing the one tool which is likely to give the required output at the lowest cost in the foreseeable future requires both technical knowledge and a shrewd judgment of relative costs and efficiencies. The wide range of choice now available in tools implies that people may make the wrong choice, and run into debt, while only a few successfully master the possibilities of a new invention. This kind of risk becomes more common as the scientists and engineers invent new methods of production, offering more alternatives between which choice must be made.

CAPITAL AND FIXED COSTS

Fourthly, the use of capital involves the user in fixed costs. We began the discussion on commercial farming by assuming the existence of a fixed input for each productive unit, and that this fixed input might be either land, or the farmer's own powers of management. Let us now assume that our productive unit has some piece of capital equipment—a team of work oxen, or a tractor and its implements. This capital enables the farmer to double his output from the same inputs of the variable factor, but the improvement involves the farmer in some fixed costs, as defined on p. 45. For work oxen, these costs may be the cost of purchasing the animals and their implements, the cost of feeding them, and of repairing their harness. Further, although this piece of capital will, or should, outlast more than one year's output from the farm, it will eventually need replacement, so that the farmer must, at the end of its working life, have money in hand to buy a replacement. Some of this cost he can obtain from the sale of the oxen for meat, but much must be obtained from the sale of the annual output of the farm. A tractor, with its implements, will have a falling market value during its working life, and a large sum must therefore be set aside from each year's income for replacement, as well as meeting the costs of repairs, or insurance and tax, and the cost of petrol and oils when the tractor is working. If the farmer has borrowed money to buy his capital equipment, his fixed cost must also include the interest and repayment of his loan.

Let us now see how the introduction of a fixed cost of this sort affects the planning of output. Table 9 repeats the basic information of table 8, but adds in col. 4 the fixed cost of 20 units of local currency. The output has been doubled for all units of input and we assume that the same price still holds for this larger output; col. 3 shows the total receipts. Average costs are recalculated to take into account the new elements of fixed cost and of greater output.

In the first place, we note that total costs will now exceed total receipts for the smallest size of business, and will leave only a small margin of profit for two units of the variable factor. Unless the farmer can acquire three units, the new tool will be of no use to him. Secondly, the level of output for which marginal cost equals price has now risen to absorb 8 units of input and involves the sale of about 250 units of output. Can the farmer find a market at our

TABLE 9. *Fixed and variable costs*

1 Units of variable input	2 Total output	3 Total receipts	4 Fixed cost	5 Variable cost	6 Total cost	7 Average cost (per unit	8 Marginal cost of output)
1	6	18	20	10	30	5	
2	16	48	20	20	40	2·5	1·0
3	30	90	20	30	50	1·67	0·71
4	46	138	20	40	60	1·30	0·62
5	60	180	20	50	70	1·17	0·71
6	70	210	20	60	80	1·14	1·0
7	78	234	20	70	90	1·15	1·25
8	84	252	20	80	100	1·19	1·67
9	86	258	20	90	110	1·28	5·0
10	86	258	20	100	120	1·40	—

NOTE. Cols. 1, 2, 3 and 5 are taken from table 8, using the same assumptions, that the output is sold for a fixed price of 3 per unit, and that the units of the variable input cost 10 each. Col. 3 is then col. 2 multiplied by 3. Col. 6 is the sum of col. 4 and col. 5. Col. 8 is obtained, as before, by dividing the increase in total cost by the increase in the output; thus for 6 units of the variable input, the marginal cost is calculated by $(80-70) \div (70-60)$ which equals 1.

assumed price for this increased output? If he is selling cotton to a marketing board, he need not bother about this problem, but if he is selling onions in the local market, he may well need to consider the disposal of so much extra production. And there are other matters which have also changed with the introduction of the fixed costs of a piece of capital.

Consider for instance the introduction of oxen and a plough into an area hitherto cultivated in scattered plots by hand tools. The land to be ploughed must be of a size that allows for working in straight lines or gentle curves, without frequent turnings; plots must therefore be consolidated into fewer but larger fields. The ground must be cleared of termite mounds and tree roots, which are left embedded by hand tools; having performed this heavy work, the farmer will want to cultivate his farm continously after clearing, instead of moving his plots every three or four years. His oxen must be hand-fed while working; the farmer must therefore have some improved grazing for them, and grow some kind of fodder crop, both for feed and for litter in stalls, for he will need the animals' manure, as well as fertilisers, on his fields in order to continue cropping on some rotation. A plough-team therefore implies the control of some 15–30 acres of land, in which the farmer will have invested much labour. Even where land is available freely, such consolidated holdings may upset the existing patterns of cultivation and the existing ideas about land tenure. Where land is scarce and families do not usually cultivate more than a few acres each, farmers who accumulate land enough for a plough team may incur dislike and envy. Further, a man with twenty or thirty acres of land, half of it under crop in any one season, will need to employ hired workers for planting, the later weeding and harvesting; he must find the resources to pay these workers for many weeks before the crops are sold. Only farmers with a certain size of farm and of income are therefore likely to be able to afford to buy a plough-team, and if they make a success of their investment, there will be a still greater difference between them and their poorer neighbours in the same village, who may find themselves working on a large farm for wages. The efficient operation of a piece of capital, such as a plough, may therefore require changes in the lay-out of fields, in the type of farming, in the traditional patterns of land tenure, and in the social structure of rural communities.

MECHANISED FARMING AND ITS COSTS

In table 9, it was assumed that the fixed costs of the piece of capital were added on to the existing inputs of some variable resource to produce a greater output; capital is here *complementary* to land and labour, enabling the total combination to increase output. But some types of capital are *competitive* with labour, since they enable fewer men to do more cheaply what could otherwise only be done by more men at higher cost. The kind of problem here being considered is shown in graph 6, which indicates, for Uganda in the 1950s, comparisons of the cost per acre of cultivating coffee farms of various sizes by hand labour, by a small tractor and disc harrow, costing 12,000*s*., and by a standard tractor and disc harrow, costing 17,400*s*.

At the costs then ruling, hand labour was thought to be the cheapest method for plots of less than five acres; a small tractor with disc harrow was the cheapest method for plots above five acres in size but was more expensive for the smaller plots; the standard tractor was probably the cheapest method only on plots of 40 acres or upwards. It was also thought that work oxen might have proved cheaper than tractors or hand labour for plots between two and five acres in size. Such comparisons would need to be recalculated if the current level of wages rose, or the output per man fell, or if costs of buying and operating tractors changed appreciably.

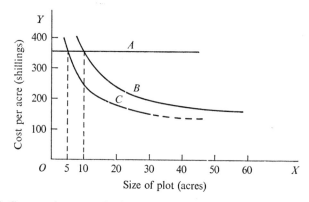

Graph 6. Comparative costs of using hand labour and field machinery. (NOTE. The line *A* shows the cost of cultivating plots of different sizes by hand labour; the curve *B* shows the estimated cost of the same work by standard tractor and harrow; the curve *C* shows the estimated cost of the same work by a small tractor and harrow. For the assumptions on which these estimates were made, see L. Joy (ed.) *Symposium on Mechanical Cultivation in Uganda* (Kampala, 1960).

The example given above shows that the lowest-cost combination of resources will vary with the scale of output, and with the type of tool chosen. Cultivation by hand labour takes the form of variable costs, if the workers can be hired for this work alone; if only a few acres are cultivated, the total costs will be low, but they rise in proportion to the area worked. But the use of tractors involves the farmer in both fixed and variable costs. The fixed costs, the purchase price of the tool, its licence, insurance and maintenance, do not vary with the area cultivated, but they must be paid somehow. If these costs are charged upon the output of a few acres, the cost per unit of output or per acre is extremely high, but it falls as the output increases. Costs of petrol, oil, the driver and sundry repairs, are of course variable costs, like those of hand labour. The total average cost of using machinery is thus composed of two parts, as in graph 7.

With hand labour, the costs per acre of cultivating land do not appreciably vary with the size of the business, until the farm becomes too big for the farmer to exercise efficient supervision. The same can be said of the running costs of the tractor, but the average fixed costs fall sharply as the area cultivated increases from a low level, and they continue to decrease appreciably with each additional acre, for some further expansion in the area worked.

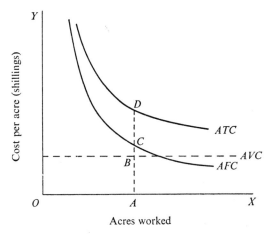

Acres worked

Graph 7. Fixed and variable costs. (NOTE. The line AVC is the average variable cost of the tractor per acre worked; the line AFC indicates the average fixed cost per acre. The line ATC represents the addition of the other two, making up the average total cost per acre. Thus AB plus AC equals AD, and similarly for all points on the curve ATC.)

It will be seen that the introduction of a capital tool into the productive process complicates the structure of the costs which set the ultimate limit to output. Total costs, which must be covered if the business is not to become unprofitable, include fixed costs, but fixed costs are not included in the marginal cost which determines the scale of output of the existing combination of resources; marginal cost, it will be remembered, is defined as the change in cost caused by producing one more unit, and thus excludes the fixed costs.

Take the case of a farmer who has acquired a plough-team or a tractor, which he finds he cannot keep fully employed on his own land, and is asked to cultivate a plot for his neighbour. What is a suitable charge for such work? Clearly, the minimum charge the farmer can make, without losing money, is the marginal cost of this work, the addition to total costs made by this extra output, which is composed of the variable costs of the petrol, oil, the driver's time, and minor incidental costs. But this leaves the farmer with no contribution towards the fixed costs of the tool, and he would normally be well advised to charge something above the marginal cost. If he is advised to charge the average total cost, the question then arises, how is this average to be calculated? If the capital is not fully employed, then the average cost will be higher than if it was, since the fixed costs are being averaged over a smaller quantity of output; at the same time, the farmer will be in greater need of extra income to meet the fixed costs and it will pay him to accept outside work if he can charge only a little above the marginal cost.

If the capital is already fully employed on the farmer's own land, at the time his neighbour asks for assistance, then other considerations come into play. Going back to graph 3, p. 40, and assuming that the capacity of the tool is the limiting factor in the output for the second and third months of the season, we can see that the farmer should only undertake outside work at this period if he charges a sum, over and above the variable costs, which would recompense him for having a smaller area under crop on his own farm for that season; he should charge the opportunity cost, the total benefit he might have obtained from the next most profitable opportunity for using his capital. But if the outside work can be carried out when the capital is not fully employed, as for instance in the dry season, then the farmer will gain if he obtains anything above the variable costs of the operation.

In any short period of time, therefore, the output to be obtained from a piece of capital equipment is limited by the variable costs associated with each operation, and these variable costs are likely to rise sharply if the tool is worked beyond the capacity for which it is designed. But unless the tool, over its working life, earns enough to pay for its fixed costs, including *depreciation*, (the fall in the market value through use and age), the farmer will eventually find himself without his capital, and with a lower level of output. So that for the longer period of time, output is limited by the total cost of the capital tool, averaged over the output it has produced in the course of its life. The introduction of capital, with its fixed costs and varying degree of use, thus introduces into the concept of cost a certain vagueness, or indeterminacy, linked with this question of time. We shall take up this point again in the next chapter (p. 68), and also in the discussions about the price policy of large firms (p. 155).

Finally, it is important to realise that the efficiency of complicated forms of capital, such as tractors, depends on a number of complementary resources which are not always present in any one environment—facilities for repair and servicing, adequate supplies of other inputs, experienced management, suitable tracts of land under one control, and the like. Particularly in farming, the management of large units combining expensive tools with many workers and the biological factors can only be learnt by experience, either personal or by watching other managers. The previous accumulation of capital and of credit is also difficult where incomes are low, and there may also be problems of marketing a greater output for local consumption in conditions of rural poverty.

IMPROVED FARMING

The dominant business unit in African agriculture remains the family farm, with several plots of land scattered among the village lands, and cultivated by hand tools; in pastoral areas, there are the migratory herds of cattle, sheep and goats, including animals belonging to a group of related families following the customary pattern of seasonal grazing. Most farmers sell some product in local markets, and also grow some crop for export outside their own territory, such as cotton, groundnuts, or tree crops. Output per man and per acre remains low, there is little surplus over the subsistence of the family, and the rural population therefore buys little in the way of industrial goods, or of foods not grown locally. Nevertheless, there are wealthy farmers in most areas, and it may be helpful here to look at some examples, to discover how the constraints upon production have been overcome.

TREE CROPS FOR EXPORT. The early plantations of cocoa by farmers in Ghana and Nigeria represent the use of surplus land and labour to produce a crop for foreign markets. The initial stimulus to this type of investment came therefore from the countries rich enough to consume large quantities of chocolate and cocoa butter, and their merchants generally organised the trade and the processing. In Africa, the investment took the form, firstly of applying labour to land, and secondly, of a long period of waiting before returns began to accrue. As noted above, this form of investment carried the risk of a high degree of specialisation; the incomes of cocoa growers have fluctuated widely, partly because of changes in prices, and partly because pests and diseases found the cocoa trees conveniently close for their own multiplication. Nevertheless, substantial incomes have been secured by cocoa growers in West Africa and by tea and coffee growers in East Africa which they have used partly in greater consumption, partly in paying taxes to their governments, and partly as a source of further investment in their farms.

PLOUGH TEAMS. In certain parts of Uganda and Northern Nigeria, where cattle can be kept free of tsetse fly, the use of oxen has enabled some farmers to plant and cultivate larger areas of crops than is possible with hand labour. This increase in output depends on two pieces of investment—the purchase of the trained animals and their implements, and the investment of labour in thoroughly clearing land from obstructions which hinder the passage of the implements. Moreover, the area of land which such farmers cultivate must usually be weeded and harvested by hand; the cost of wages and the supply of pre-harvest credit therefore set limits to the area of crops which can be grown. Recently, a few farmers and some Departments of Agriculture have also established tractor services for hire, enabling those who control enough land, labour and credit to employ machinery for the work of clearing and cultivating, without the need to buy it.

INTEGRATED CROP AND STOCK FARMS. Farmers in temperate climates have secured a high output per acre by combining fodder and cash cropping with livestock, and a high output per man by mechanisation. The use of clover and sown grasses, in rotation with other crops, improved the supply of nutrients to the soil; fertilisers and the manure of the animals further increased the capacity of the land to provide high yields of crops, both for sale and for fodder. In Africa, this type of farming is only possible where the rainfall permits good pasture, where cattle can be kept fairly free of disease, and where farms have been consolidated under some form of crop rotation. Such techniques involve disturbance to existing systems of land tenure, since scattered plots must be brought together and fenced; it involves capital investment in livestock, fertilisers, fencing, water supplies and control of animal diseases; it requires management of a high order both of crops and of livestock; and its success depends on the existence of profitable markets for the improved quality of the meat and milk produced.

INTENSIVE CROP FARMING. In many African villages there are two or three men who have become successful and relatively wealthy commercial farmers, in circumstances where the majority of families remain confined to subsistence farming with a small area of a cash crop. These men are often recent immigrants, or they have had experience, and accumulated capital, in government posts or in transport. They have brought to farming the commercial habits of weighing costs against prices, and of looking for cheaper methods of performing traditional tasks; they also had the initial capital to break through the constraints limiting the purchase of inputs such as hired labour, fertilisers or implements. They are likely to consult the local advisers from the Ministry of Agriculture over fertilisers and crop sprays, improved varieties of plants, the inoculation of animals against diseases, and possible grants or loans from the Ministry. They adapt their farming to supply the needs of a growing market for foods in a town recently made accessible by cheaper transport, or itself rapidly expanding because of new factories. Such men are the innovators of new types of intensive farming, planned for the maximum profit from using available resources in new combinations; they provide the links between the growth of export crops, which provided over much of Africa the initial stimulus to economic development and to the growth of towns, and the transformation of local farming to cater for the expanding domestic demand for foods in more varieties and in greater quantities. Such men need to be encouraged and imitated, since they pioneer economic development at their own cost, working out new patterns of farming, the most successful of which can be copied in due course by the less venturesome.

SPECIALISED PLANTATIONS. In many parts of Africa, large farms have been introduced for the cultivation of one crop, usually for export, and usually employing foreign managers and foreign capital; because these were originally concerned with tree crops, such as rubber and oilpalms, they became known as plantations. Growing a single crop simplifies the problems of management, the machinery and implements required, and the routine of work to be learnt by the staff employed. Many of these plantations—for rubber, oilpalm, sugar, groundnuts, sisal and cotton—have been abandoned, since it was found either that the receipts from the output did not cover the high fixed costs, or that diseases became too concentrated and successful; moreover, the occupation of large tracts of land by foreign companies aroused local mistrust. Since independence, African governments have taken over some old plantations, and they are also experimenting with new types of mechanised farming in large units by putting into consolidated blocks the scattered plots of many farmers. Many of these new settlements, such as those in Eastern and Western Nigeria, in Kenya, and in Tanzania, have again shown that field machinery generally tends in Africa to increase costs more than output, though there are some operations—such as clearing bush—which can be carried out more cheaply by machinery than by hand labour, if sufficiently large areas can be tackled in an orderly fashion.

5. The theory of the firm

INTRODUCTION

In studying the economics of commercial farming, we found that the constraint upon further output was set by the level of marginal cost compared with the market price obtained by the farmers for their output. Costs paid by the farmers represent the resources used in production, resources of land, labour and capital which cannot be used for other purposes while engaged in farming; the prices obtained by farmers represent the value placed by the market on the output of those resources used in that particular way. Farmers will try to produce at the lowest possible cost, in order to increase their output and maximise their own incomes; they will try alternative combinations of resources and of outputs according to their abilities and technical knowledge, in order to find those combinations which offer the highest income.

In turning to the study of the economics of industry, we find that these basic principles still apply. The constraints upon production, whether of individual products or of output in total, are set by the level of cost in relation to the price received for the output in the market that is, by the cost of the resources used in relation to the value of their output. At any one time, the resources available for production in any one country or district are in units called businesses or firms, and produce a variety of outputs. Some of the goods and services provided—the use of a road or of a hospital—may not be sold against a price; it may be desirable, for various reasons, to pay the cost of certain services from taxation, but even so, some decision has to be made about the quantity of resources to be devoted to such uses, the cost of providing such services in comparison with the benefits to be derived from them, and with the value of those other services which the same resources might have provided.

COSTS IN THE SHORT PERIOD

For the purpose of this analysis, we continue to assume that we have a static economy which is not undergoing substantial change in the period under consideration; we shall also assume that the business units consist mainly of independent firms, concerned primarily with earning the largest possible incomes—that is, with maximising their *profits*, defined as the difference between total receipts and total costs.

Our firms may be considered to control a certain amount of capital, in the form of buildings and machinery; the manager engages workers

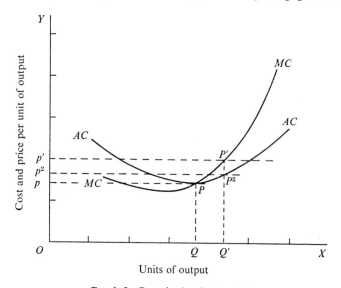

Graph 8. Costs in the short period

of various types, and also buys services such as transport and electricity; raw materials are required which are processed in various ways into a number of products—different kinds of furniture, or steel, or cloth, or bottled drinks. We assume that each firm has two fixed factors which cannot be substantially altered in a short period of time, its capital equipment and its management.

The capital equipment (or *plant*) of each firm has been designed for a certain level of output; the firm can of course operate at less than the designed output, and by working overtime it can produce a little more than the designed output, but there is a maximum output set by the plant. In this short period, therefore, firms will have cost structures resembling that shown in table 9 (p. 54), and in graph 8. Marginal and average costs will at first fall as output is increased towards the designed level of the plant, since the fixed costs are being averaged over a larger output; but once that level of output has been reached, variable costs will tend to rise for further expansion in output. At any given moment, the level of output will be set by the relation between marginal cost and the price received, which we may assume will not be affected by any change in the output of any one firm. If the market price is at P, the output corresponding to this level of marginal cost will be represented by OQ; at price P', the output will be OQ'.

At price P and output OQ, both marginal and average costs for this firm equal price; the firm's total cost is therefore covered by its total receipts, indicated by the rectangle $OpPQ$. If we assume that the manager has included in costs, as he should, his own salary, depreciation of his equipment, and the market rate of interest on his capital, the firm can continue producing indefinitely at this level of output. The interest on capital and the salary of the manager together represent a *normal profit*, defined as a profit just adequate to maintain the business at a constant size, with no inducement either to expand or to contract.

But if the market price rises to Op', the firm can expand its output to OQ', for which the marginal cost equals price. It is then making profits above the normal level, for its average cost for this quantity is represented by Op^2, which is smaller than the average price Op'. Yet the firm will find that it cannot expand output further in the short period, since at any higher level of output marginal cost will exceed the price obtained. However, from these above-normal profits, the firm could extend its factory, or order a larger plant designed to produce more. But such changes take time, and we are at the moment confined to the short period, in which firms cannot appreciably alter their present structure.

But if the price falls below the average cost of such a firm, even at its lowest point, then its future becomes doubtful. It may be able to continue in production for a time, provided the price still covers the variable costs, but the manager may lose part of his salary, or the capital will not earn a market rate of interest, or funds are not available for replacing the equipment when it wears out. But if prices stay below the average cost, and costs cannot be reduced, the firm will eventually go out of business, setting free its buildings and workers for some other use.

In an industry composed of many small firms, a rise in price for the final product will therefore encourage all to expand output, up to the limits set by the existing plant and by the rising marginal costs

3

of the extra production; a fall in price induces a contraction of output, as the firms with the highest marginal costs, or the lowest financial reserves, cut back their production. In both cases therefore, firms react so that the changes in output, taken together, tend to counteract the change in price. In a static society, where demand is fairly stable and cost-reducing innovations are rare, we can imagine for each industry a *position of equilibrium*, in which average costs for most firms roughly equal price, and there is no inducement for either output or price to change. Any small change in such a market sets in force reactions among the firms which tend to restore this position of equilibrium by small changes in output, in price and in costs.

ELASTICITY OF SUPPLY IN THE SHORT PERIOD

Let us assume that we have an industry composed of many small firms, producing a single commodity whose price increases because of an increase in demand. Firms will react to this change by increasing output, according to the pattern of their individual curves of marginal costs. If we add up all these increases in output, we obtain a *supply curve*, showing how the supply of this commodity reacts to a change in its price, as shown in graph 9.

The economists have invented the term *elasticity of supply* to describe the reaction of supply of any commodity to a change in its price. The elasticity of supply is defined as the percentage change in supply divided by the percentage change in price which caused that change in supply, all other things remaining unchanged. In graph 9, the elasticity of the supply curve $S'S'$ is measured (for the part between P and P') by the ratio of $\dfrac{OQ'-OQ}{OQ}$ to $\dfrac{Op'-Op}{Op}$. This particular curve indicates that the supply is highly elastic to a change in price; the increase in supply is proportionately greater than the rise in price which caused that increase in supply. Such a pattern implies that the marginal cost curves of many firms in the industry rise slowly for an increase in output. On the other hand, S^2S^2 shows a low elasticity of supply in response to a change in price; a change in price produces a proportionately smaller change in supply.

We have assumed that, in the short period, changes in output are limited by the equipment and management in existence at the beginning of such a period; within these limits, output can be varied by the employment of more or less of the variable factors, and in real life by minor improvements in management which slightly lower costs, and shift the curves. The length of this theoretical short period will vary considerably between different commodities, according to the technical conditions of their production. Farmers can shift their

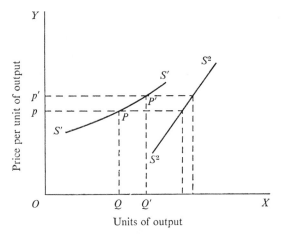

Graph 9. Elasticity of supply. (NOTE. In this graph, supply, measured in units of output along the X axis, is the dependent variable. $S'S'$ and S^2S^2 show two different patterns of the reaction of supply to price, measured on the Y axis. At price P, on the curve $S'S'$, supply will be measured by OQ; at price P', the supply will be measured by OQ'. As long as the pattern of supply remains unchanged, a change in the price offered brings a movement along the supply curve. If there is a change in the pattern of supply, as for instance would follow a technical innovation reducing costs, then we must draw a new supply curve to the right of the old supply curve, indicating that more will now be supplied for any given price, as is shown by the supply curve S^2S^2. As drawn in this graph, S^2S^2 indicates that more will be produced for a given price than under the pattern of supply shown by $S'S'$, and also that the elasticity of supply has fallen; with the new pattern, supply is less elastic to price changes.)

resources from one annual crop to another between two seasons, while there is a time lag of several years between the decision to plant tree crops and the first harvest from them. A textile factory may be able to change quickly from one type of cloth to another, according to the relative profit margins, while it may take several years to plan, order, build and equip a new factory. Where the short period in which output cannot be substantially changed is fairly long, prices can diverge considerably from the level which gives normal profits to the majority of firms. If demand suddenly increases, pushing up prices, there may be several years of abnormally high profits, before the capacity of firms can be extended, or new firms can enter the trade; a low elasticity of supply in the short period can thus lead to prolonged periods of high profits for firms already established.[1] Again, industries vary greatly in their reaction to a fall in demand which results in lower prices.

Farmers can adjust their output of annual crops within a year, but they will continue to harvest tree crops as long as the prices cover the variable cost of this work, even though the resulting incomes are lower than those expected when the trees were planted. A factory producing several commodities may switch from one to the others; but where the capital is highly specialised, firms may have to choose between running at a loss, or closing down some or all of their plant. Here again, a low elasticity of supply to a fall in price may lead to prolonged periods of abnormally low profits, or losses, for those firms remaining in the trade.

In discussing the expansion of agricultural output (p. 48), we noted the costs of acquiring variable inputs might themselves rise under an expanding demand; workers and raw materials might have to be attracted from other occupations by the offer of higher prices or better working conditions. Within the short period, such rising prices for inputs may intensify the constraint upon supply at any given level of prices for the final output. If prices rise, because demand is expanding, output may increase to some extent within the existing capacity, and this rising output itself helps to check the rise in price when the extra output reaches the market. Meanwhile, some firms may be making profits above the normal level, and these profits will eventually encourage such firms or others outside the industry, to expand their capital equipment. On the other hand, if prices fall so that some firms cannot cover their costs, then output will fall or costs be reduced; eventually some firms may go out of business, and the resulting fall in output will restore profits to a normal level for the remaining firms.

COSTS IN THE LONG PERIOD

We can therefore define 'the long period', in distinction from the short period, as that period of time in which the firms composing an industry have adjusted their output to a change in costs or in prices.

---

[1] Such temporary high earnings, caused by a low elasticity of supply of resources, are sometimes called *quasi-rents*.

The U-shaped pattern of marginal and average costs in the short period thus gives us the clue to the manner of change in output in the long period. As long as prices are above average costs, and profits are above normal, management and capital will flow into the industry, taking with them a greater input of labour and raw materials of all kinds; either firms will expand from existing profits or new firms will set up in the business. In this long period, therefore, it is the relationship between average cost and price which determines the level of output; while in the short period, it is the relationship between marginal cost and price which is important. Therefore the elasticity of supply over the long period depends on the movement of average costs in the industry as a whole, in response to changes in prices for the final output.

Graph 10 illustrates the elasticity of supply in the long period for an industry which, at a given point of time, was selling an output OQ', with price p' and average and marginal cost curves in the short period of AC' and MC'. A rise in price for the final output leads to an increase in output set by the pattern of marginal costs MC'; the resulting profits encourage the expansion of the capacity of the industry, and in the long period there may be a new equilibrium between prices, costs and output with price p^2, an output OQ^2 and a new curve of average costs A^2C^2. The two points of equilibrium lying on the curve SS indicate the elasticity of supply in response to the original rise in price, given a certain length of time.

We have here assumed that the long-period supply curve, like the supply curve in the short period, is likely to rise with increase in output; that as the community demands more of a commodity, the price which must be paid for it will tend to rise not only in the short period but also in the long period. This assumption derives from an earlier assumption that we are here analysing small changes in output which occur in a static economy in response to changes in price, all other conditions remaining unchanged. If one industry expands, it must draw larger supplies of various resources, and this in turn implies taking them away from other uses. If farmers grow more cotton because the price of cotton rises relatively to the price of other crops, then it is reasonable to assume that, at some stage in the expansion, the land newly brought into the production of cotton is less suitable for this crop than the land already growing cotton, that as less maize, for instance, is grown in competition with cotton, its price on the local market will also rise, and so on. In the

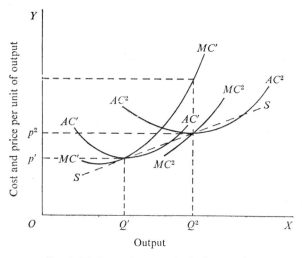

Graph 10. Increasing costs in the long period

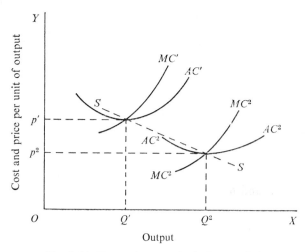

Graph 11. Decreasing costs in the long period

same way, it is reasonable to assume that firms making furniture, for instance, may have to pay higher prices for their labour, their wood and their transport as they all expand output. One farmer, one small firm, may be able to acquire more land, labour and raw materials without much rise in costs; but the expansion of one firm in a small town, or of a whole industry, is likely to cause a rise in the costs of its inputs, if the economy as a whole is fully employed. Even in the long period, therefore, some industries in a static society may be working under increasing costs of the sort shown in graph 10. The economists' distinctions between the short period and the long period, between movement along a supply curve in response to changes in price, and a change in costs which produces a new supply curve, attempt to show the nature of the changes which may be found operating together in the real world. At any one time, the price of a product may be tending to rise because of an increase in demand, while the efforts of firms to expand output lead to a rise in costs for some necessary raw material which pushes up marginal costs, and so keeps down the expansion in output. A fall in price occasioned by a fall in demand may lead to improved management among the firms selling that product, so that costs fall with prices, and again output is little changed. New techniques may reduce costs, increase supply and thus reduce prices.[1] The particular circumstances of each industry at each time determine the method by which a position of equilibrium is again attained, after an initial change; it is the task of the economist to ascertain what are the particular circumstances which in each case will exercise the dominant constraint upon output.

ECONOMIES OF SCALE

We must now relax our assumptions about a static society so far as to allow it to acquire some industrial techniques which provide *economies of scale*, or the economies of large-scale production. This term may be defined as the possible reduction in average costs of output associated with an increase in the scale of production. We have already come across one form of such economies of scale—the use of a tractor to cultivate plots of coffee (p. 56). Here we have a piece of capital which, when combined with the appropriate quantities of other resources such as labour and land, can produce a large quantity at lower cost than hand labour alone. But these economies of scale can only be obtained if other resources are available; if the plots of coffee are small, steep or scattered, if servicing facilities do not exist, if there are no skilled drivers and mechanics, then hand labour may be cheaper than machinery, even on large farms.

---

[1] P. Kilby, 'Competition in the Nigerian Bread Industry', in *Readings*, vol. I.

Economies of scale are usually derived from a piece of capital whose fixed costs of purchase, maintenance and depreciation can be spread over a large output with comparatively low variable costs. We normally think of such output as consisting of a large quantity of a single product such as cement, but a chemical firm produces a wide variety of products from oil, a railway provides transport for people and for commodities of all types, a large dam supplies water for irrigation as well as hydro-electric power for industry and for domestic use.

The economies of scale derive from different sources, not all of which are available in any one case. We may note the following:[1]

1. Indivisible costs associated with a single piece of equipment, or a building. A tractor or blast furnace cannot be split, and is only economic if worked nearly to its full capacity. The costs of setting up a book for printing must be incurred, however many copies are subsequently sold.

2. The costs of increased dimensions of any container increase proportionately to its surface area, but its cubic capacity increases more rapidly than its surface area. A large silo thus costs less, per ton of maize stored within it, than a small silo.

3. If successive processes require heat, then costs are reduced if all the processes are continuous within one plant, so that materials do not need re-heating.

4. The larger the output, the greater the opportunities for specialisation of routine processes, both for men and for equipment.

5. The costs of buying, transporting and storing raw materials may be lower per ton when handled in bulk lots, than in small quantities. It costs less, per ton, to send a truck-load of groundnuts from Kano to Lagos by railway than to send them in separate lots, each of which must be handled, documented and delivered separately. Economies of bulk may also affect the supply of capital and of credit.

6. Large firms are likely to attract superior management at all levels, leaving the small firms in charge of the less efficient managers.

7. Finally, there are some economies of scale which can only be obtained by individual firms expanding their output—*the internal economies of scale*, usually associated with single pieces of equip-

[1] C. Pratten and R. M. Dean, *The Economies of Large-Scale Production in British Industry*, Department of Applied Economics, University of Cambridge, Occasional Papers no. 3 (Cambridge, 1965), pp. 17–18.

ment; but there are also *external economies of scale*, obtained by all firms in an expanding industry, through the falling costs of some input which they all use, such as electric power, transport, skilled men or specialised machinery. Economies of scale which are external to one industry are thus internal to some other industry, such as electricity generation, or the railway, or a training school.

Now, if an industry can secure economies of scale as it expands its output, we can expect that the long-period supply curve will tend to fall over time, not continuously, but in a series of jerks associated with sudden changes in the type of equipment and the average size of firms. In such a case, if average costs fall as output expands in response to a rising demand, what are the constraints upon production? Can we not expect an indefinitely large output of such commodities, as shown in graph 11 (p. 70)?

The answer is no, for three main reasons, which we may take in turn—rising marginal costs in the short period; imperfect competition in the markets; and the expansion of costs with the size of firm.

Looking first at the pattern of costs shown in graphs 10 and 11, we can see that whether costs increase or decrease in the long period, an industry or firm is likely to have rising marginal costs in the short period, even though a larger firm may have lower average costs, when working to capacity, than a smaller firm. The larger firms may be able to drive their smaller competitors out of business, but having adjusted capacity to serve the new market, they will again be subject to rising marginal costs from new plant. Each step in the expansion along the long-period supply curve, involves the risk and uncertainty of setting up a new plant and finding a market for its output; only if demand is expanding rapidly, or there are large economies of scale from a small increase in the size of plant, will a few firms be able to expand rapidly and smoothly with falling average costs. Such combinations of expanding demand and of technical change recently occurred in the industrialised countries with commodities such as cars, radios, refrigerators and the like, known as *consumer durables*. As the techniques of mass production became applied to the output of these commodities, there was fierce competition among firms to obtain the economies of scale, output rapidly expanded, prices fell, the weaker firms went bankrupt, and a few large firms survived. This kind of change, based on economies of mechanisation, also occurred in the bread industry of Nigeria.[1]

[1] Kilby, 'Competition in the Nigerian Bread Industry', in *Readings*, vol. I.

LARGE FIRMS AND IMPERFECT COMPETITION

The second restriction upon output occurs from the effects of imperfect competition between a few large firms serving the same market. We have so far assumed that, in the markets in which farmers and firms sell their output and buy their requirements, there is *perfect competition*. Perfect competition can be defined as a state of business in which no one buyer or seller can influence the market price for the commodity in question by altering the amount which he himself buys or sells at any one time. Later we shall look more closely at the degrees of competition in markets, but here we need only discuss the effects of imperfect competition upon the growth of firms.

Imperfect competition exists in any market when any one buyer or seller can, by altering the amount bought or sold in a unit of time, influence the price at which he buys or sells. Probably most markets have some degree of imperfect competition at one time or another; many markets for industrial products are dominated by a few firms only; a few markets have either a sole seller (*monopoly*) or a sole buyer (*monopsony*).

Let us consider the selling policy of a firm as it grows in an expanding market, under the influence of economies of scale, from one among many sellers to one of two or three. At first, the firm has only to consider how much it can sell at the current market price; it chooses that combination of resources which gives the lowest average cost, and it produces in the short period that amount for which its marginal cost equals price per unit of output. If this price yields above normal profits, then, in the long period, supply will increase and prices tend to fall; but as long as the individual firms are small relatively to the total output of the commodity, each firm need not take into account, in deciding its profitable output, the effect of its own action in adding to total supply.

Let us now assume that there is a technical innovation in this industry, offering considerable economies of scale to larger firms. After a period of fierce competition, a few firms emerge, each supplying an appreciable proportion of the total demand; a change in the output of any one firm will therefore affect the price it receives for all its output, on the pattern shown in Table 10.

In these circumstances, a firm must consider its marginal costs in relation to its *marginal revenue*, defined as the change in total receipts

TABLE 10. *Marginal revenue to a seller*

1 Units offered for sale	2 Price per unit	3 Total receipts	4 Extra revenue per 10 units	5 Marginal revenue
70	11½	805	—	—
80	11	880	75	7·5
90	10½	945	65	6·5
100	10	1,000	55	5·5
110	9	990	−10	−1·0

NOTE. Col. 4 is the increase in total receipts obtained by adding 10 more units of output, and col. 5 is the addition to total receipts obtained by adding 1 more unit of output, col. 4 ÷ 10.

caused by changing the amount offered for sale by one unit. If at some stage an extra unit can only be sold by lowering prices sharply, then the marginal revenue may be low, or even negative; the extra receipts obtained by selling one more unit may be smaller than the loss in revenue from the fall in price over the whole output. In table 10, this point occurs with an output of 100 units; beyond this point, the total receipts fall, and the marginal revenue becomes negative. Clearly, no firm will wish to expand its output to the point where it suffers a fall in total receipts; it will tend to adjust its output to the level for which marginal cost equals marginal revenue, the addition to its total receipts caused by adding that final unit of output.

In a competitive market, the output of each firm is determined by the interaction of marginal cost with price, which in the short period may be above or below average costs for the majority of firms; in the long period, output becomes adjusted to that level for which average cost, in the industry as a whole and for the majority of firms, equals price. With imperfect competition, however, output tends to that level for which marginal cost equals marginal revenue for the successful firms. Since marginal revenue partially reflects the fall in price brought about by an increase in output, it will in some circumstances keep output below the level which it would have attained if firms only considered the interaction of marginal cost and price.

This statement must be qualified, for in fact the average and marginal costs of a few large firms may be lower than the costs of the larger number of smaller firms which existed before the technical innovation which offered economies of scale. We cannot therefore legitimately compare the level of output before and after the change in the structure of the industry, and say that output would be higher if the few large firms operated in conditions of perfect competition which existed when there were many small firms; a technical innovation has changed both the structure of costs and the structure of competition. Nevertheless, imperfect competition may promote the maintenance of abnormally high (or abnormally low) profits for considerable periods of time. As the size of firms increases, in relation to the size of the market for the final product, so it becomes more difficult for new firms to enter the industry and compete with those already established. If there are substantial economies of scale, only a large firm can hope to compete successfully with those already established; but a large addition to total output is likely to lower market prices considerably for all firms and thus lower the expected revenue for the newcomer as well. A large firm also implies the investment of a large amount of capital, with all the risk and uncertainty involved in the face of competition from the existing firms, and the unknown reaction of demand to an increase in total supply. Under imperfect competition, therefore, increases in output and outbreaks of competition based on the economies of large scale production are likely to occur only rarely; established firms are likely to come to agreement among themselves to limit competition in various ways, in order to maintain their profits at what they regard as a satisfactory level.

Such agreements are almost inevitable if the industry is one in which variable costs are only a small part of total costs, and demand is not likely to increase much for a fall in price. Fixed costs in one of the Nigerian cement firms were thought to comprise between 35 and 50 per cent of total costs.[1] On the Nigerian railways in 1964, average costs of transport from the north to the southern ports were calculated at 2·2d. per ton-mile, while the variable cost was reckoned at 0·4d. per ton-mile, since the railway had spare capacity for much of each season.[2] A firm with excess capacity and a low proportion of variable costs is strongly tempted to lower its price in order to attract customers away from its competitors, and thus spread its fixed costs over a larger output. But if all the firms copy

[1] S. Ugoh, 'Nigerian Cement Industry', in *Readings*, I, 104.
[2] Ministry of Trade and Industry, *The Industrial Potentialities of Northern Nigeria* (1964), chap. 42.

the price-cutter, the total effect may be lower prices all round, causing lower profits, but little increase in demand for any one firm.[1] Industries with high costs of capital equipment, such as steel, man-made fibres, oil refineries, cement, have a long history of restricted competition among a few firms.

If such large firms must consider the effect of changes in their own output upon the price received for their sales, so they may also have to consider the effect of changes in their demand upon the costs of their inputs. A family firm making furniture or clothes or running one truck between two market towns can engage another few workers, rent an adjacent piece of land, buy another sewing machine or another truck, without affecting the market prices of these inputs. But a cotton ginnery in a small town trying to engage 100 men at the start of the season, a bottled-drinks factory trying to buy an acre of land to extend, when it is already hemmed in by other buildings, a sugar refinery extending the area of its purchases, may all find that as they increase the scale of their output they must pay more for their inputs. Sometimes the higher cost relates only to the marginal units, in the sense that sugar cane from the more distant farmers can be purchased at the same price though the transport costs to the factory will be higher. But if higher wages have to be paid to attract another 100 men to one factory, the existing workers will certainly claim to be paid the new level of wage, and the costs of expansion will be correspondingly raised. Imperfect competition can be frequently found in the markets for inputs, particularly, of course, where those inputs are the outputs of other firms, supplying a market in conditions of imperfect competition.

Some of these factors which affect the size of firms and the structure of their costs are illustrated in the following feasibility study made in the early 1960s for a desiccated coconut factory in West Africa:[2]

The factory should be planned to produce about 720 tons of desiccated coconut (dry weight) per annum. This size is based largely on the machinery specifications, but probably represents a suitable sized unit for the following reasons:

1. a smaller unit would not be able to bear the overhead cost of a responsible manager (costed at £1,000 per annum);

[1] Decisions about output and price taken by large firms in conditions of highly imperfect competition resemble in some particulars decisions taken in games of chance. See H. A. Simon, 'Theories of Decision-Making in Economics and Behavioural Science', in *Surveys of Economic Theory*, vol. III (London, 1966).
[2] Federal Ministry of Commerce and Industry (Nigeria, 1964).

2. a larger plant might experience difficulties in obtaining an adequate supply of coconuts.

It is suggested that two or three further coir fibre factories, at least one rubberised coir fibre plant, and one or more of the desiccated coconut factories could well be established in one area, under common management. Integration of these related industries is obviously desirable, as the waste product (husk) from the desiccated coconut plants would be used as a raw material for the manufacture of coir fibre. The enlarged scale of the operation would, by increasing turnover, permit a higher level of management to be employed than could be supported by a desiccated coconut industry working in isolation. Other overhead costs, such as transport and staff amenities, could proportionately be reduced, by sharing between the different branches of the coconut-exploiting industry.

		Estimated costs of one desiccated coconut factory	
Capital		£	
Land		?	
Buildings, 10,000 sq. ft		15,000	
Machinery, installed		21,000	
Working capital, 3 months		13,000	
		£49,000	
Fixed costs			
Manager		1,000	
Skilled and permanent workers		3,276	
Depreciation and insurance		5,200	
		£9,476	
Variable costs			
6 million lb coconuts at £5½ per 1,000 delivered		33,000	
Electricity and water		3,800	
Packing materials		1,600	
Casual labour		1,500	
Miscellaneous		1,450	
		£41,550	
Total costs			£51,000
Estimated annual output:	Tons	£	
(300 working days, 2 shifts)	720	64,800	
paring oil	70	4,200	
cake	35	700	
Total receipts		£69,700	

Expected profit of £18,700, or 30% on capital of £49,000.

EXTERNAL ECONOMIES AND COSTS

This feasibility study for a coconut factory reveals several types of economies of scale. In the first place, there is the cost of the manager and the amenities of the staff; secondly, there is the use of the waste product of one factory as a raw material for a second which could therefore be conveniently put alongside the first. Thirdly, a factory set up in a rural area requires a hard road, telephones, electricity and water; the supply of these amenities might cost less, per unit of output, if they were installed to service several factories than if only one had to bear the full cost. Here we have the economies of scale which are internal to these public services, but external to the industries making use of them.

Such external economies have an important influence on the location of new industries and firms. If a new firm opens in the suburb of a large town, it may well find transport, water, electricity and telephones already available; there may be a pool of unemployed men who are accustomed to factory work; there may be garages to service vehicles, schools and hospitals for the staff. A new firm may therefore save some fixed costs in providing these amenities, and it may obtain external economies from sharing in those already established. The advantages of such amenities draw new firms and new industries to the well-established industrial centres, and discourage new industries from settling in rural areas which lack these external economies.

At the same time, 'external costs' may often be inflicted upon existing firms by a further expansion of industry or commerce in an area which is already overcrowded. A firm may decide to open in a town already provided with public services, in order to save the capital cost of installing them for itself in a country area. But if the amenities of the town are already over-loaded, the arrival of another firm may cause electricity supplies to be subject to cuts, water may have to be rationed, there may be greater overcrowding in schools and hospitals and on buses, further delays on telephones and transport, more damage to inadequate roads. The new firm may share in these inconveniences, but the costs of congestion are borne by all the firms and inhabitants, of which the new firm and its workers are only part. Its own costs do not therefore fully include the real costs of the resources used, since the firm only includes the costs which it pays itself.

In the long run, of course, more firms and expanding trade may enable the public amenities to be themselves expanded, in order to keep pace with demand. Yet the experience of all large towns and industrial centres in the last few decades has shown that the costs of congestion, such as the delays in transport, the pollution of air and water, the general overcrowding of streets, buses and catering facilities, may collectively out-balance the external economies obtained by each individual firm or factory or shop when it starts in business or expands in an area already congested and urbanised. However, firms continue to develop in such areas because the external economies to each firm outweigh the costs which each firm bears on its own accounts.

Among the costs of such congestion must be included the costs of such scarce resources as land for building sites. Here we have a case of a resource whose supply, within any one area, is rigidly fixed. There is only so much land within one mile of a port, or a railway station, or the junction of two main roads. There are certain trades whose profitability depends on attracting large numbers of people— department stores, banks, cinemas, cafés, lorry parks and the like. Competition among such buyers for a site within small areas pushes up prices[1] almost indefinitely, gradually raising costs for all who either buy land of this sort, or who rent office space in town centres.

Such rising prices, whether for purchase or for leasing, have of course a useful function. Given that the area of land in a certain situation is limited, competition transfers the scarce resource to those buyers who can pay the highest price, because of the nature of their business, or the efficiency of their management, or of their willingness to build skyscrapers and blocks of flats, and thus to economise in land itself. From the point of view of production as a whole, high prices for land in such situations are of importance in so far as they do secure the most profitable use of a scarce resource, since the supply of land is itself not affected by the price paid for it. But the control of such scarce resources can lead at times to incomes which have little connection with useful output; and growing congestion intensifies the rising costs of acquiring land and buildings for many firms.

Many external economies and costs are thus inadequately reflected in the accounts of small firms which individually have only a

---

[1] Prices for land and buildings may be either purchase prices for the ownership of the property, or annual payments (*rent*) for the use of the property for a specified period of time. See also graph 22, p. 153.

small effect upon their environment. The larger the firm, in relation to the industry and to the town of which it is a part, the larger the proportion of such costs and economies which are reflected in its own accounts, and which influence the decisions of its managers about output and prices. Thus the final constraint to the output of large firms is set partly by the market for the output, since increases in output bring about falling prices, partly by rising costs for scarce resources, and partly by the limitations of management, dealing with ever more complex organisations.

THE COMBINATION OF INPUTS

We have so far assumed that firms can only alter their costs by changing the scale of their output. This of course is far from true, since there are often several methods of producing a given level of output, and the choice between them depends on the cost and efficiency of the resources available in different circumstances. We must now look more closely at the problems of combining resources to obtain a given level of output at lowest cost.

We have already met the basic principle, in discussing the combination of resources in farming. No farmer, or manager of a firm, will employ resources unless the cost is less than the probable receipts obtained from the resulting output. If the cost of employing a man is 60s. a week, the manager must expect extra sales of at least this amount, before he engages the man. Similarly, if a farmer can borrow 100s. for a year at 10 per cent, an investment is only worth while if he can reasonably expect to earn at least 110s. from his investment; to allow for risk and uncertainty, there should be a reasonable expectation of a return considerably greater than this. The amount of each resource employed therefore depends upon its *marginal productivity* in particular uses, in relation to its marginal revenue. The marginal productivity of a resource is defined as the change in output caused by employing one unit more or less; marginal revenue has already been defined[1] as the change in receipts brought about by a change of one unit in output. The three factors taken into account here are therefore the cost of one unit of each resource, its output when employed in certain combinations, and the value of that output in the market. A change in any one of these three factors for any resource may alter the amount of it employed in any one use.

[1] See p. 74–75.

As we noted earlier, resources are both competitive and complementary to each other in most uses. In the short period, we assume that the capital structure of a firm is fixed, and that the combination of resources is varied only by changing the inputs of labour and raw materials and current services. But in the long period, factories can be equipped with new and larger plants, and new factories built, and it is when such decisions are taken that the combination of resources is determined, within narrow limits, for some future period of time. Let us consider, for instance, the effects of a rise in wages upon the employment of labour in combination with other resources.

In the first place, industries employ differing proportions of the main resources, and so they will be affected to differing degrees by a rise in the price of any one resource. Consider for example the comparative employment of capital and labour in certain industries in Nigeria and in the United Kingdom, as shown in tables 11 and 12.

Capital-intensive industries, such as hydro-electric power, will be less affected by a rise in wages paid to the operating staff than industries using little machinery or credit, but a quantity of labour. If wages account for half the total costs of one industry and for three-quarters of the total costs of another industry, a rise of 10 per cent in wages will increase costs by 5 per cent in the first but by $7\frac{1}{2}$ per cent in the second.

Secondly, industries vary in the degree to which resources can be substituted for each other, according to the production functions available at the time. Labour-saving machinery which formerly was not economic may become so with a certain rise in wages. After such a change has been made, a firm may find itself with fewer men at the higher wage, with more machinery and a higher proportion of machinery costs; its total costs may be only slightly higher than those which existed before the change in wage rates, and rather lower than those which would have existed if the same number of men had been employed at the higher wage. It will then find a new balance between marginal cost and marginal revenue with a slightly higher cost, a slightly lower output, and fewer men employed.

Thirdly, a rise in costs which threatens a firm or farmer with loss of income may cause an improvement in management to enable each man to increase his output sufficiently to earn the higher wage. Men may be more thoroughly trained in their work, the flow of materials may be improved so that there are fewer delays, the farmer may spend more time on his farm and less at the market. As a

TABLE 11. *Estimated capital requirements per worker in Nigeria* (At 1962 prices)

	Annual output	Capital per worker £
Textiles	32 m.sq. yards	2,000
Jute estate and factory for bag-making	4 m. bags	3,000
Asbestos-cement roofing sheets	?	5,000
Flour mill	25,000 tons	6,000
Fibre board mill	12,500 tons	10,000
Fruit canning	?	300
Leather goods	30,000 cases	400
Sugar estate and mill	?	2,000

NOTE. Ministry of Trade and Industry, *The Industrial Potentialities of Northern Nigeria* (1964); the estimate for sugar is taken from *West Africa* (23 Dec. 1967), p. 1649, where the initial capital of the Nigerian Sugar Co. at Bacita was given as £6 m. and employment in 1967 as 3,000 persons.

TABLE 12. *Average net assets per worker in British nationalised industries, 1966–7*

	£
Coal industry	1,600
Post Office	3,700
British European Airways	5,000
British Railways	5,350
Gas industry	7,800
British Transport docks	8,600
Electricity—England and Wales	17,000
Hydro-electricity—Scotland	64,500

NOTE. Net assets taken as capital at cost less amounts written off. *National Industries*, Cmnd. 3437, (London, 1967), p. 17.

result, productivity may rise sufficiently to keep pace with the rise in wages, so that the cost of labour per unit of output does not appreciably change. A claim for a rise in wages is often supported by this argument, of its effect in improving management and productivity per man, which thus pays for the higher wage. This sequence undoubtedly does occur in some situations, but improved management takes time and is not always forthcoming, while a sharp rise in the costs of employing labour may equally lead to substitution of machinery for men, and the loss of employment for some of the labour force.

Fourthly, the effect of a rise in costs is also influenced by the market for the final product—by the extent to which demand may fall for a rise in price. At one extreme, a rise in wage rates in government services may cause, not a fall in employment, but a rise in taxes, so that the same volume of services is provided as before but taxpayers have less to spend on other things. Firms selling direct to the government—the construction industry, suppliers of telephones and office equipment—may also obtain a corresponding rise in the prices of the things they sell. Other firms may find that demand falls sharply for a small rise in price, so that a rise in wages must either be offset by substitution of labour by cheaper resources, or output must be cut back. Generally speaking, a rise in the price of any resource will normally lead to a fall in its employment for two reasons—the rise in costs will cause a fall in the final output, the *output effect*, and other resources will gradually be substituted for the dearer one, the *substitution effect*. The output effect is likely to take place immediately, while the substitution effect takes time to develop, and may not show its full effect until new plant must be ordered based on the new level of costs.

Lowest-cost combinations of resources thus depend on the relative marginal productivities and marginal costs of the different resources used in production. There are therefore considerable dangers in transferring particular combinations from one country to another, where productivities and costs may vary. The costs of installing, maintaining and operating machinery are generally higher in Africa than in many European countries, for instance, so that the lowest-cost combinations may also differ between the two continents[1]. Such international comparisons of costs are not easy, since the straight comparison of wage rates, for instance, tells nothing about the output per man, and therefore the labour cost per unit of output, against the local prices for the final output. High wages can be accompanied by low costs, if productivity is high, and low wages can be combined with high labour costs, if the men are inefficiently employed. Thus importing the newest techniques from some other country, with differing relative costs for its resources, is no guarantee of efficient low-cost production in another part of the world.

---

[1] See International Labour Office, 'Economic Development, Employment and Public Works in African Countries', in *Readings*, vol. II.

INVESTMENT AND RETURNS

The investment of capital always involves risks and uncertainties. The feasibility study given on pp. 77–8 shows that the expected profits would be wiped out if the required quantity of coconuts cost £8 per 1,000 instead of £5½, or if the price of the product fell from the expected £90 per ton to a little under £70. The study gave no indication of the probability of such changes occurring in costs and in prices, nor did it make allowance for the inevitable delay between incurring the first cost and the arrival of receipts which exceed the variable costs and thus allow for some return on the capital investment.

Economists and accountants have devised various methods of comparing investments with returns accruing over different periods of time and with differing degrees of uncertainty. In the first place, it is customary to calculate a *rate of interest*[1] upon the costs incurred until the receipts accrue, on the assumption that the investor (the person making the investment) could have lent the money to some borrower who would have paid the market rate of interest. Thus if the market rate of interest is 10 per cent, and there is a delay of one year between making the investment and obtaining the expected return, then the costs should be increased by 10 per cent; a delay of five years would increase the estimated cost of the investment by more than 60 per cent. The same principle may be applied, but in reverse, to the expected receipts, assuming that the present value of any sum of money which will not be received until one or more years in the future should be reduced by the rate of interest each year, or *discounted* at the market rate of interest (see Appendix 2). Such a discount makes some allowance for the uncertainty which attends all expectations about future income, an uncertainty which increases with the length of time involved.

In addition, any study of the comparative benefits to be expected from different investments should properly include some estimate of the degree of uncertainty over the costs and the probable receipts. Looking at past statistics, it might be possible to deduce, to take an

---

[1] Interest is the sum paid for the loan of a specified value for a specified time. The rate of interest normally assumes that the loan was of 100 units of currency for one year. A rate of interest of 10 per cent thus implies that the borrower will return 110 units at the end of a year for each 100 units borrowed; if the loan was for six months, the interest would be 5 units, representing a rate of interest of 10 per cent for half a year.

imaginary example, that the price of desiccated coconut was above £70 per ton in fifteen years out of the last twenty years, and above £100 per ton in two of those years; a further study would be needed to ascertain whether the market conditions that ruled in the previous twenty years would be likely to continue in the near future, or whether some large change could reasonably be expected, either because demand was increasing faster than supply, or because supply from other areas was already increasing faster than demand.

The probability of costs not exceeding certain levels may be even more difficult to estimate. A small factory coming into a rural area might be able to obtain its supplies both of coconuts and of un-skilled labour without much effect upon the current prices paid for these resources. But if other factories did develop in the same area, then competition might well push up the level of wages. Some farmers might find it more profitable to grow vegetables and other foods for the new market provided by the factory workers than to supply coconuts to the factory; the opportunity costs of the necessary supply of coconuts might thus be raised, and the factory would have to pay a higher price to maintain full production. The larger the investment in relation to its environment, the more difficult it becomes to estimate its long-term effect upon local costs, incomes and prices, and hence the greater the degree of uncertainty.

APPENDIX 1: LOWEST-COST COMBINATIONS OF RESOURCES

Graph 12 shows a geometric solution to the problem of obtaining the lowest-cost combination of two resources to secure a given output of one product. Assume that each resource (here capital measured on the vertical axis and labour on the horizontal axis) can be divided into small identical units and that all combinations of resources are possible. The curve AA is drawn to represent all combinations of these two resources which give the same output, measured by the rectangle drawn from any point on AA by lines at right angles to the axes. AA is known as an isoquant—a line showing the same quantity. The line PP represents the relative prices of the two resources, here indicating that 3 units of capital cost the same as $1\frac{1}{2}$ units of labour. Then the point C, where the line PP touches (or is tangential to) the curve AA, represents the lowest-cost combinations of resources for the output AA. The larger isoquant $A'A'$, with the same relative prices PP, shows the lowest-cost combination at M'.

If the price of labour falls relatively to the price of capital, indicated by the line P^2P^2, then the lowest-cost combination changes to C^2 and M^2, indicating the use of more labour and less capital for the same output. This graph therefore only shows the substitution effect of a change in relative prices; it ignores the output effect of an immediate change in costs.

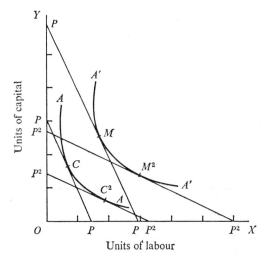

Graph 12. Lowest-cost combinations of two resources

APPENDIX 2: APPRAISAL OF INVESTMENT BY DISCOUNTED CASH FLOWS

Assume that two investments, each costing £1,000, can be made; it is required to estimate the relative profitability. Assume further that the expected future costs and future incomes for each of the next ten years will be as in table 13, p. 88, and that the rate of discount is taken at 15 per cent—£100 accruing one year from now is discounted at 15 per cent and its present worth is therefore only £87 ($\frac{100}{115} \times 100$); £100 deferred for two years is therefore worth $\frac{87}{115} \times 100$ = £75·6 (D.C.F. stands for discounted cash flow).

Allowing for discount at 15 per cent per year, both these projects would yield a positive return on the expenditure, but because the high yields occur soonest in project *B*, project *B* has a higher return than project *A* within ten years. Summing the expected costs and incomes without D.C.F. would not distinguish between them.

With any rate of interest at or above 10, discounted cash flows accruing after year 10 have little value, as is shown in the table 14, p. 88, taken from National Economic Development Council, *Investment Appraisal* (H.M.S.O., London, 1967).

TABLE 13. *Discounted cash flows*

	Investment A				Investment B			
Year	Out flows	Income	Net flow	D.C.F.	Out flows	Income	Net flow	D.C.F.
0	500	—	−500	−500	1,000	—	−1,000	−1,000
1	500	—	−500	−500	25	300	270	234
2	50	200	150	113	25	350	325	246
3	50	250	200	132	50	400	350	230
4	50	300	250	143	50	400	350	200
5	50	350	300	150	50	400	350	174
6	50	400	350	151	50	400	350	151
7	60	400	340	128	60	400	340	128
8	60	400	340	111	60	250	190	54
9	75	400	325	92	75	125	150	14
10	75	400	325	80	75	75	—	—
	1,520	3,100	1,580	+100	1,520	3,100	1,580	+431

TABLE 14. *Present value of £1 deferred one to ten years*

Rate of discount ...	5	7	10	12	15
Year 1	0·952	0·935	0·909	0·893	0·870
2	907	873	826	797	756
3	864	816	751	712	658
4	823	763	683	636	572
5	784	713	621	567	497
6	746	666	564	507	432
7	711	623	513	452	376
8	677	582	467	404	327
9	645	544	424	361	284
10	614	508	386	322	247

6. The market for labour

INTRODUCTION

The majority of African families derive their living from the crops they grow on their land, supplemented by occasional paid work, by trading, or by the sale of some handicraft. Full-time paid workers are relatively few, and many of these may spend most of their lives on family farms. The resource which economists call labour consists of all persons gainfully employed, and thus includes wage-earners, members of farm families, the traders and craftsmen found in villages and towns. The market for labour is of particular importance for two reasons. Firstly, the poverty or wealth of a country depends greatly on the efficient use of the available labour, in conjunction with the existing natural resources. In the second place, the patterns of income within a community are partly determined by the market for labour, offering prices in terms of incomes, of goods and services, and of status. Here we study the market for labour primarily as a device for securing the flow of labour into those combinations of resources where it adds most to the national output of goods and services, and thus earns the highest income; in this book, we must exclude from consideration many non-monetary aspects of the market for labour which are yet so closely connected with human happiness.

THE STRUCTURE OF THE MARKET FOR LABOUR

The market for human energy and skills in Africa differs in several respects from the markets in industrialised countries.[1] In the first place, the number of workers in paid employment is a small proportion of those gainfully employed, most of whom work on farms. In a sense, therefore, the number of people seeking paid employment

[1] W. Elkan, 'An African Labour Force', and T. Yesufu, 'The Shortage of Skilled Labour', in *Readings*, vol. I; K. C. Doctor and H. Gallis, 'Size and Characteristics of Wage Employment in Africa: Some Statistical Estimates', *International Labour Review*, XCIII (1966), 149–73; K. Taira, 'Wage Differentials in Developing Countries': A Survey of Findings', *International Labour Review*, XCIII (1966), 281–301.

is capable of a large expansion in short periods, not merely from the pools of unemployed and half-employed to be found in most towns, but also from persons still engaged in the cultivation of crops for themselves and their families.

Secondly, much of this resource called labour has no experience of working with machinery or of the routine of a factory whose capital equipment needs to be regularly employed in order to yield profits. The conditions of working in a large factory or office are different from the seasonal variations in effort and leisure found in agriculture, and from the informal discipline of the family group. From the point of view of the manager of a large factory, workers taken straight from rural districts have to be trained in punctuality, regularity of work, observance of regulations for safety, and so on, in addition to the training in the actual work to be done. Further, many unskilled workers are illiterate, so that there are peculiar problems in training them and in explaining day-to-day changes in routines.

Thirdly, recent economic development has expanded the number of jobs demanding specialised skills faster than the facilities for providing them. Any large organisation requires a variety of managers at all levels, from the director down to the foremen in charge of small groups of workers engaged on particular jobs; each machine requires maintenance and repairs, as well as operation; buying, selling and the payment of wages require scrupulous honesty in the handling of large sums of money and the keeping of detailed accounts. The scarcity of such skills and the current high costs of those who possess them reduce the chance of securing economies of scale from large firms in Africa, and favour the family businesses, where management and finance can be controlled by one or two people.

Fourthly, the professionally trained scientists, managers, university staff, engineers and accountants are still drawn partly from foreign countries, because of the shortage of Africans with similar qualifications. Consequently, the salaries of such posts (and supplementary benefits such as pensions, housing and leave) are influenced by the standards of the wealthy industrialised countries. As a result, there is an exceptionally wide spread in African countries between the earnings of professional workers and unskilled workers. A university assistant lecturer in Britain or America at the start of his career may earn less than a skilled mechanic of the same age working in a factory; a professor in charge of a large faculty may earn four or five times as much as a moderately skilled worker (with income tax considerably reducing the initial disparity), and considerably less than successful farmers running large farms. In contrast, professional salaries in African countries may be fifty or a hundred times the average earnings of farm families. The structure of government, of education, of social services and of the engineering trades is thus more expensive in Africa than in most industrialised countries, relatively to the majority of taxpayers.

MOTIVES AND WORK

The basic purpose of work is to provide food and shelter for oneself and one's family, but there has been much argument over the motives which lead people to work with differing degrees of intensity. It may be that a person wants only the basic minimum of food, clothing and shelter, and that once he has these, he prefers leisure to further effort. In such cases, the higher the rate of pay per unit of work, or per unit of time, the fewer will be the days or weeks that will be devoted to work, above a certain minimum amount. It has often been stated that many African workers for wages (and also peasant farmers) have supply curves of work of this pattern, usually described as *backward-sloping supply curves* and illustrated in graph 13.

It has commonly been supposed that such workers wish to earn a particular sum of money, in order to pay their taxes, buy a bicycle or accumulate a bride-price; once they have achieved their target, they will probably return to their villages. Undoubtedly, such *target workers* do exist in all communities; there are always some people who prefer few material possessions and much leisure to hard work and a multitude of belongings.[1] And the very poor will work very hard if the alternative is starvation, and may reasonably consider that some rise in income per unit of effort justifies a reduction in the output of effort. But for people above the level of immediate hunger, it is reasonable to expect that there is a customary amount of effort given in return for the customary wage for unskilled labour, and that a higher rate of pay may lead some workers to assume more responsibility and to work harder, up to a certain

[1] E. J. Berg, 'Backward-Sloping Labour Supply Functions in Dual Economies—The Africa Case', *Quarterly Journal of Economics*, vol. LXXV (1961).

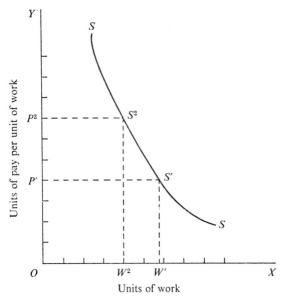

Graph 13. Backward-sloping supply curve of work

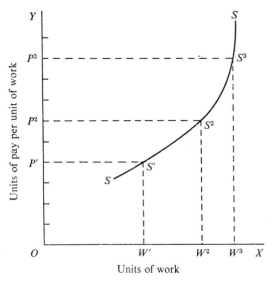

Graph 14. Ordinary supply curve

point where no extra effort will be offered by the existing employees for a further rise in pay. Further, if one firm or farm increases the rate of pay offered, there may well be resulting increases in the number of workers offering effort to that firm. For any individual employer, or for one industry, we can therefore normally expect the supply of labour to follow the pattern shown in graph 14.

THEORY OF WAGES

If we could assume that all persons seeking employment, all the units of labour, were both mobile and identical, we should expect that labour would be distributed among the various uses so that it secured equal marginal returns in each major use. Men would take paid employment if by so doing they could earn more than they could obtain by working on the family farms; they would move between farms, factories and shops seeking the highest level of earnings. There would then be a rough equality of incomes, based on equal marginal productivity of the resource labour in all its uses.

Even in this world of identical and mobile units of labour, we must allow for some non-monetary factors in this concept of income. Earnings might be higher in mines than in similar occupations as compensation for the dangers and discomforts of working underground in conditions of heat and dust. Some firms may pay salaries during short periods of sickness and pensions after retirement, while other firms may offer higher direct earnings and no such benefits. Some farmers may offer food as well as a wage to men working for them, or may allow seasonal workers to grow a patch of cotton or of food crops on their land, in addition to a cash wage. Grown sons working on the family farm may expect to draw on their father for periodical benefits, which they would not get if they worked by themselves in a town. And workers induced to work in towns by the lure of higher earnings may find themselves poorer than at home, partly because they must buy food out of their earnings, partly because rents must be paid for accommodation, and partly because of periods of unemployment between spells of work. In comparing earnings between occupations, some allowances must be made for these varying ingredients in the concept of 'income'.

We know, of course, that labour is not perfectly mobile between regions and between occupations, and its units are not identical. Nevertheless, people do move between employments and between regions sufficiently to exert a continuing pressure towards less inequality of earnings. Thus the rich farming areas of Uganda, growing cotton, coffee, bananas and vegetables, import workers from the northern and eastern districts where rainfall is lower and farming less productive. The cocoa-growing regions of West Africa draw workers from the drier savannah regions to the north. Here we see the geographical mobility of labour flowing into those areas with higher incomes based on higher marginal productivities.

Let us suppose that there is some interruption to such movement between different regions, so that fewer people are available for employment in the more fertile areas. In the regions of emigration, there will therefore be more people working, with a lower marginal productivity and lower incomes than they could have obtained elsewhere; they will therefore be poorer because of the barrier to mobility. Moreover, if diminishing returns already exist to the input of labour in their own district, the pressure of more people working on the farms may reduce the average output per person, so that most families may be worse off than before. Here we have an example of indirect damage inflicted on persons not directly concerned with a particular balance of cost and benefit.

In the receiving area, a more complex situation may develop. Here we may suppose that the farmers who formerly employed the migrants now have fewer people working for them; there will therefore be a greater demand for those already in the area, and the average level of wages paid to them may rise to equal the higher marginal productivity of the smaller number. These workers will therefore benefit from the barrier to migration. But the rise in costs will mean that less will be produced for market, so that buyers of food and other crops find that prices rise, until price and marginal cost again balance at a higher level of prices. Although the incomes of townspeople have not changed, these incomes will now buy less food because of the rise in prices; the reduction in the number of workers will thus cause a net loss to the buyers of food and other agricultural products in the area where they used to work. In between the two groups of gainers and losers come the farmers, who may either gain or lose from the smaller output with higher costs and higher prices, but who probably will have slightly lower incomes as a group.

This simplified analysis of the effects of restricting geographical mobility reveals that the group likely to gain is that of the competitors in the local market—the people seeking paid employment who find fewer competitors and therefore higher wages for their services. A restriction in the number of competitors benefits those who sell the commodity in question, whether the commodity be cotton or labour; the remaining sellers obtain a larger volume of demand for their product, and therefore will probably obtain higher prices, while the rise in the costs of the final product is likely to have only a small effect on their purchasing power. Secondly, the people who are made poorer are firstly, the would-be migrants who may have no political power in the area to which they wish to move; secondly, the large group of purchasers of the final products who may hardly notice the rise in prices, if this occurs gradually.

This distribution of the benefits and the costs of limited mobility explains why almost all the richer countries, and the richer areas within a country, discourage the immigration of people from poorer areas. Leaving aside the questions of political power and social cohesion of multi-racial countries, the immigration of unskilled workers can be regarded as tending to reduce the earnings of similar workers in the richer countries, regarded as relatively poor in comparison with other taxpayers in their own country. International barriers to the free movement of labour are only the most obvious example of the barriers which most groups of people try to erect against their competitors, in order to improve their own incomes.

MARGINAL PRODUCTIVITY AND WAGES

In chapter 3, we noted that varying inputs of labour, with fixed quantities of some other resource, yield varying returns; the marginal output of labour varied with the number of units employed in such combinations, as well as with the technical conditions controlling the production functions. The number of units of labour employed was determined by the relationship between marginal cost and the value of the marginal output, or the marginal revenue. Marginal revenue is thus composed of two elements—change in the output and the change in the price obtained for that output in the market. For the purpose of this section, we may assume that there is a constant price for such output, so that changes in marginal productivity reflect only changes in output, not changes in its price.

Apart from exceptional cases where the fixed resource is not fully employed, we can generally expect that marginal productivity of

labour will fall with increases in the amount used in combination
with fixed quantities of other resources; in the short period, the
curve of marginal productivity of labour for each firm will normally
slope down from left to right as the curve *MP* in graph 15.

If the supply of labour to this firm is measured by *OQ*, then the
marginal productivity for that supply is shown by the point *W*,

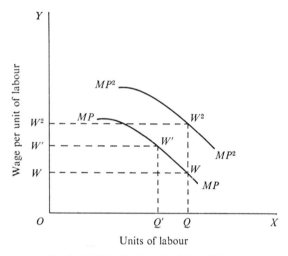

Graph 15. Marginal productivity of labour

indicating the maximum wage appropriate to that supply. If the
supply of labour then falls to *OQ′*, there will be a rise in the marginal
productivity to *OW′*. Alternatively, if a minimum wage is imposed
equal to *OW′* when the current wage in this firm equals *OW*, then
there will be a fall in the volume of employment from *OQ* to *OQ′*;
no firm will continue for long to pay a wage in excess of the marginal
productivity of its supply of labour. Nevertheless, marginal productivity may be higher than the wage paid, for various reasons.

First, there may be costs incurred in employing people in addition
to the wage paid in money—food supplied, insurance against sickness and unemployment, pensions on retirement, housing, leaves,
medical services, canteens and the like. These costs must be included
in the earnings of the workers enjoying such benefits. Secondly,
there may be 'exploitation' in the strict sense, when an employer is
paying less than the marginal productivity of his workers, because
of their ignorance or weak bargaining power; in such a case, an

employer with a number of workers equivalent to OQ' in graph 15 only pays a wage equal, say, to OW.

Thirdly, there is often a certain vagueness about the marginal productivity attributed to any one unit of resources in combination with others, such as a group of unskilled men working under a supervisor, or a farm tractor and its driver. The marginal productivity of a group depends very largely on its supervisor, and a driver without his tractor is reduced to hand labour. These are joint costs which employers must incur together; the amount they must pay for each unit of the combination will be determined roughly by the market price for each component, but the actual price paid will be determined by individual bargaining within the limits set by the marginal productivity and the current profits of the employer. It is even less easy to assign a marginal productivity to small groups of office workers or minor administrators in a large business or government department, even though some value may be given to the services provided by the whole.

Fourthly, individuals vary greatly in skill, strength and industry, and a uniform wage may both over-pay the weaker workers and under-pay the stronger, in proportion to their output. This variation between individuals is one reason for the variety in methods of payment which complicate comparisons of earnings between occupations and between individuals. Employers may pay *time-rates* offering a fixed sum for each hour, day or week of a stated number of hours. The employer then takes the responsibility for seeing that the workers are properly occupied during the stated hours, and may have to provide close supervision to ensure that the allotted tasks are carried out. In industrialised countries, time rates are often combined with higher rates for time worked in excess of the agreed hours, or worked at night or on Sundays; earnings of individuals may therefore vary greatly, according to the number of hours worked, or the incidence of night shifts and Sunday duty when a process has to be continuous. Alternatively, workers may be paid *piece-rates*, an agreed sum for each unit of output. Farmers may thus pay workers for each basket of cotton picked, or for each plot weeded; the workers can then take their own time about the job, and the fast workers may either earn more, or enjoy more leisure, than the slow workers. Here again, close supervision may be necessary to see that the work is done properly, since the workers have an obvious advantage in speed, rather than accuracy; their output may also be affected by

4

interruptions in the supply of raw materials or tools whose provision is properly part of the employers' responsibility. Payment by piece-rates probably leads to more disputes between workers and between employers and workers than time-rates, but it does offer scope for quick experienced workers to earn substantially more than the unskilled or those with little interest in the job; piece-rates may therefore enable employers to match marginal productivity to earnings more closely than under time rates.

Fifthly, a peculiar situation may develop in industries which are monopolies, or working in conditions of highly imperfect competition, and which are enjoying above-normal profits as a result.[1] Some of these profits may be passed on to the workers, through the bargaining of their trade unions, so that they obtain higher wages than they could earn in similar occupations in other industries. The value of the marginal productivity is then inflated by the existence of monopoly profits, and marginal costs rise to correspond. Such a situation is shown in graph 15, where a wage OW^2 might be paid from monopoly profits which have raised the curve of marginal productivity from MP to MP^2. Indeed, one of the dangers of monopoly or of highly imperfect competition is this inflation of costs above a competitive level through the sharing of excessive profits throughout the industry; trade unions then become supporters of monopolies on behalf of their own members.

Sixthly, the general level of productivity is itself conditioned by the whole social and economic structure, of which monopolies are only one part. In most African countries, there is a sufficient flow of labour between a variety of unskilled occupations to equalise marginal productivity over this wide field of employment, and the general level of productivity of unskilled labour is therefore set by the low level of output and of earnings obtained in the ordinary family farms worked by hand tools. Given this dominant influence, differences in earnings between different occupations can often be explained by the relative scarcity of different skills, by the length of training required, by other barriers, natural or artificial, which restrict the flow of persons between occupations and between regions, and by the persistence of differentials which are sanctioned by custom, even when they no longer correspond to current events. But we are still faced with the established facts of high productivity and high incomes in the United States, for instance, compared with

[1] See Appendix, p. 104.

most European countries, and with still lower productivity in most African countries. Here, we are dealing with the fundamental problems of macro-economics, arising from the relative scarcity of capital, of education, of business enterprise, of natural resources, scarcities which maintain a low level of productivity right through the economic structure of some countries, including agriculture, industry, commerce and the public services.

TRADE UNIONS AND WAGES

Within these differing environments, however, it still remains true that relative scarcities of labour can exert an appreciable influence upon relative wages within one country. And, as we noted above, it is always in the interest of small groups of workers to restrict the numbers of their competitors, so as to force up their own earnings as far as possible, and this is the primary purpose of *trade unions*.

In Britain, a trade union may represent all the workers in one factory in their bargaining with the management, the *company union*. More usually, however, unions represent workers with one particular skill employed either in one industry, such as engine drivers employed on railways, or in many industries, such as electricians, carpenters, laboratory technicians, engineering draughtsmen, statisticians and other professional workers. These are the craft unions and professional unions. There are also the *general unions*, which cater for the unskilled workers employed in large numbers in building, transport, the docks, the public services and in distribution.

The extent to which trade unions can raise the level of the wages of their members depends upon a number of factors, some affecting supply, some affecting the demand. On the side of supply, there may, in the first place, be a natural scarcity of certain skills in relation to the demand for them. This has occurred in all African countries, where the importation of foreign technology and administration created a demand for a variety of technical and managerial skills, before the local educational systems had been organised to provide them. Once high wages and salaries have been established by a natural scarcity, the trade unions commonly resist any reduction, either absolutely or in relation to other wages which formerly were much lower. Differentials in earnings, once established for reasons of history, often become unjustified by subsequent changes in demand

and in supply, but they are often maintained by the pressure of the trade unions of the higher paid workers concerned.

Where natural scarcity is beginning to give way, the craft unions may try to create artificial barriers to the supply of competing persons. They may restrict the number of apprentices or learners that employers may take; or press for restrictions upon the immigration of foreigners with such skills; or try to restrict employment to members, by threatening to strike if non-members are employed; or insist that certain jobs can only be done by members and must not be done by non-members. Many disputes in Britain take place over such demarcation lines between craft unions, each trying to keep for its own members particular types of work, a process made more difficult by the constant changes in technology. In some African countries, certain occupations have come to be dominated by particular tribes, who try to exclude from that occupation all except their own group; the ordinary processes of economic competition are then aggravated by ill-feeling between groups of different ethnic origin.[1]

On the side of demand, we must note the special circumstances which limit the power of any trade union to raise the wages of its own members. The main restraint is, of course, the fear of unemployment which might result from a sudden rise in wages in a particular trade or occupation. The conditions in which the demand for a particular type of labour will not fall appreciably after a rise in wages may be listed as follows:

1. The cost of the wages concerned is a small part of the total costs of the final product. Wages can therefore be raised more easily in industries employing large quantities of capital than in occupations such as farming, where wages form a high proportion of the total costs paid in money.

2. The work concerned cannot easily be carried out by other people, or by further mechanisation; there are few possibilities of substituting cheaper resources for the resource made more costly. One of the difficulties of the trade unions representing unskilled workers is the presence of alternative workers who might easily fill the place of workers called out on strike, while there is less possibility of such substitution in the case of workers in the craft unions.

3. A firm which sells its product in a market with imperfect competition, or is a monopolist, may be induced to share its monopoly

---

[1] A. Cohen, 'The Politics of the Kola Trade', in *Readings*, vol. I.

profits by pressure from its workers, with little effect on the volume of employment.

4. If there is competition between firms in the market for the final product, a trade union which has members in all firms may be able to raise wages by bargaining with the industry as a whole, rather than by bargaining with individual firms. In Britain, trade unions have tended to develop national federations for this reason, so that bargaining over wages could take place throughout one industry, such as mining, or cotton, or building; firms were thus protected from competing in their final market with a burden of higher costs not inflicted on their competitors.

5. Demand for the final product does not fall appreciably for a rise in prices induced by a rise in wages, so that the cost of higher wages does not result in unemployment caused by falling output.

6. (*a*) Higher wages lead quickly to higher productivity of the workers, either because they can afford a better diet, or because the threat of higher costs compels the managers to organise the workers more efficiently; and (*b*) the higher output from the existing workers can be absorbed by the market without a fall in prices and profits which would cause unemployment.

For any individual trade union trying to raise wages for its members, we can summarise these conditions under the headings first of possible substitution between the competing resources, and secondly of changes in output for the final market, which influence the total volume of employment at one time.

TRADE UNIONS IN AFRICA[1]

In Europe and America, trade unions were generally formed by workers to counteract the bargaining power of the employers, and were regarded with suspicion and hostility by employers and governments alike. It was only in the present century that the government in Britain began to encourage the formation of trade unions among the lower paid workers, and to institute trade boards, or committees of appointed people, to undertake for such trades the functions of trade unions. The two main reasons for this action were, firstly, the existence of widely varying wage rates because of the ignorance and

[1] T. M. Yesufu, *Introduction to Industrial Relations in Nigeria* (London, 1962); International Labour Office, 'Evolution of Labour Disputes Settlement Procedures in Certain African Countries', *International Labour Review*, XCI (1965) 102–20.

weak bargaining power of certain groups of workers; and secondly, the cumulative effect of exceptionally low wages in perpetuating ignorance, inadequate diet, low productivity and low earnings. In Africa, trade unions were generally encouraged by the former colonial governments, for the same reasons. They have developed chiefly among the workers engaged in government service, partly because governments are generally the largest employers, outside agriculture, of all types of paid labour, whether unskilled, skilled, technical, clerical or professional. Moreover, although labour forms a high proportion of government expenditure, the final output takes the form mainly of services provided free or at controlled prices and financed wholly or partly from taxation; productivity in such services cannot easily be measured against the wages paid to individual groups of workers. Even where the services are sold, as for instance electricity, railways, schooling, the government is often virtually a monopolist. Consequently, trade unions have more success in government service than in other occupations in pushing up the level of wages and of salaries for clerks and for manual workers, above the earnings commonly secured for similar work in commercial firms and family businesses, which sell their output in competitive markets.[1]

One result of this higher level of wages in government service is the custom of buying employment from those who control it. We have here a market in which the price, expressed as the official wage or salary, creates a supply in excess of demand; since all cannot be employed who wish to be, the unofficial payments decide who shall be employed, and they also help to equalise the level of incomes between the different occupations.

In most African countries, the trade unions are still few, weak and short-lived, often becoming effective only in connection with one particular dispute over wage rates or conditions of work, and then breaking up with internal strife.[2] Such organisations are clearly required, however, with the growth of large firms employing numbers of workers of different types and skills in a common task. Apart from bargaining over wage rates, there are a multitude of decisions to be made daily over the details of work in a large firm, decisions in which the workers need to be represented by someone who knows

---

[1] T. M. Yesufu, 'The Shortage of Skilled Labour', in *Readings*, vol. I.

[2] 'Nigeria's Unions in Transition', *West Africa* (9, 16 and 23 March 1968). Callaway, 'Labour in the Nigerian Economy', October Lectures, Nigerian Broadcasting Company (Ibadan, 1967).

the details thoroughly and understands how individuals may be affected. Raising the general level of productivity involves both management and the workers; the existence of educated and honest officials representing the workers could do much to improve both earnings and productivity in many occupations, and thus to alleviate the poverty of so many families in Africa.

UNEMPLOYMENT AND UNDER-EMPLOYMENT

An economy of self-supporting farms, with land available for all who ask for it, does not have unemployment—the problem of people unable to earn an income and thus unable to buy food. It may, of course, suffer from seasonal variations in the volume of employment, and many African farmers engage in crafts, or in trading, or seek employment in other districts, during the months when there is little work on their own farms. But they may also accept the fact of a slack season, and spend it in visiting relatives, in family ceremonies and in other forms of leisure; many farmers seem to prefer alternative spells of work and leisure to continuous work and a higher income.

But even in areas where land is freely available, unemployment has become a distressing feature of many African towns, developing alongside the growth of a class of paid workers. A fuller discussion of this trend must be deferred until we turn to a study of macro-economics in Part 4, but some aspects must be discussed here.

Firstly, there are various reasons why young men leave villages in search of paid employment, even though they could find land to farm at home. There may be a tradition of travelling to see the world before a man settles down to marriage and the farm; many of those employed in mines or in towns do, in fact, eventually return to agricultural work in their original villages. Many young men are attracted to towns by the reports of high earnings which may indeed be available for limited numbers in favoured employments, such as government service; those who fail to get such employment accept casual work with low and intermittent earnings in the hope that something better may eventually turn up. Again, there is little variety of employment to be found in rural districts, where the cultivation of crops and occasional trade are the chief methods of earning money; youths who have had some education in a primary school feel that any form of manual work is beneath them, and do not wish to return to their families without the prestige of an office job, for which they are often poorly qualified. Without earnings, such young men cannot embark on the further training which might qualify them for the posts they feel themselves entitled to occupy. In areas where land is scarce in relation to the demand for it, a man without capital to acquire land may have little choice in his employment. He may continue partially employed on the family farm, sharing in resources which are not adequate to support an increasing family; he may obtain seasonal work on some other farm; or he may seek casual employment in the nearest town, or in some distant mine where he has relatives to help him to get established. Once he has obtained paid employment, he may be able to accumulate the cash which will enable him to buy the rights to occupy land.

Secondly, employment in many occupations requires the existence of capital, to provide tools and buildings and raw materials. Table 11 on p. 83 indicated the amounts of capital which were thought to be required for each worker in various occupations. If there is a scarcity of capital, then there is also a scarcity of this sort of employment. A hundred years ago, economists in Britain were emphasising the lack of accumulated capital as a constraint upon the volume of employment offered in an economy where unemployment was common; and lack of capital remains in many African countries as a similar constraint today.

Thirdly, the low level of most incomes in Africa obviously sets another limit upon employment, in the face of rapidly increasing populations. The lack of markets which is the result of low incomes limits production, whether by commercial firms or by Governments financed out of taxes; the majority of families in rural areas can only afford to spend a few pounds a year upon industrial goods and services, and therefore offer little opportunity for business enterprise.[1] Low incomes resulting from low productivity, high costs and lack of markets set interlocking constraints upon economic development which cannot be removed by easy remedies at any one point.

APPENDIX. IMPERFECT COMPETITION AND THE LEVEL OF WAGES

An employer facing conditions of imperfect competition (as defined in chapter 8, p. 132) may be able to act as a discriminating monopolist, paying each worker, or small groups of workers, the lowest wage which

---

[1] S. P. Schatz, 'The Capital Shortage Illusion', in *Readings*, vol. I.

will induce them to work for him. The wage rate for each separate group then becomes a matter of individual bargaining. The formation of a trade union, negotiating wage rates for all workers, may then succeed in levelling up wages to the marginal productivity of the group as a whole. Alternatively, an employer may find, firstly, that as he expands employment he must raise wages to attract workers from other employers and

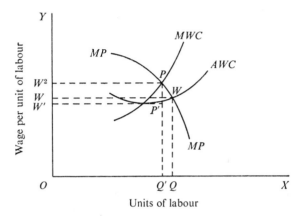

Graph 16. Imperfect competition and the level of wages. (NOTE: *MP* represents the curve of marginal productivity of labour in a particular use; *MWC* and *AWC* represent the marginal and average wage costs of employing the units of labour measured along the horizontal axis.)

from more distant areas; and secondly, that his existing workers insist on being paid the higher wage accorded to the newcomers. In this case, the marginal cost of employing more men rises sharply, above the average cost, as shown in graph 16 by the curves MWC and AWC.

In conditions of perfect competition, when the employer can engage as many workers as required at the market wage *OW*, employment will be determined by the intersection of *WW* and *MP*. With imperfect competition, the employer will engage that number for which marginal wage cost equals marginal productivity, here *OQ'*, and he will pay a wage *Q'P'* (=*OW'*) determined by the intersection of *AWC* with the vertical line *Q'P'P*. If a trade union manages to negotiate a standard wage at *WW*, then this type of imperfect competition will disappear; both the level of wage and the volume of employment will increase, from *OW'* to *OW* and from *OQ'* to *OQ* respectively.

PART 3

Markets and prices

7. Demand, prices and supply

DEMANDS

In all countries, goods and services are being produced, traded, transported, bought and sold and consumed; people are earning incomes which they spend on food, clothing, bicycles, education, housing, and imported goods—all the many things which make up the standard of living of a nation. Though supply and demand may change from week to week and from year to year, they are connected with each other through the structure of markets and of prices.

In the subsistence sector, wants must be satisfied from the output of each small group of families, supplemented by a few traded commodities. Both wants and the methods of satisfying them are therefore limited in range to those things which can be grown locally, or which can be cheaply moved. Food preferences naturally develop from the customary diets obtainable in each district; they persist, even within the exchange economy, because people are generally conservative in their food habits, and only slowly develop a liking for new flavours and new methods of preparing food. What people want is therefore largely conditioned by their customs and traditions, together with the opportunities they see about them. One of the principal results of a monetary system and of economic development is the awakening of new wants, and the provision of a wider range of alternative methods of satisfying them.

Wants, when expressed in money, are called demands by the economists, and commercial supply exists to satisfy demand. A poor family may have as many wants as a rich one, but because its income is less, it has fewer goods and services with which to satisfy its wants; its effective demand is less in the markets where goods are bought for money. Again, there are many wants which are not directly expressed in money, such as wants for happiness, or for immortality; these wants become effective demands when people buy transistor radios or build pyramids. But since the supply of food to satisfy hunger, the basic want, is still the largest industry in African countries, employing more people in production, transport and distribution than any other activity, it is reasonable to begin the analysis of markets by looking at the markets for the output of agriculture.

DEMAND AND PRICES

The usual relationship between demand for a commodity and its price is expressed in the statement that 'demand for a commodity will normally increase as its price falls, but will fall if the price rises, other things remaining unchanged'. There are three reasons why this relationship generally holds.

We assumed earlier (p. 4) that people spend their incomes so as to obtain the greatest satisfaction of their wants. It follows that, with a given income and a given set of prices for the available commodities, a person will buy such quantities of goods from those available for purchase as will give him equal satisfaction from the last, or marginal, shilling spent on each commodity. He will not buy a second yam for one shilling if his want for food would be better satisfied by buying a third bundle of beans for the same price. But if the price of beans rises relatively to the price of yams, so that one shilling now buys a smaller quantity of beans but the same size of yam, some people may prefer to buy more yams; the demand for beans will fall, because the price has risen, and the demand for yams will increase, because the price has fallen relatively to the price of beans.

Secondly, the more a person has of one commodity, the less he normally values another unit of it, and the lower the price at which he will buy more units, within a given period of time. If the price of a commodity falls, therefore, some people may buy more of it since the lower price now matches the lower *marginal utility*, or value which they attach to the extra unit bought.

Thirdly, any large group of people will have different incomes and different tastes. As the price of a commodity falls, more of the poorer people will be able to buy some of it, in addition to the richer people buying more of it. The extent to which demand for a commodity changes with its price partly depends therefore, on the number of possible buyers in each income group, on the distribution of incomes within the community, as well as upon their personal tastes and habits. If a high proportion of families in any community have low incomes, demand may not increase much with a fall in

TABLE 15. *Price-elasticity of demand*

Price-elasticity	0·99 or under	1	over 1
	has low p.e.; is inelastic to change in price	has p.e. of one, or has unit p.e.	has high p.e.; is elastic to change in price
Total expenditure:			
with a rise in price	increasing	constant	falling
with a fall in price	falling	constant	increasing

price until the price comes down into the range of possible purchase by the majority of households.

The relationship between price and demand for a commodity is described as the *price-elasticity of demand*, which may be defined as the ratio of the percentage change in demand for a commodity to the percentage change in price causing that change in demand, other things, including incomes and other prices, remaining unchanged. If the price changes by 10 per cent (from 10d. to 9d. per unit) and demand changes by 10 per cent (sales in a unit of time increase from 100 to 110 units), then the ratio of the percentage change in demand to the percentage change in price is one

$$\left(\frac{(10-9) \times 100}{10} : \frac{(110-100) \times 100}{100} \right).$$

In this case, the total expenditure by buyers and the total receipts by sellers will be almost unchanged in spite of the change in price and in the quantity sold; 100 units at 10d. each totals almost the same as 110 units at 9d. each. Demand is then said to have a unit price-elasticity. If the percentage change in demand is greater than the percentage change in price, then demand is said to have a high price-elasticity, greater than one; if the percentage change in demand is smaller than the percentage change in price, demand is said to have a low price-elasticity, or a price-elasticity less than one. These definitions are set out in table 15 which shows the relationship between price-elasticities and the change in the total expenditure on a commodity.

These relationships are also illustrated in graph 17. On this graph, the price-elasticity of demand (the ratio of the percentage change in demand to the percentage change in price) is shown on $D'D'$ by the ratio of QQ'/OQ (the change in demand) to pp'/Op, the change in price. The graph shows at a glance that at high prices, this demand is elastic to a change in price—the change in demand is proportionately greater than the change in price. At low prices, demand is inelastic, for the change in demand is proportionately less than the change in price.

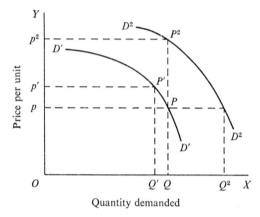

Graph 17. Demand curves. (NOTE. The quantity demanded of a given commodity is measured along the horizontal axis, and the price per unit of the commodity is measured on the vertical axis. The lines $D'D'$, and D^2D^2 then indicate two *demand curves* for the commodity, indicating the amounts which will be bought at the corresponding prices, for two patterns of demand. At price Op, the quantity OQ will be bought if demand follows the pattern shown by $D'D'$; if the prices rise to Op', then demand will fall to OQ'.)

Further, the total expenditure at any price, the quantity bought multiplied by the average price, is shown by the area of the rectangle bounded by the vertical and horizontal lines showing the quantity demanded at that price. Thus at price Op, the total expenditure is shown by $(OpPQ)$; for any substantial change in price, it is easy to see whether total expenditure will increase or decrease.

Such a graph can be read in two ways, since it gives information to both buyers and sellers. With competition between all parties, sellers will find that if they wish to sell the quantity OQ in a unit of time, the average price will settle to about Op, which makes demand equal to the supply. If sellers ask for a higher price, some quantity will remain unsold; if some sellers start at a lower price, competition among the buyers should quickly push prices up again to the equilibrium level. Alternatively, if the buyers collectively wish to buy the quantity OQ, they must expect to pay a price of about Op for this quantity.

We are here looking at demand as a *dependent variable*, something which varies only because the market price for this commodity has changed; any other reason for a change in demand has been ruled out of this calculation by the assumption that other things remain unchanged, while the price of this one commodity changes. If we want to show the effect of a change in demand (caused for instance, by a rise in income) upon price, thus treating price as the dependent variable, then we must draw another demand curve, as at D^2D^2; this particular curve shows a demand which is larger than that of $D'D'$ for all prices. Thus at the price Op, the quantity now bought will be OQ^2; alternatively, if the quantity OQ is now brought into the market for sale, the price will rise to Op^2, higher than Op, the price which would have ruled if demand had remained at $D'D'$.

Consider now the effects of price changes upon total expenditure by consumers, and total receipts by sellers. If demand is inelastic to price changes, as in the lower part of $D'D'$, then total expenditure will increase as prices rise, since demand will fall proportionately less than the rise in price; this will continue for each rise in price, until demand becomes elastic to a further change. On the other hand, if demand is elastic to price changes, as in the upper part of $D'D'$, total expenditure will increase with each fall in price, since demand increases proportionately more than the fall in price.

Consider this graph in relation to the village markets for the basic food in any African community—such as yams, cassava, maize or guineacorn (sorghum). For such commodities, demand is likely to be inelastic to price changes in normal times. People without adequate supplies of their own must have a minimum quantity of the basic food each day; they will, if necessary, pay a high price for that quantity. On the other hand, they do not want to buy much more than the normal quantity for each day, however low the price; they will tend to spend the extra money on other foods, if they can buy their basic food very cheaply.

Moreover, supplies of such foods in village markets commonly vary much, from week to week, and between seasons of good or bad harvests. A variable supply meeting a demand which is inelastic to price changes, as in the lower part of both demand curves in graph 17, inevitably leads to prices varying widely over time, as sellers either compete to sell large quantities, or buyers compete to buy the small quantities upon offer. Consequently, total expenditure by consumers and total receipts by sellers will also vary widely.

Farmers selling foods in local markets are well aware of this type of demand. They often find that an exceptionally good harvest of the basic crop can only be sold at prices which bring them a smaller total sum than they receive in years when the crop is rather poor but prices are high. If supplies are exceptionally large, there may be virtually no price at all, at which the total quantity offered will all be sold in a short space of time—there will be a glut, and total receipts by sellers may be very low, in spite of the larger quantity brought to market. Such a glut is a common occurrence in markets for perishable foods, whose supply varies over short periods of time and must be sold when ready for market. On the other hand, if the supply of a basic food is short, prices may rise to extreme levels very quickly, before the poorer buyers cannot afford to buy their usual quantity; a scarcity will greatly increase both the price and receipts by the sellers.

In such markets, the effect of changing prices upon the buyers can be divided into a *substitution effect* and an *income effect*. When the price of one commodity rises, buyers will, if possible, switch some of their purchases to the most suitable substitute which may serve to satisfy their demand and which has now become relatively cheaper; by so doing, they mitigate the rise in price of the original commodity by transferring part of their demand to some other commodity, in order to equalise marginal utility and marginal cost. However, substitution is limited for the basic food in any rather isolated community, since good and bad harvests are likely to affect most of the local foods at the same time; it is this difficulty of finding substitutes for the small group of basic foods that makes the demand for them inelastic to price changes. Secondly, a change in the amount of expenditure required to secure the normal quantity of food immediately affects the *real income* of any family which habitually spends much of its cash income on such purchases. Real income can be defined as the quantity of goods and services which can be purchased with a given sum of money income; a rise in the prices of the basic foods is equivalent to a fall in real income for families with a given level of cash income. And since it is the poorer families who habitually spend the highest proportion of their cash income upon the basic foods, it is also the poorest families whose real income is most reduced when food prices rise; richer families may be able to transfer some of their purchasing power to more expensive foods, and in any case they are likely to spend a lower proportion of their normal income upon the basic food.

After one or two poor harvests, governments often attempt to prevent such reductions in real income among the poorer families by imposing maximum prices for the main foods, considerably below those which equate demand with the reduced supply. Without other measures to relieve the shortage, however, such price control is more likely to reduce the supplies coming on to the ordinary markets than to improve the position. Turning back to graph 17 (p. 112), let us suppose that D^2D^2 represents the normal pattern of demand but that owing to a poor crop of the basic food, the supply has fallen from the normal level OQ^2 to OQ. The price which then equates demand with this reduced supply is Op^2. If the government then imposes Op as a maximum price in this market, demand will exceed supply by a large quantity, and many buyers will be willing to pay more than the official prices in order to satisfy their wants. In these circumstances, it is impossible to prevent buyers from dealing with sellers outside the official markets and the official prices, and supplies to the regulated markets are reduced even further. To be effective, maximum prices must be supported by measures to bring supplies under control, and to distribute them on some basis of need, rather than by ability to pay.

In a free market, the level of prices tends to move to the point at which demand is equal to the immediately available supply, so that the supply is distributed among buyers in proportion to their demands expressed in money. But if demand is inelastic to price changes, and if the supply varies greatly, price may not be able to achieve this function at either end of its range of variation. A glut in supplies may bring low prices, and low total receipts to the sellers, without stimulating demand sufficiently to clear the market; an extreme shortage of supplies may cause such high prices, and involve such a high total expenditure by consumers, that the distribution of the basic foods cannot be left to price alone. With these exceptions, however, the movement of prices in a competitive market does normally effect a balance between demand and the immediately available supply.

DEMAND, PRICES AND SUPPLY

We have so far assumed that consumers and sellers deal directly with each other in village markets. But traders play an important part in this matching of supply and demand through markets and the mechanism of prices. Consider for instance the matching of supply and demand for the food crops of African communities.

Even in country districts, there are a few families which may regularly buy most of their food, and in towns such families provide a regular market on a large scale. In addition, many farm families eat their own food crops early in the season, but become buyers if their stocks are exhausted before the new crops are harvested. Demand therefore usually increases throughout the season, as more farm families become buyers; demand early and late in each year may be represented by the two curves in graph 17 (p. 112). In order to match this demand, the supply from the farms should therefore increase from month to month in each season.

In many areas, however, the supply sold from the farms tends to be concentrated in the months immediately after harvest. Some farmers may have incurred debts in the course of planting and cultivating their crops; they must pay their taxes; they possibly have no stores in which to keep their crops. The need for ready money just before and after harvest leads many farmers to sell at once a quantity that may leave them insufficiently supplied later in the season, when they may have to buy in the local market. The supply of food crops is therefore often largest in the months immediately after harvest, when demand for immediate consumption is the lowest, and falls later in each season, when the demand normally increases. How are these trends reconciled in practice?

Part of the answer is contained in the price mechanism; prices fall to their lowest point immediately after each harvest, and rise throughout each season to a peak immediately before the new crops are ready for consumption.[1] Low prices immediately after harvest encourage consumers to buy freely then, while high prices later enforce economy in purchases until the new harvest becomes available.

But a more important part of the answer comes from the effect of these price variations on the activities of traders. Traders buying for

---

[1] An example of this trend in market prices is shown in H. A. Luning, *Socio-Economic Survey in N. Katsina* (Kaduna, Nigeria, 1961), p. 137, for millet and guineacorn at Katsina market in Northern Nigeria.

later resale represent a *derived demand*, a demand derived from expectations of future prices when they resell to ultimate consumers (or to other traders who in turn will resell). Traders' expectations of prices are, in turn, derived from previous experience of price relationships between seasons and between markets; a trader with many years of experience behind him is likely to be more accurate in his current expectations than a newcomer into the trade, and this knowledge is an important part of his professional skill. The usual margin between low prices after harvest and high prices at the end of each season induces traders, and some farmers, to undertake storage, so as to even out the flow of supplies.

Storage can be regarded as transport over time. Traders buy a product when its value is low, because supply is large in relation to demand; they store it, and resell when the price is higher, when demand has a tendency to exceed supply. They have thus added to the national output of goods and services a volume of utility or usefulness, corresponding to the margin in price. The transport of, say, 100 tons of grain over six months removes from the market produce which, perhaps, can hardly be sold because of the seasonal glut in supplies; it adds extra supplies later, bringing down prices at a time when the poorer purchasers of food may be meeting a real scarcity.

Such storage involves costs and risks. The produce must be transported to a store, probably dusted with some kind of insecticide, put into a store which someone must have built and roofed, and then taken back to market at some later date. Even if produce is stored in the open, as groundnuts are stored round Kano in Northern Nigeria, it has to be put into bags, the bags built into pyramids, guarded from theft and vermin, covered with tarpaulins, and eventually taken out of store for final sale. Further, a trader buying for storage locks up in store a quantity of his capital which otherwise he might use to buy and sell a greater volume of produce over the period of storage, making a profit on each transaction. A farmer who builds a mud store and fills it with maize or guineacorn might in the same time earn money by collecting firewood and selling it. This is the concept of opportunity cost which was discussed earlier in connection with the economics of production (see p. 44); people will not devote their labour and capital to providing a certain service unless they expect a return roughly equal to what they could earn in the next most profitable enterprise.

In addition to these costs, there are the risks associated with storage. All stored produce may deteriorate in condition, so that of the quantity put into store only a fraction may be sound enough to sell several months later. There are also the risks that the traders' expectations of future prices may sometimes prove to have been wrong, so that the final receipts do not cover their costs of buying produce, storing it and selling what is sound. Traders and farmers undertake storage for resale because, on the average of years, the seasonal rise in prices is large enough to pay these costs and to leave them a profit adequate to induce them to risk their capital and labour in this service. The expected difference in prices over the season thus influences the amount of crops stored for later resale; the amount stored and the timing of the purchase and of the resale in turn influence the seasonal trends in market prices.

In African conditions, and especially in the wetter climates, the risks of storage are high for most foods, since infestation by insects, fungi and bacteria is common. Capital and credit are scarce; a high price must usually be paid for loans and there are many alternative opportunities for using them. All these factors taken together imply that storage is costly, and will only be undertaken when there is normally a high margin between prices over each season. Any improvement in techniques which would reduce these costs and risks would encourage a greater volume of storage, and thus reduce the range in prices over each season, and the period of pre-harvest hunger which is a feature of many African communities. It is especially the poorer farm families that suffer from the existing price variations, for they are often compelled by debts to sell much of their output immediately after harvest, and then to buy food later in the season, at the high prices of the period of greatest scarcity.[1] It is the scarcity that must be tackled, if the high prices at the end of each season are to be reduced, and the low prices immediately after harvest improved.

The price which equates demand and supply thus also influences the volume of supply available in each month from the annual crop, encouraging traders to move produce from the period of low prices for resale in the period of high prices. In the same way, price differentials between markets reflect the costs of transport over space, and influence the flow of supplies between markets. Consider, for instance,

---

[1] O. Oloko, *Study of Social Economic Factors affecting Agricultural Productivity in Annang Province, E. Nigeria* (N.I.S.E.R., unpublished report, 1963), p. 81.

TABLE 16. *Costs of different methods of transport*[1]

Method	Miles	Time	Max. wt.	Approximate cost
Donkeys	60	3 days	1–2 cwt	9s.–10s. per donkey
Bullock cart	60	3 days	2–2½ cwt	20s. per load
Headloads	20	1–2 days	½ cwt	3s.–4s. per day per man
Railway	—	—	—	2d.–3d. per ton per mile for ton lots
Lorry–laterite road				7d.–10d. per ton mile
tarred road				6d. per ton mile

the estimates of costs of different methods of transport, given in Table 16 in relation to the building of a new railway through the eastern provinces of Northern Nigeria.

As long as crops can be moved only by headload or bicycle or donkey, the cost of transport is high in relation to the prices likely to be obtained for each load. Local production will be offered for sale in the nearest market; prices here can get out of line with those in other markets before it pays sellers to move from markets where prices are low to markets where prices are higher, or for buyers to move themselves in the opposite way. High transport costs thus lead to small markets in which prices vary widely and demand generally has a low price-elasticity; gluts alternate with scarcity, caused by local variations in supply. In Northern Nigeria, the opening of new roads suitable for lorries, in connection with the extension of the railway, enabled foods to be moved more quickly and more easily than had formerly been possible. As a result, producers in the more remote areas obtained higher prices for their output, since more traders bought for sale in other markets, and it became worth while for more farmers to grow crops especially for market.[2]

Such a rise in local prices, caused by a fall in transport costs, may not suit local buyers; sometimes it is local sellers who oppose such improvements, because they fear that cheaper transport will bring extra supplies into a local market where prices tend to be relatively high. But such changes are part of the wider process of increasing the national output of goods and services by reducing costs and linking up local markets. Both buyers and sellers are likely to benefit eventually from the greater volume of production and of trade, and

[1] *Report on Agricultural and Natural Resources in Bauchi and Bornu* (Kaduna, Nigeria, 1957), p. 47.
[2] *Movement of Local Foodstuffs* (Kaduna, Nigeria, 1957), para. 118.

from the reduced variability of prices, but some time may elapse before people experience these benefits.

One of the most striking examples of the effect of prices in matching supply and demand is the movement of cattle from the northern regions of West Africa through the tsetse-fly belt (where cattle cannot be reared) to the meat-consuming towns near the coast. Prices here are often twice as high as they are in the collecting markets in the north, such as Niamey, Kano and Fort Lamy; this difference in price induces hundreds of traders to incur the costs and risks of buying cattle and moving them, either by rail or by road, across a thousand miles of Africa. The demand for meat generally has a high price-elasticity, and the demand for it is also rising with rising incomes; better transport and cheaper transport is therefore likely to assist the growth of an already important trade.[1]

The supply of goods thus tends to flow in the direction of the higher priced markets, while demand tends to flow in the direction of the lower priced markets; small changes 'at the margin' in the volume of produce offered or demanded cause prices to rise in some markets and to fall in others, until there is a rough equality between them, allowing for transport costs and risks. Improvements in transport reduce these costs and risks, and thus increase the volume of trade and the level of consumption.

One function of price is thus to equate demand with the immediately available supply. A second function of price is to indicate, by its relationship with costs, what adjustments in supply would increase its value and the satisfaction of consumers' wants. These adjustments in supply can take the form of storage over time; or transport over space; or conversion into some other form, as ground nuts are converted into oil; finally, the pattern of production can be changed given a long enough period of time.

STAGES IN MARKETING

We can describe the structure of markets either by the size of business, or by function. If we look at the size of business, we can distinguish farmers' markets, where the growers sell to local consumers or to

[1] J. Mittendorf and S. G. Wilson, *Livestock and Meat Marketing in Africa* (F.A.O., Rome, 1961), chap. VII; P. Hill, *Landlords and Brokers, A West African Trading System* (University of Ghana, Legon, 1965); A. Cohen, 'The Politics of the Kola Trade', in *Readings*, vol. I; A. M. Hay and R. H. T. Smith, 'Preliminary Estimates of Nigeria's Inter-regional Trade and Associated Money Flows', *Nigerian Journal of Economic and Social Studies* (March 1966)

traders; wholesale markets, where traders sell to each other, or to processors; and retail markets, where traders or shop-keepers sell to the final consumers. In the first and last type of market, the quantity involved in each transaction may be small, since each grower and each consumer may only be concerned with a few pounds; in wholesale markets, transactions may involve a tin of palm oil, or a ship-load of coffee.[1]

Many of the traders in farm produce operate on credit allowed to them by the bigger firms, for credit is perhaps one of the scarcest commodities in Africa. Such traders can therefore only buy a small quantity which they must resell quickly; they cannot hold stocks or pay for transport over long distances. This scarcity of credit implies that many traders are involved, each for a short time and for a small quantity, in the chain of transactions that leads from a head-load of produce to the assembly, or bulking, of supplies for sale to a marketing board for export, or for transport by rail or lorry to a distant market. And again, the process of breaking bulk, of buying a lorry-load of produce for resale to the ultimate consumers, may involve a large number of traders, because each trader can only operate within the limits of his credit.[2]

There is usually one stage in the marketing of any commodity where the aggregation of demand and supply is the greatest, and where, therefore, a price level is set which dominates the other markets in the chain of distribution, in both directions. For internationally traded commodities, we must look for these dominant prices in the great produce markets at Chicago and New York, Manchester and London, Rotterdam and Hamburg, where traders from many countries buy and sell. Such aggregation of supply and demand is only possible, first, when the commodities can be graded, and therefore bought and sold by description, without having to be physically present in the market; and secondly, when traders are well informed on the current trends in all the markets concerned. Trade journals exist to provide detailed information about the demands and

---

[1] P. Bauer, *West African Trade*, (Cambridge, 1954) pp. 59, 60, gives examples of the various stages in the marketing of imported matches and cigarettes in Nigeria in 1950. He noted that some traders obtained a profit only because the empty container itself had a market price, after the contents had been sold.

[2] Bauer, *West African Trade*, chap. 2; I. Livingstone, 'Marketing of Crops in Uganda and Tanganyika', in *African Primary Products and International Trade*, ed. I. G. Stewart and H. W. Ord (Edinburgh, 1965).

supplies of internationally traded commodities such as cocoa, coffee, cotton and petroleum.

For commodities which are not exported, the dominant price must be sought in the large wholesale markets regularly attended by many traders, whose connections extend back to the growers and forwards to the ultimate buyers. These markets usually develop at some centre well served by transport, either road, river or railway; their positions and relative importance thus change with developments in transport. Because most of the produce flowing through local markets is not graded, it has to be present in the markets at each sale, and this itself limits the volume of trade which can be carried out by one buyer. If therefore we want to know how prices are determined in the local markets for maize or cassava or beans, we should begin by studying supply and demand in the nearest wholesale market of any size; from there, we should work backwards to the markets in which farmers sell, and forward to the shops in which, perhaps a hundred miles and several weeks away, other families buy their food.

Looking at the functions of markets, we can distinguish the following:

1. Assembly, or the bulking of small lots;
2. Grading and packing;
3. Transport over space;
4. Transport over time, or storage and preserving;
5. Processing;
6. The provision of credit to cover the time between sale by the producer and purchase by the final buyer;
7. Risk-taking—(a) of physical deterioration or loss; (b) of unexpected price changes.

Not all commodities go through all these stages, and a large quantity of local foods may be sold by the farmers, or by their wives, in the local market direct to the consumers. When the grower is widely separated from the consumer, some of these functions are taken by specialists, applying specialised knowledge, and adapting methods of trading and size of business to secure the appropriate economies of scale and the lowest degree of risk. When a function becomes specialised in this way, another market develops between the specialists. Thus the traders buying cattle in Northern Nigeria sell to a wholesaler who can arrange transport by road or rail to the southern towns; the northern traders in kola nuts buy the services of a 'mai gida', resident in the south, who collects and packs the nuts and organises their transport north.[1] In carrying out such functions, traders alter the place, time of sale, appearance or use of a commodity so as to make it more convenient to the next buyer; they are producers of utility, or usefulness. Like other producers, traders may at times produce something which the next buyer does not value at the costs incurred, for this is the inevitable risk of all production. But over a period of time, a group of traders carrying out a function in a market must earn enough to allow them a reasonable profit over such losses, if this production of utility is to continue. With strong competition in a market, we can expect that the average profit earned by a group of traders, over and above occasional and individual losses, will be just sufficient to keep in business the number of traders required for that function; the average costs incurred will roughly balance the price received, here expressed as the *traders' margin* the difference between the average selling price and the average buying price over a period of time.

THE EQUILIBRIUM OF DEMAND, PRICE AND SUPPLY

The two functions of price so far stated are firstly, to equate demand with immediately available supply; and secondly, to indicate, by its relationship with cost, what changes in supply are desirable. These two functions relate to different periods of time, since it takes a longer period of time to bring about changes in the supplies reaching any market than for people to change the quantity they buy with a given change in price. But if we ignore, for the present, this difference in the time periods, we can represent these two functions of price on graphs.

In graph 18, the curve DD represents the demand of buyers in one unit of time when faced with various prices; the curve SS represents the volume of supply which will flow into this market in the same unit of time, in response to various prices. There will be a certain price, here Op ($= QP$), at which demand and supply will be equal. Individual buyers and sellers may, of course, at times misjudge the market, and transactions may take place at prices higher or lower than Op, but if we assume well-informed traders buying

---

[1] Cohen, 'Politics of the Kola Trade', in *Readings*, vol. I.

and selling a uniform commodity in conditions of competition, the average price paid will tend to settle at the equilibrium level, *Op*, at which demand is equal to the supply *OQ*.

Let us now suppose that, for some reason, demand increases to the curve *D'D'*, so that at all prices more will be bought. Immediately,

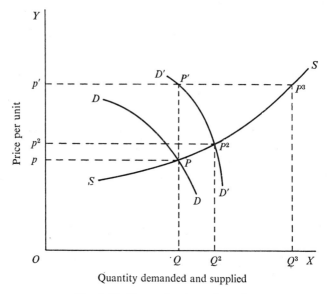

Graph 18. Demand, price and supply

only the quantity *OQ* is being supplied, and the price will therefore rise to *Op'* ($= QP'$), equating demand with the immediately available supply. But at this price, supply will begin to increase, and would eventually increase to OQ^3, given time. But as supply rises, price will begin to fall again under the pressure of competition among sellers, and it will tend to settle at the new equilibrium level of Op^2 ($= Q^2P^2$), at which demand again equals supply for the quantity OQ^2. In this process of change, demand, price and supply have mutually determined each other, and the price which now equates demand and supply is rather higher than before for the larger quantity.

Given the increase in demand, the extent to which the equilibrium price will change depends on the way in which supply reacts to the change in price, that is, on the price-elasticity of supply (defined on

p. 66). In graph 18 the price-elasticity of supply is measured by the ratio QQ^2/OQ (the proportionate change in supply) to pp^2/Op (the proportionate change in price).

A graph of this sort enables the reader to see at once how supply curves with different price-elasticities will give different prices after an increase in demand. If supply has a high price-elasticity, that is, there is a large change in supply after a small initial change in price, the new equilibrium price will be not much higher than the old, and the equilibrium quantity will be considerably greater. On the other hand, if supply changes only slightly in response to a large change in price, that is, supply is inelastic to a change in price, then the new equilibrium price will be much higher than the old price, and the new equilibrium quantity will be only slightly larger than the old quantity. In the first case, the supply curve, SS at the left side in graph 18, has a small slope in relation to the X-axis; in the second case, as at the right side of the graph, SS rises sharply in relation to the X-axis.

We have so far ignored the problem of time, but clearly the price-elasticity of supply for any commodity will vary over different periods of time. In a village market, day-to-day changes in the demand for certain foods may lead to large changes in price, since supply for each day may not be much affected by recent prices but may be influenced more by conditions of weather, and the need of farm families to consume certain quantities of their own crops. On the other hand, if prices are consistently high for some days or weeks, traders may begin to move supplies in from other markets, and eventually farmers may decide to plant more of this profitable crop for the next season. Price-elasticity of supply may therefore be almost nil if we are taking a time period of one day; it may be appreciable if we allow a week; and it may be quite high if we consider changes in supply over a year or more. We shall consider later the effect of these changing price-elasticities in creating large variations in the prices for many agricultural products.

The student is advised to draw a number of graphs with supply and demand curves of differing price-elasticities, in order to show the effect on the equilibrium price, after a change in demand. It may also be helpful to draw graphs showing the changes in the equilibrium price which follow from changes in the conditions of supply, given the demand curve, such as DD. A reduction in transport costs, for instance, may mean that, at any given price, the supply to an inland market may be greater than before; the new supply curve will lie below and to the right of the old supply curve, cutting the demand curve at a lower price. On the other hand, an increase in transport costs, such as occurs during the rainy season in many parts of Africa, may imply that, at any given price in the inland market, supply will be lower; the new supply curve lies to the left of the old supply curve, cutting the demand at a higher price, and leaving more buyers unable to purchase. In these exercises, it is important to distinguish between a shift in the demand or supply curve, which causes a change in the equilibrium price regarded as the dependent variable; and a change in the quantity demanded or supplied in response to a change in price, that is, the movement *along* a demand or supply curve; here, demand or supply is the dependent variable.

Further, these graphs relating demand and supply assume that all other things in the economy remain unchanged, except for the particular, small, change we are studying. We are dealing here with *partial equilibrium*, with the forces which tend to restore equilibrium within a static economy after a small change in one part of it. We have therefore assumed (for example) that a change in price, which causes a change in demand or in supply, has no further influence on the economy, and that the resulting changes in demand or in supply are caused solely by the original change in price. In Parts 4 and 5 we shall take up the problems of general equilibrium in an economy, when we must recognise that a fall in the price of cocoa or coffee may have effects on an economy extending beyond the confines of the markets for these products.

FLUCTUATING PRICES, SUPPLY AND INCOMES

In the discussion about seasonal changes in prices, it has been assumed that prices of agricultural produce fluctuate each season about a 'normal' level, and that there will be a seasonal pattern in prices appropriate to years of good, average or poor harvests. But what prices are farmers likely to take as guides for their plans for production?

A general answer to this question is that farmers and traders generally expect that the recent prices will continue into the near future, with some allowance for events which are clearly abnormal. This assumption may not always hold, for various reasons—changes in demand, expectations about imports and so on, but prices in the last year or two in local markets probably have the dominant influence when farmers are planning their crops.

Now, the wider the fluctuations in prices, the greater the chance that the 'average' price which each farmer has in mind will not correspond to that realised in any one year, and that the planned production will also diverge from that which would give, at average

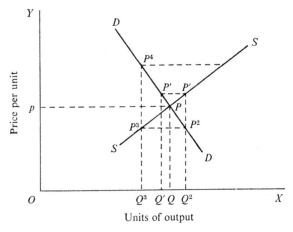

Graph 19. The cobweb theorem

yields, the greatest satisfaction to consumers from the available resources. For if a bad season follows two or three good ones, farmers may have planted less of a crop because prices have recently been low, and thus intensify a shortage. This effect of fluctuating prices upon planned production is known to economists as the *cobweb theorem*.

In graph 19, the quantity produced, assuming average yields, is related to the price of the preceding season. A poor harvest (OQ') causing prices to rise during the season to $Q'P'$ will then result in the next season in an increase in planned output to OQ^2; this in turn, assuming normal yields, will reduce the average price in the next year to P^2, which will cause a shortfall in production in the next season, to OQ^3. Experiments with curves of different price-elasticities will demonstrate that if demand and supply are equally elastic to price changes, than, after an initial disturbance, prices and planned supply will oscillate indefinitely between two points; if demand is more elastic than supply, then an initial disturbance will produce an oscillation which tends, year by year, to diminish towards an equilibrium level; if supply is more elastic than demand, as in graph 19, then prices and planned supply spiral outward indefinitely, until the elasticities change.[1]

In practice, such violent fluctuations are usually prevented by unforeseen changes in yield and other accidents of nature, but in some agricultural crops there is a strong tendency for production and prices to follow some sort of cycle. This is the more likely to happen the longer the time lag that exists before the decision of farmers to produce more or less results in changes in the supply on the markets. This time lag varies from perhaps three months for some vegetable crops to seven or ten years for tree crops; once planted, farmers may continue to harvest from them as long as prices cover the variable costs of harvesting.

A variable supply, such as is common in agriculture, thus automatically produces variable prices. But prices which vary with the state of the harvest are also those which guide the future pattern of production; the most economic use of available resources might be easier if prices did not vary so widely. Moreover, prices which equate demand with variable supply, and which guide planned production, also distribute incomes. To some extent, indeed, price fluctuations help to stabilise the incomes of farmers, in the face of unplanned variations in the yields of crops. If the sales of one crop fall by ten per cent in any season, the resulting rise in price compensates, in whole or part, for the fall in the quantity sold. Again, farmers usually sell more than one crop, so that fluctuations in any one price cause smaller fluctuations in total incomes. Families can also carry over income from one season to another, putting aside some reserves from the high income of a moderately bad year to meet the low incomes resulting from a glut, or from a harvest failure, when many farm families may themselves become buyers of food. In practice, however, it seems likely that the majority of the poorer farmers incur debts when incomes are low, which they endeavour to pay off in a season of higher incomes. They thus incur a cost in the form of interest charges, and a risk to the continued occupation of their land, which may be handicaps towards expanding production in future years. There are therefore various undesirable results of incomes which fluctuate widely from year to year, and there is a general

[1] F. G. Hooten, 'Risk and the Cobweb Theorem', *Economic Journal*, vol. LX (1950).

assumption that such fluctuations should be reduced, in the interests of greater efficiency in production and in distribution. But before we turn to consider measures of price control adopted in various countries it will be useful to look briefly at the theory of competition in the markets for agricultural products.

APPENDIX: ANALYSIS OF DEMAND BY INDIFFERENCE CURVES

Indifference curves provide an alternative method of analysing the relationship between demand and price, (see graph 20, p. 130). Assume that the consumer has a certain level of income which must be spent at current market prices upon one or other of two commodities, or on a combination of them. Assume further that the various combinations which can be bought with the given income can be chosen so as to give equal units of satisfaction to the consumer—e.g. 4 units of x and 2 of y give equal satisfaction with 3 of each. With demand for x on the horizontal axis and demand for y on the vertical axis, draw an indifference curve ii representing all the combinations of x and y which give equal satisfaction and which absorb all the given income.

Movement along the curve involves the buyer in gaining more of one commodity by giving up some quantity of the other. Thus by moving from P to P', the consumer obtains xx' more of X by giving up yy' of Y; the ratio xx'/yy' (which equals CP'/PC) measures the value attached to these units of the commodities. As the consumer moves towards Y, he gains more units of Y in return for 1 unit of X, whose marginal utility rises as the quantity possessed falls; conversely, as the consumer moves down the curve, he gains more X for every unit lost of Y.

Draw a line to indicate the relative market prices of the two commodities; e.g. if $2x$ can be bought for one unit of y, the relative prices are 1/2. Where the line touches an indifference curve, the price ratio and the preference ratio of the consumer are equal; this point therefore indicates the quantities which the consumer is willing to buy, given his income, his preferences and the relative market prices. If his income is increased, then a new indifference curve must be drawn further from the origin O, indicating that the consumer can now buy more units; a new price line drawn parallel to the former line and tangential to the new indifference curve $i'i'$, will again indicate the equilibrium demand. If the market prices change, then the new price line will touch the appropriate indifference curve in a different place, indicating a change in the equilibrium demand, as at P' in the second graph.

5

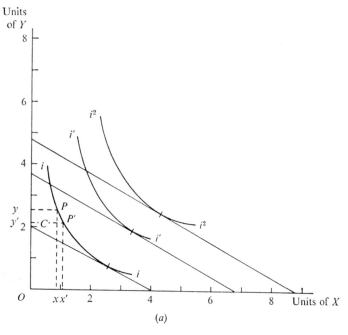

(a)

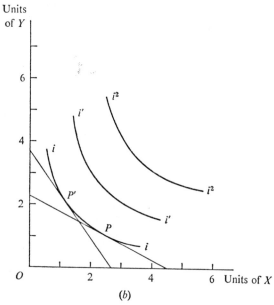

(b)

Graph 20. Indifference curves

8. Markets, competition and price control

COMPETITION

The force of competition can be seen in any African market, where trade is a trial of skill between buyer and seller; the buyer tries to obtain what is wanted at a price lower than that he would pay rather than go without the commodity, and the seller tries to obtain as high a price as possible and still sell all he has brought to market. Buyers and sellers shift their custom between rival traders until prices for the same commodity are approximately equal. In this trial of skill, competition is affected both by the number of buyers and sellers, and by the amount of information each possesses about the market situation as a whole.

Perfect competition was defined on p. 74 as occurring in a market when no one buyer or seller can by his own action appreciably alter the equilibrium price which equates demand with immediately available supply; to this definition we should now add that all buyers and sellers are well informed about the trade in general, so that they know when a price offered to them is out of line with market trends. In such circumstances, each seller finds that demand appears as an infinite quantity at or just below the ruling price, while above this price there is no demand at all. For if he tries to sell above the ruling price, which is known to all buyers, they will turn to other sellers, and this loss of custom will force the seller to lower his price again, rather than to leave his supplies unsold. Similarly, every buyer finds that he can buy any quantity wanted at the ruling price, but that no one will supply at any lower price. For each seller, the demand curve becomes a horizontal line at the ruling price, and this also represents the supply curve to each buyer.

Perfect competition and a uniform price for a commodity at any one time are quite compatible with a range of prices for what ordinary people without expert knowledge call a commodity. The expert trader distinguishes between qualities and grades which may not be apparent to the casual enquirer. There are several types of yams grown in West Africa and many different methods of cooking cassava which is often bought as a ready-to-eat meal; buyers are willing to pay different prices for the particular product they each fancy. Cotton is sold on international markets graded by length, strength and lustre; Sudan long-staple cotton normally commands a higher price than Nigerian Allen which approximates to American 'middling' cotton in quality and price. For some uses, groundnuts and palmoil may be regarded as alternative types of vegetable oil with common trends in price, but groundnuts also have a separate market as edible nuts with a different price level.

In conditions of perfect competition, traders are 'price-takers' and 'quantity-fixers'—they must each decide what quantity they will buy or sell at the ruling price which cannot be changed by the deliberate action of any one trader but which is determined by the total demand and supply in the market. Expectations of future supply may also influence the ruling price at any one time, since the earliness or lateness of the next harvest, or its probable size, affects the volume of demand to be met from the current harvest; in the European markets for tropical produce, the quantities afloat also exercise an influence on current prices, which are concerned with matching demand, over the next few days or weeks, with the supply likely to be available.

IMPERFECT COMPETITION IN THEORY

There are many markets in Africa and many international markets for agricultural produce in which conditions could generally be described as those of perfect competition. But imperfect competition is also found in most markets at times, and in some markets for most of the time. Imperfect competition ranges from almost perfect competition on the one hand to monopoly on the other, the two extremes being special cases in the theory of markets and price formation. *Monopoly* strictly means a single seller in a market, and *monopsony* means a single buyer in a market, but monopoly is often used to describe either of these conditions.

Where competition is less than perfect, then by definition some buyers and sellers can affect the price by changing the quantities which they individually buy or sell. We noted earlier (p. 74) that a seller in a market with imperfect competition will normally match his marginal cost to his marginal revenue, to the change in revenue which results from changing the scale of his operations by one unit. Such changes in revenue are the result of opposing trends. If a seller lowers his price, he will attract buyers away from his competitors, but as he increases his sales, there is a fall in the equilibrium price which matches total supply and demand. To each seller therefore,

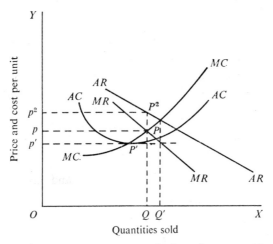

Graph 21. Marginal revenue under imperfect competition

the demand curve will tend to slope down from left to right, instead of appearing as a straight line at the ruling price; the larger the proportion of sales accruing to each seller, the more nearly his demand curve approximates to the demand curve for the commodity as a whole. Each seller will increase his output until he reaches the scale where his marginal cost equals, not the average price, but his marginal revenue.

In graph 21, the curves of marginal and average costs are assumed to be of the normal type for a firm in the short period. The curve AR, drawn as a straight line for simplicity, represents the demand curve for this seller, that is, the average price which is obtained for the quantities sold, which are measured on the horizontal axis; marginal revenue is shown by the line MR, which cuts the curve of marginal cost at a price P, for a quantity OQ. For this level of output, the average price OP' allows the firm excess profits measured by the rectangle $p'P'P^2p^2$, representing the difference between average price and average cost, multiplied by the quantity. For any given pattern of costs, then, output is likely to be lower, and price therefore likely to be higher, under imperfect competition than under perfect competition, when for each firm the lines of average and marginal revenue tend to come together into a horizontal line.

We have so far assumed that each seller sells all his output at a single price, but under imperfect competition a seller may be able to sell to isolated groups of buyers at different prices, maximising profits from each market according to the price-elasticity in each. One afternoon, three small girls were sent at intervals to the village seller of sugar with a penny each; they returned with three, five and eight lumps, quantities which roughly corresponded to their ages. The market woman was here acting as a *discriminating monopolist*, adjusting the quantity she sold for one penny to obtain the maximum profit from buyers with differing degrees of bargaining ability; if the markets had been combined, with all three girls buying at once, she might have had to allow eight lumps for each of them. As a general rule, traders operating in several markets tend to maximise their profits by maintaining low prices where demand is elastic to a rise in price because of competition; they charge higher prices to buyers where demand tends to be inelastic, possibly because there are no alternative sources of supply. Conversely, they may buy at higher prices in markets where there is competition and buy at lower prices where farmers are ignorant or have no alternative market.

IMPERFECT COMPETITION IN PRACTICE

Why does imperfect competition occur in markets and in the distributive trades which are concerned with the sale of all kinds of raw materials and intermediate goods?

One common cause of imperfect competition is the high cost of transport which separates village markets and keeps down the number of traders operating in each. Secondly, there is the general ignorance of illiterate farmers about current prices and alternative markets; even a schedule of official buying prices posted in the market is of little use to men who cannot read and who are unfamiliar with the official weights and measures. Traders operating in several markets and in touch with wholesalers are likely to be better informed than most farmers; to some extent they may act as discriminating monopolists, buying or selling at different prices in different villages, over and above the difference in costs of transport.

The existence of kinship groups which dominate particular trades has often been alleged as a cause of imperfect competition. The West African trade in cattle from the north to the southern cities is generally in the hands of men of the Hausa group, who also dominate the return trade from south to north in kola nuts.[1] In many parts of Africa, the wholesale trade both in imported products and in exports has been mainly conducted by Indians, Syrians and European firms, which had the international connections and the capital and credit required for long distance trade.[2] Managers in these firms tended to take as employees or partners only persons speaking the same language, so that it has been difficult for other groups to enter these trades. There may be fierce competition between the existing firms in such groups, but potential competitors tend to regard all the businesses as a single unit which indulges in various monopolistic practices and enjoys excess profits in consequence. For this combination of kinship groups and commercial rivalry stimulates ill-feeling, in excess of the normal dislike of competitors. Every trader, every farmer, wants to limit competition in his own occupation; he wants to limit the number of people who compete with him, while seeing an increase in the number of buyers for what he has to sell, or of sellers when he wishes to buy. By reducing competition with his own activities, he may be able to reduce the price-elasticity which he faces in his market as a seller, and thus obtain for himself higher profits. Equally every trader who finds that a competitor has bought something at an exceptionally low price for resale tries to break into this imperfectly competitive market; by so doing, his action tends to improve competition and thus to raise prices where they are unduly low.

The new governments in Africa have often promoted competition, in order to reduce excess profits resulting from imperfect competition, whether clearly established or only suspected. The Uganda government has encouraged the farmers' co-operative societies selling cotton to take loans in order to buy ginneries, and thus to compete with the Asians who formerly dominated this trade; marketing boards have awarded licences to trade in export produce to struggling local firms, assisting them with guaranteed overdrafts, as in Nigeria.

[1] A. Cohen, 'The Politics of the Kola Trade', in *Readings* vol. I.
[2] I. Livingstone, 'Marketing of Crops in Uganda and Tanganyika', in *African Primary Products and International Trade*, ed. I. G. Stewart and H. W. Ord (Edinburgh, 1965).

On the other hand, there has been a strong influence towards the suppression of competition in favour of regulated monopolies, especially in the trade in agricultural exports. Here there have been various strands of official thought. One has claimed that the multiplicity of small firms organising transport and maintaining buyers has led to excessive costs, and that a single authority could enjoy such economies of large-scale business that farmers could obtain higher prices. In practice, such economies of large scale trading by monopolies do not seem to have led generally to lower costs in Africa, for various reasons, including the high overhead costs of centralised offices, the risk of theft and corruption, the difficulties of communication, the lack of experienced management at all levels, and the slowness of adjusting to the many changes in local conditions and in world trade.

The second reason for the attempts to suppress competition, or at least to regulate it, arises from a different argument, that competition tends to accentuate the fluctuations in agricultural prices and in agricultural incomes. In the last chapter, we noted that the combination of variable supply and of demands which are inelastic to price changes causes fluctuations in the prices at which farmers sell and consumers buy. Consequently, the incomes of farmers also fluctuate widely and so may the real income of the final buyers. These trends may, it is claimed, be intensified by the action of traders, buying and selling in anticipation of future changes in price. In times of scarcity, some rise in price is inevitable, in order to attract supplies of acceptable substitutes and to encourage consumers to transfer their demand. But traders intensify the current scarcity by buying and storing for a further rise in prices, so that the original rise in price leads, perversely, to a rise in immediate demand, thus intensifying both the current scarcity and the rise in price. In the opposite direction, large numbers of traders, anticipating a fall in price with a good harvest, may intensify the fall by the policy of selling their stocks quickly, and by refraining from their usual purchases.

Thirdly, there have been the large fluctuations in the prices received by farmers for their exported crops, which have led to large changes in their incomes. Some of these fluctuations have arisen from the normal variations in harvests, affecting the volume of supplies; others have been due to sudden changes in demand, often associated with the trade cycle in industrialised countries. Over the period from

1901 to 1951, the world markets for fourteen agricultural products showed average changes in price between successive years ranging from 9 per cent for tea to 21 per cent for rubber; within single years, the average change in monthly prices, expressed as a percentage of the highest price, ranged from 19 per cent for sugar to nearly 40 per cent, again for rubber.

For the foods traded on international markets, the price and volume of exports tended to move in opposite directions, suggesting that it was changes in supply which often caused the change in price; year-to-year fluctuations in the volume of exports from all sources were frequently twice as large as the fluctuations in price. For raw materials used in industry, price and volume of exports tended to move in the same direction, indicating that changes in demand were the more important influence in causing price changes than the level of supplies, which tended to follow price changes.[1] The total value of these exports thus fluctuated more than either the volume or the price, and these fluctuations in the value of exports had serious effects, not only on farm incomes, but on the economies which depended on two or three crops for their receipts of foreign exchange.

Further, these fluctuations in world markets had at times an intensified effect on producer prices, because the costs of transport and collection remain stable; a fall of 10 per cent in price on the international market (say from £100 to £90 per ton) may become a fall of 20 per cent (from £50 to £40 per ton) in the price paid to up-country buyers, and therefore an even greater fall in the price paid to farmers for their small lots. The greatest falls of this sort occurred during the world-wide economic depressions of 1920–3 and again between 1929 and 1933, when incomes of almost all farmers connected with international markets were drastically reduced. Such sudden and apparently inexplicable changes in prices and in incomes in short periods serve no economic purpose; they resulted in strong pressure, both in African countries and in Europe and America, for some control over markets and prices, in the interests of greater stability, and, if possible, of higher incomes for the farmers who supplied food and raw materials to world markets. It is not possible here to describe the various schemes of price control adopted by African countries, but it may be useful to analyse the types of problem which they have encountered.

[1] United Nations, *Instability in Export Markets of Underdeveloped Countries* (New York, 1952).

PRICE-AVERAGING SCHEMES FOR EXPORT CROPS

The centralised marketing board has been a common device for reducing the effect of fluctuations in prices on world markets upon the prices paid to African producers. These boards usually have a legal monopoly of buying specified crops for export; they licence the first buyers, arrange sales at port or in overseas markets, organise the shipment, and collect the receipts from which they pay the farmers previously announced prices. The main objective of such marketing boards was to remove or reduce random fluctuations round the trend in prices, so that farmers could plan their production rationally to the trend, without the distractions of year to year changes. 'If stable prices could be achieved, this would encourage production and safeguard the producer against the short-term fluctuations of the world market'.[1]

Now this objective assumes that the managers of these boards can distinguish in advance between 'random' fluctuations, and changes in the long-term trends in prices, which should be allowed to influence the production plans of farmers. Unfortunately, even experts are liable to mistake forecasts about the immediate future of prices, and marketing boards have at times found themselves with quite inappropriate prices, which have had to be changed abruptly. Thus the Western Nigerian Marketing Board reduced its buying price for cocoa by £15 per ton in the middle of the 1960/1 season, causing much confusion in local markets, and especially in markets bordering other regions where prices changed much less.[2]

Secondly, a price-averaging scheme implies that farmers will get higher prices than those paid by the market when market prices are low, and lower than market prices when market prices are high; in some years, there will be an accumulation of funds, and in other years, a spending from reserves. But if some years have elapsed between accumulation and its dispersal, the farmers receiving the additional sums will not be the same as those who contributed to the reserves; there is a transfer of incomes not only over time but also between persons, and possibly between regions of contracting and expanding production.

[1] Northern Nigeria Marketing Board, *Fourth Report, 1957/8*, p. 8; *Statement on the Future Marketing of West African Cocoa, 1946*, Cmd. 6950 (London, 1946).
[2] Western Nigeria Marketing Board, *Report* (1961).

Thirdly, the instability of prices resulting from the instability in crop yields does in part help to reduce fluctuations in the incomes of farmers; a price-averaging scheme may therefore intensify the instability of incomes arising from varying harvests.[1] The ultimate effect of such schemes upon farmers' plans for production is also uncertain. We know too little about the decision-making of African farmers to judge what effects upon output can be expected from a price-averaging scheme for one or two crops. Do farmers plan output by absolute prices, by relative prices for the different crops, or by expected income per acre? Evidence from Egypt indicated that Egyptian farmers between 1899 and 1956 (omitting years of war) planned their production of cotton more by the relative prices between cotton and competing crops than by changes in the market price of cotton itself; one stabilised price might therefore distort the pattern of production as much as short fluctuations in prices which affected most crops at the same time. It has also been argued that crops which require substantial investment, such as cocoa, palm oil, rubber, may be more easily extended out of the occasional profits of high prices than from a steady price; supply is little affected by temporary low prices, since, once planted, the costs of harvesting are low.[2]

Fourthly, the monopoly exercised by these marketing boards over the internal trade in the exported commodities has often disturbed the normal flow of supplies, and created pockets of imperfect competition. In buying at fixed prices at inland markets, the boards must prescribe buying and transport allowances for their buying agents at levels which allow for the collection of crops from the most remote areas; it is open to question whether the results have reduced costs or inflated profits for the traders concerned. Thus in Uganda, the zoning of cotton deliveries to the ginneries effectively created local monopolies for the existing merchants, and denied farmers the choice of buyers for their crops. One of the Nigerian marketing boards was asked by its buying agents to prescribe the quantities they each could buy, in order to prevent the traders from competing among themselves by offering higher prices to farmers than those officially prescribed. Remarkably, the board tried to comply, but found that

[1] A. A. Suliman, 'Stabilization Policies for Cotton in the Sudan', in *African Primary Products and International Trade*, ed. I. G. Stewart and H. W. Ord.

[2] R. M. Stern, 'Price Responsiveness of Egyptian Cotton Producers', *Kyklos*, vol. XII (1959); R. H. Green and S. H. Hymer, 'Investment in the Ghana Cocoa Industry', *Economic Bulletin of Ghana*, vol. IX (1965).

the agents would not accept the quotas allocated; it did however sharply reduce the buying allowances for the next season, having realised that they must have been unnecessarily generous to the traders.[1]

Again in Kenya, the Maize Marketing Board controls the trade in maize for conversion into posho, as well as exports, when there is a surplus, or imports, when there is a deficiency. The board bought from farmers at stated prices, designed to encourage the production in Kenya of a supply which would normally satisfy home demand; it sold maize to the posho mills at a price that covered the costs of transport, storage and the loss on exports. One result has been that relatively high prices have been charged to the mills in years of a good crop when exports were sold at prices below those in the home market; the board has then found difficulty in preventing the mills from buying direct from farmers.[2]

Finally, whatever the purpose of these boards when first established, those dealing with export crops have operated largely as tax collectors for their governments, whether national or regional. Export taxes, produce taxes, loans, grants, have all provided funds for the governments, funds accumulated by holding down the prices received by farmers, irrespective of the prospect of future low prices which might require payment out of reserves. As one marketing board reported in 1963:

at the same time as world market values have been declining, the Board has had imposed upon it the duty of achieving a high annual profit to assist in development...This can only be done by fixing producer prices which it is known inflict hardship on the producing communities and which are likely to result in reduced purchases for export.[3]

Stabilisation of prices to farmers has therefore led, in the case of export crops, to prices considerably lower than those in world markets, not only when prices were rising, from 1947 to 1952, but also when prices were stationary or falling. This policy has thus reduced farm incomes from these crops and reduced also the incentive to expand their production, as well as holding down the consump-

---

[1] C. Ehrlich, 'Some Social and Economic Implications of Paternalism in Uganda', E. African Institute of Social Research, Conference, 1959; Eastern Nigeria Marketing Board, *Eighth Report, 1963*.

[2] M. P. Miracle, 'Economic Appraisal of Kenya's Maize Control', and A. A. Haller, 'Kenya's Maize Control', *East African Economic Review*, vol. VI (1959).

[3] Eastern Nigeria Marketing Board, *Eighth Report, 1963*, p. 45.

tion of farm families. On the other, side, farmers' costs have presumably been reduced by the government's investment out of these funds in research, advisory services and roads; it is difficult to estimate the effect of these opposing influences upon the output of the exported crops.[1]

It must be noted that marketing boards themselves have provided a variety of services to their farming communities. They have financed research into crop diseases, storage and plant breeding; they have developed processing equipment; they have built stores and improved transport facilities; they have bargained with railways and shipping companies for better freights; they have improved grading and the quality of the products. Their powers of licensing have been used in Nigeria to Africanise the internal trade in export crops, which until about 1950 was largely in the hands of foreign firms, employing local people only for unskilled work. These are the permanent advantages derived from the compulsory centralisation of the receipts from export crops.

REGULATION OF INTERNATIONAL MARKETS

Just as many countries have attempted to reduce the fluctuations in prices and incomes for their farmers, so attempts have been made by governments and by international institutions to exercise some stabilising control over the prices in international markets. International regulation has faced much the same problems as those encountered by national boards, only on a larger scale.

If price fluctuations arise from variations in the size of harvests, then the accumulation of *buffer stocks* is an obvious remedy, but the practical difficulties of such a policy are great. Firstly, stocks have to be accumulated, presumably at a time when prices are low. Producers wish to be paid for their output, whether it is moving into consumption or into storage for later sale. Secondly, therefore, storage requires the provision of capital on an enormous scale, both to accumulate stocks and to build stores. Thirdly, storage also involves continuous costs, and to avoid deterioration the stocks must be sold and renewed in a regular pattern. Finally, the setting up of buffer stocks implies some agreed decision about the 'normal' variations in price which are to be allowed, and the 'excessive'

[1] G. K. Helleiner, 'The Fiscal Role of the Marketing Boards in Nigerian Economic Development', in *Readings*, vol. II.

variations which are to be prevented by the purchase or release of stocks. Yet the effects on price of variable harvests and of cyclical changes in demand cannot always be disentangled from the price changes which result from more fundamental changes in supply and demand.

The International Tin Council has been one of the few international organisations which has operated buffer stocks for any length of time; it has the advantage of dealing with a product which is cheap to store and exported by only a few countries. Nevertheless, the finance available for storage was exhausted in 1956 in an attempt to maintain a minimum price which eventually had to be abandoned, and the same thing also happened in 1958. In 1963/4, the accumulated stocks proved inadequate to prevent an upsurge in demand from pushing the price to record levels. In the ten years 1955–64, the price of tin on the London market fluctuated between £570 and £1,600 per ton, though the existence of the buffer stocks did modify the smaller changes in prices.[1]

The costs of storage on a scale sufficient to keep prices within approved limits inevitably led to attempts to control production whenever prices fell outside the lower limit. The international agreements for tin, sugar and coffee all embodied provisions for the restrictions of exports or of production whenever prices fell below certain levels. But there have been great difficulties in securing agreement among the exporting countries on the allocation of the desirable volume of exports. Among a number of exporting countries, there will be some whose output is expanding rapidly at low costs, while others may be willing to restrain high-cost production if the resulting rise in price will increase total receipts. Further, the relative importance of different sources of supply may change rapidly within a few years, so that export quotas based on previous sales rapidly become out of date.

The prices of some commodities in international markets have been supported in the last decade by the stocks accumulated by the American Government, in order to maintain the prices and incomes of its own farmers. At times, stocks of wheat held by the American Government have been nearly equal to the annual world exports, while stocks of cotton have amounted to about two-thirds of world exports. Stock-piling on this scale is only possible for wealthy countries, and even in America it has had to be supported by restrictions upon output, and by selling in separated markets.

[1] *The Economist* (12 Dec. 1964), p. 1275.

The international trade both in wheat and in sugar has developed some of the characteristics of discriminating monopoly, in selling at different prices to different markets with differing price-elasticities of demand. The International Wheat Agreement, supported by the principal importing and exporting countries, prescribes a certain range of prices within which the bulk of the trade is carried out between the selling and buying agencies for these countries. Outside this agreement, the exporting countries sell on specially low terms to undeveloped countries, and to countries with exceptional needs. The incomes of wheat growers are thus maintained by the sales within the agreement, where the demand for wheat is generally inelastic to a fall in price; the excess production goes to those countries where incomes are lower, and price elasticity probably higher. For sugar, both the United States and the United Kingdom buy a large part of their imports at prices required to maintain their domestic industry, based on sugar beet, at approved levels. The agreed prices apply only to stated quantities from certain countries; the remainder of the required imports comes from these and other countries at prices determined by the free market, where the fluctuations are intensified by the concentration of all the marginal changes in demand and supply. The French government agency also buys certain quantities of produce from associated countries in Africa at prices considerably higher and more stable than those ruling in the international markets.

The relative stability of prices in such protected markets has thus been secured partly by intensifying the fluctuations which have occurred in the 'free' or outside markets, which have been compelled to take the surplus supplies that were kept out of the higher-priced markets. Import controls have also been required to maintain the separation between free and controlled markets; domestic prices tend to diverge widely and permanently from those in countries which trade in the unprotected markets.

In recent years, discussions have centred not so much upon fluctuations in international prices, but upon the general trend for prices of foods and raw materials exported from undeveloped countries to fall relatively to those for the manufactured products which these countries buy from the industrialised countries. There are three main reasons for this trend. In the first place, the countries of Europe and North America, which are the principal buyers of tropical produce, now have low price- and income-elasticities[1] for

[1] See p. 232.

most foods; increases in demand are likely to come chiefly from increases in population, but these are areas with relatively low birth rates. Secondly, there has been a great development of synthetic substitutes for many raw materials, such as rubber, wool, leather and cotton, and there has consequently been a slackening in the growth of demand for them. Thirdly, these industrialised countries also support agricultural structures where supply is increasing rapidly, and where the prices and incomes accruing to farmers have been supported by progressive restrictions upon competing products, mainly sugar, cereals and livestock products. The downward trend in the relative prices of foods and raw materials is thus partly the inevitable result of trends in the demand and supply for these commodities, but partly also the result of the intent of the industrialised countries to support the incomes of their own farmers at levels judged to be politically desirable in their own communities. Much has been said at international conferences about the need to reverse this downward trend in the relative prices of tropical produce, or to provide some form of compensating finance,[1] but so far the ingenuity of economists in devising schemes has not been matched by agreement among the governments, each concerned to obtain the greatest advantage for the particular groups of mankind over which it exercises authority.

[1] G. Blau, 'International Commodity Arrangements and Policies', in *Readings*, vol. I.

9. Business and the state

INTRODUCTION

One of the basic assumptions of economic theory is the existence of governments which maintain law and order and which follow some kind of economic policy. Part 5 is devoted to the analysis of policies intended to stimulate economic development, but here we may consider various ways in which governments influence the conduct of business and the flow of incomes within the territory under their control.

THE LEGAL STRUCTURE OF BUSINESS

The most common form of business unit in Africa is the family farm, in which land, labour, capital and management are combined by a small group of relatives, with the older members taking decisions on behalf of the others. Many traders operate in the same fashion, drawing credit perhaps from a wider circle of kinsmen, and employing one or two young relatives as assistants and learners. But these simple units cannot cope with the complicated types of production, requiring the combination of many persons with different skills, much capital, management at varying levels, and facing large risks in anticipation of a market for the output. Such businesses require legal powers to enable them to act as a unit in dealing with others— in incurring debts, claiming payment of debts or dealing with tax collectors; they need regulations about the rights and responsibilities of the individuals providing the various resources within the firm. The main types of business unit are the partnership, the company with limited liability, the co-operative society, and the public corporation, the last three depending upon a legal framework provided by government.

PARTNERSHIPS. A partnership requires a formal agreement between a small number of persons to undertake a common business or trade. Normally, all partners are legally liable for debts incurred by any of them, and for all actions done in the name of the partnership; hence this form of business unit is commonly found in the professions, in trade and distribution, where a few people who know and trust each other can take active parts in the business. A partnership can be dissolved by agreement, and disputes between the partners must be settled by them, or taken to a court of law for settlement on the basis of the original agreement.

COMPANIES. A company is a legal unit, registered with the Registrar of Companies and subject to the company law current in the territory of registration, as well as to the company law in other countries where it operates. The legal owners are the *shareholders*, who have provided the capital in return for a *share* in any profits made by the enterprise. Shares have various *nominal values*, say five or twenty shillings each, and profits, if available, are divided annually among shareholders in proportion to the number of shares which they hold in the company. The capital lent by shareholders is not normally repaid by the company, but individual shareholders can recover their capital by selling their claim to a share in the profits on the *stock exchange* to some other buyer. Companies can also borrow by the issue of *stocks* (or *debentures*) at fixed rates of interest; the interest on these loans must be paid before the shareholders receive profits. Company law requires the annual presentation of properly audited accounts at an annual general meeting of the shareholders; holders of fixed-interest stocks do not usually have the right to attend or vote at this meeting, so long as their interest has been duly paid. The shareholders elect the auditors and the board of directors, who manage the company in accordance with company law and the articles of association, drawn up when the company was formed. Shareholders are themselves liable for debts of the company only to the extent of their holding of shares, and this limited liability is indicated by the word 'limited' normally found after the title of company.

Shareholders in a company provide capital in return for annual *dividends* which will vary with the profits made by the company; if there are no profits, there is no dividend, and if the company becomes insolvent, the shareholders may lose their capital as well as the expected dividends. The price of a company's shares on the stock exchange therefore reflects the expectation of profits in the near future. If a company is making high profits, investors may bid up the price of the shares considerably above the nominal value of the capital originally lent; thus a five-shilling share may be worth six shillings on the stock exchange if buyers expect that dividends will be high for the next few years. Conversely, the shares of an unprofitable company may be quoted at prices considerably lower than the nominal value. Prices of shares, or *equities*, are therefore likely to vary more than the prices of fixed interest stocks, such as company debentures or government loans.

The limited liability company has proved a flexible device for bringing together in a common enterprise labour, management of different kinds, and capital owned by persons who may not want to engage in trade and manufacture themselves. Moreover, companies often invest in the stocks or shares of other companies, sometimes to gain control over competitors or over suppliers of their requirements, sometimes to obtain the economies of scale in the marketing or in the provision of finance, sometimes as an investment for surplus profits. African governments have themselves set up companies for specific enterprises, supplying some capital in the form of debentures or shares, and joining with a foreign firm which provides management, technical knowledge and the remainder of the capital; the shares can gradually be sold on the local stock exchange so that local people become investors in the business. But the power of companies to hold each other's shares has inflicted a number of frauds upon the public, who may be invited to invest in companies with hidden debts and controlled by a few shareholders retaining a majority of votes.

CO-OPERATIVE SOCIETIES. A co-operative society can be formed by a number of people, ranging from about a dozen to several thousand, who combine their capital in order to provide some service for themselves. There is usually a limit to the number of shares which any one member can hold, and the interest payable on share capital is also limited, to discourage the speculative investor. Societies are managed by a board of directors or a committee of managers, elected by the members at the annual general meeting, at which each member has only one vote, irrespective of the number of his shares. Profits when earned are normally distributed among members in accordance with the amount of business done by each member with the society; the annual 'dividend' is thus linked to the economic activity of members and not to their share capital. Co-operative societies must be registered with the appropriate government office, which has powers to regulate their affairs, inspect their accounts and help them in many ways. Co-operative societies have been used for a variety of purposes. In Uganda, they have been concerned mainly with the marketing of coffee and cotton which are sold for their members to the marketing boards. In Kenya, groups of new farmers on land settlements are encouraged to form co-operative societies to undertake the purchase of supplies, the marketing of produce, the provision of services such as cattle dips and coffee hulling. In Nigeria, their chief business has been the collection of savings from weekly wage earners in towns, though some societies process and sell palm oil and have established shops for their members. Recently groups of farmers in Nigeria and in Uganda have formed co-operative societies to hold land which is farmed by the members either collectively through a paid manager and the government tractor service, or individually as tenants of the society.[1] Co-operative societies have generally been favoured by governments since they enable small groups of people to embark on some joint enterprise for their mutual advantage; they are often lightly taxed compared with companies, and can usually obtain loans from official sources for approved purposes, to be used either by the societies in setting up processing plant or by their members on their own farms. But the successful operation of enterprises on this basis requires honesty and trust among the members as well as efficient management, and many co-operative societies have foundered because of incompetent committees, dishonesty of officials or apathy among the members.

PUBLIC CORPORATIONS. Public corporations are companies set up, not under company law, but by special legislation for specific purposes. Marketing boards, central banks, development corporations, railways, electric power, telephones, docks and harbours, universities, are examples of the enterprises which are often organised by public corporations.

Some of these corporations are designed to be run on commercial principles, selling their services to the public and earning, if possible, sufficient profit to maintain their capital and possibly to extend their plant as required. Such are the corporations which manage railways, telephones, docks and harbours; their managers are usually appointed

---

[1] E. H. Whetham, *Co-operation, Land Reform and Land Settlement*, Plunkett Foundation for Co-operative Studies (London, 1968).

by governments for a term of years. The non-commercial corporations, such as universities, usually work on annual grants from the governments, with which they must provide the best services they can, supplemented by student fees and such finance as they can attract from outside sources.

Both types of public corporation have usefully organised various enterprises, but they have two main difficulties. First, government control over appointments and selling prices has led to many forms of political corruption which has distorted the functions of the corporations. Secondly, the managers and workers have little personal interest in securing efficiency and in keeping down costs, and it is difficult for an auditor or outside investigator to assess whether unnecessary workers are kept on the payroll, or excessive prices paid for supplies or for buildings. Yet such excessive costs must be met either by raising prices to the consumers, or by cutting the service provided, or by unnecessary subsidies from the taxpayers.

THE OPTIMUM USE OF RESOURCES

In addition to providing a legal framework for the conduct of business by individuals, governments usually concern themselves also with the efficiency with which such businesses use the available resources to produce the national output. Still ignoring the problems of stimulating economic growth, let us consider how governments can improve the welfare of their citizens by improving the use made of the national resources. We assume that a higher welfare can be defined as making some people better off without putting any one individual into a situation which he considers worse than his former one.

The previous sections of this book have been mainly concerned with the analysis of an economy in which investment, production, marketing, consumption and saving are conducted by a large number of small units each seeking the largest profit for itself. Such a system is linked together by the flow of money incomes passing from consumers to traders, and from traders through the farms and firms back to the individual families whose adults provide the resources of land, labour, capital, management and enterprise. The spending of incomes by consumers has been likened to the casting of votes in a ballot, since the choices made by consumers from the variety of goods in the market determine the small changes in the flow of incomes which in turn stimulate changes in the pattern of production and in the use of resources. In the reverse direction, changes in costs reflected in changes in supply influence the pattern of demand through the mechanism of market prices, so that consumers are made aware of the relative cheapness or dearness of different commodities. For each commodity, output is limited by the relationship between the marginal costs of producing more, which reflect the scarcity of resources, and the prices obtained for the final output, which reflect the value attributed by the buyers to the quantities offered for sale in any one period of time.

If each resource consisted of small, perfectly mobile and identical units, and if all farms and firms were operating in all markets in conditions of perfect competition, then we could expect the marginal productivity of each resource to be equal in all uses, and equal also to the price paid for it (allowing for the non-monetary factors included in such prices). In consumers' markets, we should also find that the prices paid for the quantities bought would balance the marginal utility on the one hand and the marginal cost on the other. With these assumptions, a static society might then approximate to the optimum pattern of production and consumption—that is, the value of the total output of goods and services could not be increased by any change in the use of resources. In such circumstances, could government action in the conduct of business increase the welfare of consumers and producers?

We have in fact noted circumstances where the operations of some businesses inflict costs indirectly upon other units, through traffic congestion, the pollution of air or water, annoyance and damage to occupiers of neighbouring sites. In these cases, resources are presumably being used at higher total costs than their marginal productivities to the firms employing them, and welfare would be increased if these costs were diminished, or pushed back on to the firms responsible for them. Something can be done to minimise these social costs by controlling land use, so that factories and homes are kept apart, some land is left open for recreation, and food markets are brought under the control of local authorities. This is a sphere of action for town planners, city councils and medical officers of health.

Building regulations and the provision of public services like water supplies and main drainage can also prevent some of the worser forms of social costs which arise from insanitary housing and factories, but only through imposing considerable costs, which may make some enterprises unprofitable. The provision of adequate housing in large towns, in particular, has generally involved costs which put such buildings outside the reach of the poorest families, who therefore over-crowd existing accommodation. Subsidised housing has been adopted in some countries as an answer to this problem of the allocation of costs between poor families, their neighbours in congested areas, and the public health authorities which must cope with the major epidemics of disease; but such a policy is generally outside the financial capacity of town councils and local governments in Africa.

Social costs and external economies of scale also provide a second reason for government action in the markets, in order to improve the use of resources. New firms may find that their private costs are lowest in an area already industrialised and provided with transport, public services and supporting trades; they will not consider the social costs of adding to the congestion. Consequently, an established town draws new firms, while other areas, perhaps equally suitable in many ways, cannot attract them.

The problem here is to create, away from the existing congested areas, a nucleus of firms and of public services large enough to provide external economies on its own—a point of growth, as it is sometimes termed. The most important of such services are likely to be transport, communications and power. Consider for instance the building of a new all-weather road, or a railway, such as was undertaken in the 1950s in Uganda and in Northern Nigeria.[1] The advantages to be expected might be:

1. Savings on existing costs along unsurfaced roads—greater speed, fewer breakdowns, delays and accidents, less wear and tear on vehicles, more goods carried per man-hour;
2. Savings on traffic costs diverted from alternative routes;
3. Growth of new traffic resulting from the fall in transport costs—the increase in exports and in imports for the region at the further end of the new railway.

It is not easy to measure these quantities, especially the third, since it is almost impossible to foresee the pattern of costs ten or

---

[1] Adapted from A. R. Prest and R. Turvey, 'Cost-Benefit Analysis: A Survey', in *Surveys of Economic Theory*, III (London, 1966), 183–90; see *Movement of Local Foodstuffs* (Kaduna, Nigeria, 1957); E. K. Hawkins, *Roads and Road Transport in an Undeveloped Country; A Case Study of Uganda* (London, 1962).

twelve years after the introduction of cheaper transport. But an isolated area recently linked to a large market by a new road or railway may first grow cotton and fruit for export, then develop ginneries and a cannery, attract service trades for its growing population with its rising incomes, and so eventually be able to provide public services which attract other industries using local resources.

Such a policy of developing a point of growth ahead of demand implies, however, the investment of scarce resources which may not yield a full return for a long time; the present value of such investment may therefore be low, in comparison with the returns to be expected from investment in a new factory at the edge of an existing town (see p. 87). Governments faced with a variety of projects and with an acute shortage of capital need to be particularly careful before they invest in new points of growth, yet all economic change involves taking risks in the hope of future benefits which seldom can be accurately measured in advance.

GOVERNMENTS AND IMPERFECT COMPETITION

A third reason for government intervention in markets lies in the existence of imperfect competition, which permits monopoly profits to be earned in some sectors of the economy and which may restrict output below the level which might have existed with conditions of perfect competition. Here action designed to improve welfare should be based on a study of each situation.

Imperfect competition may develop from lack of information. Farmers may not know the current prices in the local market when they sell to traders on their farms; wage earners may not know what wages are being paid in some other area. The remedy may then lie in government-sponsored information, made available at markets or over the radio. Bargaining power in many markets is unequal for many reasons, and one partner to a transaction may be able to dominate the other. A legal minimum rate of wages for certain types of work may prevent some exploitation of manual workers in conditions of excess supply, though it may also intensify unemployment and be difficult to enforce. Many governments have attempted to control rents charged for housing in towns, where demand usually exceeds supply. The results have often been unsatisfactory, since the supply of rented houses may fall and over-crowding encouraged; but the existence of rent tribunals to which tenants can appeal for

assistance may sometimes check the exploitation of the weaker
party to a bargain.

In many developing countries, the pattern of land ownership has
been a source of monopoly profits and an example of output restricted below the optimum level. Where a few families own large

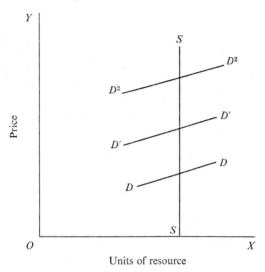

Graph 22. Price of a resource with fixed supply

estates let to tenant farmers who have no other means of earning
their living, the force of competition may push up the level of rents,
and reduce the security of tenure, until the occupiers have no margin
above subsistence to invest in improvements, and no inducement to
invest even if they could borrow the resources. This is the classic
case of unequal competition based on ownership of a resource
which is necessary for production and whose supply is fixed in
quantity. The situation can be shown graphically by a vertical supply
curve for land, whose average price, expressed in rents or in land
values, is determined by the level of demand, as in graph 22.

Where a population is increasing rapidly in an area of already
occupied land, those who control access to it inevitably obtain
rising prices for the use of their property. Rising demand for food
and for raw materials pushes up the prices of farm products; this
rise in price enables farmers to intensify output from the existing
farms and to bring into cropping the poorer land, but competition

among farmers for land also forces up the level of rents paid to the owners, transferring to them the surplus over the costs of production and the bare subsistence of the occupiers. If the owners do not themselves invest in improvements, such as irrigation, buildings, fertilisers and field drains, it is unlikely that the increase in output will match the increase in demand.

In a number of countries, therefore, reform of land tenure has been undertaken by the appropriate government. In recent years, both the Indian and Egyptian Governments have controlled farm rents, limited the size of estate which can be owned by any one family, and provided finance for the tenant farmers to buy their land and thus to become owner-occupiers.[1] The Kenya Government has purchased large estates in the highlands from European families and converted them into small farms for families from over-crowded lands.[2] Such an upheaval runs the risk of temporarily reducing the output of food and raw materials reaching the market, for a number of the large estates were efficiently run on commercial lines and might provide common services for the tenants as well. There has here been a conflict between the long-term advantages of a diffused ownership of land which gives security to the farmers and an inducement to improve their farms; and the short-term disadvantages of breaking up large units and of burdening farmers and governments with debts incurred in compensating the former owners for the loss of their property.

A second reason for government intervention in land tenure lies in the scattered plots and confused boundaries which, in many parts of Africa, impede the most economic use of land. Consolidation of plots and the granting of freehold titles to single occupiers was adopted over a wide area of Kenya from the mid 1950s, the government supplying the administrative and legal staff for the surveys, mapping, re-arrangement of boundaries and the provision of cropping plans for the guidance of the occupiers.[3] Again, schemes for irrigation and reclamation of land may involve such vast areas and so many diverse interests that privately owned capital is unlikely to take the risks involved. The Gezira scheme in the Sudan and the Volta Dam in Ghana are examples of this scale of operation.

[1] G. S. Saab, *The Egyptian Agrarian Reform 1952–62* (London, 1967).
[2] See p. 256, below.
[3] E. S. Clayton, 'Economic and Technical Optima in Peasant Farming', and G. J. W. Pedraza, 'Land Consolidation in the Kikuyu Area of Kenya', in *Readings*, vol. I.

The existence of economies of scale in many industries is a frequent cause of imperfect competition, since a few firms may dominate a series of markets. Governments have tried a variety of measures aimed at regulating monopolies, preventing their creation or intensifying competition among a few large firms. A public corporation may, of course, be the best method of providing some service where the economies of scale necessitate a single firm in a country, or in each area, as with railways or the provision of electricity. Prices charged to consumers can then be regulated to prevent the extortion of monopoly profits. But price control also raises a number of intricate problems in the relationships between costs and prices, and between different methods of raising capital. Should a firm charge all its customers average costs, even when demand is not adequate to keep the plant running at capacity and average costs are therefore high? Should consumers who add to demand only when the demand is already equal to capacity be charged the marginal costs of over-loading, a major problem for urban transport and for electricity generation? If capacity must be expanded, is the capital to be found from profits, so that present buyers provide it in their prices; or from the stock exchange, where private investors will require evidence of past profits and future prospects; or from the taxpayers through the government? Experience has shown that government control over such monopolies, while often inevitable, raises important problems of definition and price policy.

Instead of controlling prices and profits, governments may also encourage competition by various methods. In Britain and the United States, there is legislation against certain types of price agreement between firms, and amalgamations between existing firms may also require government approval. Governments in Africa have stimulated competition in distribution and in manufacturing by a variety of measures already described (see p. 135).[1] On the other hand, governments may wish to protect infant industries from the competition of established firms. By raising the price of imports through a tax, home producers can then find a market for their output by the diversion of demand from the higher-priced imports, while they build up their scale of output. In such cases, the cost of

[1] S. P. Schatz, 'The Capital Shortage Illusion, Government Lending in Nigeria' and O. Olakanpo, 'Distributive Trade: A Critique of Government Policy', in *Readings*, vol. I.

establishing a new industry is partly borne by the present buyers of the output, who pay higher prices for their purchases. Alternatively, the cost of support can be spread over the taxpayers, by providing a subsidy to the new firms, or by allowing them tax concessions for some years. These policies recognise that new firms take time to become as efficient as their competitors but that it is in the national interest to encourage business men to invest their resources and their enterprise in competition with existing firms.

THE DISTRIBUTION OF INCOMES

In an economy composed mainly of competing small businesses, the flow of incomes is effected through the markets for resources. People use, or offer for sale, their labour, land, capital and enterprise, deriving incomes from the supply of resources, of commodities or of services; many will also obtain food, shelter and a degree of social security from the family farm. The pattern of incomes derived from such an economy thus reflects the relative earnings of the different resources, as well as the efficiency with which they are used. If capital is generally scarce in relation to labour, then the owners of capital may obtain relatively high incomes from profits and interest; capital will be used only where its marginal productivity is likely to be high. Money lenders combining loans with the marketing of farm produce may reap high incomes for their enterprise. If land is scarce in relation to both capital and labour, then the owners of land obtain high rents for the use of their property. Owners of urban land, in particular, may receive very high prices for the limited number of sites suitable for building factories and houses in an expanding town.

Such high incomes in turn exert an influence upon the patterns of production and of imports, since a family with five thousand pounds a year has a hundred times as many votes in the market as a family with fifty. So the economy imports Mercedes cars and Scotch whisky, and builds air-conditioned villas with swimming pools, while many farm families are short of food in the weeks before harvest. Moreover, the ownership of capital makes easy the purchase of education and the entry into well-paid posts, and thus sets up a cumulative process of wealth acquiring wealth.

It has often been argued that governments based on some form of democracy should restrict this accumulation of wealth by a small minority of citizens. The rule of diminishing marginal utility may be taken to apply to money as to other commodities—the more money a family possesses, the lower the value of the marginal unit. A thousand pounds taken in taxation from a family with five thousand pounds a year and spent in providing education for poor families will therefore, it is claimed, cause little loss of welfare to the rich and a substantial gain to the poor. This principle has generally been accepted by governments, in spite of the difficulties of making inter-person comparisons of the marginal utility of incomes of different sizes. *Direct taxation*, taxes levied on incomes, now usually take a higher proportion of the larger incomes than of the smaller incomes—taxation is *progressive* with income. On the other hand, a *poll tax* of a fixed amount for each adult represents *regressive* taxation and it may take quite a sizeable proportion of the cash income of many farm families in Africa. *Indirect taxation*—taxes paid on the production and sale of goods—may also be regressive with income, if levied on commodities bought by most families to about the same amount.

High rates of progressive taxation, which may increase the welfare of the poor more than the loss of welfare to the rich, may at times conflict with the inducements required to secure both the most efficient use of present resources and also the highest rate of economic growth. If a manager moving from one firm to a larger firm with greater responsibilities finds that he obtains little extra income, after tax, from his higher salary, he may judge that the extra work is not worth while. Firms making profits will have their capacity for investment reduced by the amount of taxation; risky businesses with fluctuating incomes may pay higher taxes in aggregate over several years than firms with stable incomes, and this may discourage enterprise in new ventures. There has been much discussion over the effects of high taxation on the incentives to work harder and to take risks, and some economists maintain that business men, aiming at a certain net income, will be encouraged to increase their efforts if profits are heavily taxed by the state. There is no doubt however that progressive taxation of large incomes at high rates encourages avoidance and evasion, and this human characteristic may set the limit to the attempts by governments to increase total welfare by transferring income from rich families to the poorer sections of the community.

PART 4

Macro-economics

10. Money and banking

INTRODUCTION

The economy of any country is made up of thousands, perhaps millions, of independent units producing and consuming the goods and services which make up the national output and the national income. At the base of economic theory, therefore, lie the constraints upon production and consumption experienced by these units, and their reactions to changes in costs, to changes in incomes and to changes in prices. In a commercialised economy, these costs, incomes and prices are expressed in money; the flows of money link together production and consumption through the numerous markets, both in one country and in other countries. Money is one of the most useful inventions of mankind, but like many inventions it can at times cause harm. Moreover, the fact that money can be stored implies that savings in one period may influence demand in the future, when savings are spent or debts repaid. In this chapter we consider how money works through the banking system of any country, assuming, for most purposes, that there is no international trade. We then turn to the flow of government receipts and expenditure, and then to the problems of international trade and the corresponding flows of international payments by which that trade is financed.

WHAT IS MONEY?

The exchange of goods can occur in the form of barter, as when a man gives the village elder a goat in return for the right to occupy a particular plot of land, or when relatives exchange gifts at family ceremonies. Beyond this limited range, it becomes convenient to have a commodity which everyone will accept in exchange for a sale, and which can again be used to buy something else. The 'medium of exchange' needs to be fairly durable in quality, easily recognisable and divisible into small units. The Hausa word for money is 'kudi' (meaning cowry), because in the past cowry shells became a common medium of exchange; gold, silver, bars of iron and even cigarettes have served the same purpose.

In most countries today, the legal currency is some form of paper money, supplemented by metal coins of small value. Paradoxically, the paper notes which purchase most have the lowest value as objects apart from their legal use, for metal coins may have some value in industry. But people are willing to use paper notes and metal coins because they know that, within the boundaries of their country, everyone is willing to accept them in exchange for some quantity of goods and services.

One essential, however, for a medium of exchange is that its quantity should not vary greatly in short periods of time, so that prices—the quantities of other goods exchanged for it—do not vary greatly. If prices were expressed in terms of a grain crop, for instance, a good harvest or a poor harvest would alter all prices expressed in grain. Hence the issue of legal currency in any country is usually given to a monopoly, such as a central bank or a government department such as a currency board, which can print paper notes and mint coins out of metal only under strict control. It must be noted that money is not wealth for the country as a whole; more coins and paper money in my pocket means more wealth for me, because other people are willing to exchange goods and services for my notes, but it is the goods and services which constitute the national wealth, and the paper notes are only the medium of exchange between individuals wishing to buy or to sell goods and services.

But in addition to the *legal tender* of notes and coins, most countries have money in the form of bank deposits, whose supply is linked indirectly to the quantity of legal tender. Bank deposits on *current account* (and sometimes *savings* or *time deposits*) are regarded as money, since they can be used as a medium of exchange through the flow of cheques, and since they are largely additional to the stock of money, as we shall see later (p. 164). Suppose that you purchase this book with a cheque, telling the bank with which you have a deposit of five pounds to pay the stated sum to the seller of the book. Your account at the bank will go down by that sum, and there will be a corresponding increase in the account of the book seller at the same or another bank. Of course, the acceptance of the cheque depends upon confidence, the confidence of the book seller that you have the necessary deposit in the bank, that your bank will allow the transfer to be made, and that his bank will pay the cheque in legal tender if he requires it. If confidence fails about any of these matters, then bank deposits cannot be used as money, but since transactions usually

TABLE 17. *Money supply of selected countries*

1	2	3	4	5	6	7
						Col. 5
			Cash	Current account		as %
			with	deposits with	Total of	of col.
Country	Unit	Period	public	commercial banks	money	6
East Africa	£ m.	30 June 1964	54·7	89·4	144·6	62·2
Ghana	m. New Cedi	31 Dec. 1966	115·2	132·2	247·5	53·4
Nigeria	£ m.	March–June 1965	81·5	50·9	132·4	61·5
United Kingdom	£ 000 m.	average 1966	2·6	10·9	13·5	80·7
United States	£ 000 m.	average 1966	37·5	132·3	169·8	77·9

flow through all these stages without a break-down, deposits are regarded as equivalent to money.

Table 17 shows the money supply of different countries at recent dates. It will be seen that bank deposits composed about 80 per cent of the total supply of money in the United Kingdom and the United States, compared with about 60 per cent in Nigeria, 54 per cent in Ghana, and about 60 per cent in East Africa, where the European sector made extensive use of bank deposits. Such differences are important for governments trying to influence economic development through the control of the quantity of money and of bank deposits; the subsistence sector, hardly using money at all, is virtually outside such controls.

BANKS AND THE CREATION OF CREDIT

Bank deposits exist because banks are willing to store money and to lend money, and because people are willing to keep their money at the banks, rather than to risk keeping notes and coins in their houses and pockets. If a village deposited £5,000 with a local bank for safe keeping, at the end of a month the accounts of the bank would show *assets* (what it possesses) and *liabilities* (what it owes) of the same amount:

Assets		Liabilities	
Currency	£5,000	Deposits	£5,000

Customers of this bank can exchange deposits among themselves without affecting the totals. But if one customer transfers part of his deposit to someone not a customer of this bank, then both liabilities and assets will be reduced by that amount; deposits would still be covered by assets of the same amount, so that the ratio of deposits to currency would remain at one.

The bank manager will soon realise that his customers do not all take out all their money at the same time, so that he can safely lend a proportion of his deposits, and still be able to pay cheques and to repay such customers as may, from time to time, want to withdraw their deposits. He will, of course, only lend to customers considered credit-worthy, to those who will repay a loan promptly on time with due interest; the bank manager may also require a borrower to give a title to some property of his, or to find rich friends who will repay the loan in the event of the borrower's default. But having agreed to grant a loan, the bank opens an account in the borrower's name, so that the loan becomes a deposit:

Assets		Liabilities	
Currency	£5,000	Deposits	£6,000
Security against loan	£1,000		

Money has been created, since the total deposits are larger than the total of the currency owned by the bank. Consider further what happens when the borrower starts to use his loan, now called a deposit. If the *payee* (the person receiving the payment) is a customer of the bank, the deposits are merely shifted from one account to another, without altering the total. But if the payee takes his cheque in cash, or deposits his credit with another bank, the original bank has lost that sum in currency from its assets as well as from its deposits.

Commercial banks are thus torn between the need to keep a certain proportion of their assets in cash, in order to meet such withdrawals, and the need to earn a profit on assets by lending them to credit-worthy borrowers, whether private citizens, firms or governments. How much of the assets must be kept in cash depends on a variety of circumstances. Firstly, only current deposits can be withdrawn without notice; time or savings deposits can only be withdrawn after giving notice which varies from a week upwards. These deposits do not therefore count as part of the supply of money, against which cash must be held for immediate use, but some reserves must be kept for them. Secondly, small banks and banks serving only one locality will need to keep reserves adequate to meet local disasters such as a harvest failure, or the simultaneous withdrawal of a few large deposits.

Finally, the proportion of assets kept in cash depends on the *liquidity* of the assets themselves, the speed at which they can be converted into cash. In developed countries, banks may lend to the *discount houses*, which specialise in very short-term loans. Another form of fairly liquid asset is a *treasury bill*, loans to the government for 90 days; a succession of such loans can give a regular repayment week by week or day by day. Then there are similar loans made to traders to cover the period between paying for imports and selling them on the home market; these *commercial bills* may also run for 90 days. In emergency, both treasury and commercial bills can be pledged with the central bank against immediate loans of cash, though of course the central bank may charge interest for such accommodation. Banks may also lend to their government for longer periods; such loans are variously called *bonds*, or *gilt-edged securities* or *gilts*. These assets become more liquid if there is a well-developed stock exchange where a bank can quickly find buyers. However, only a few African countries have a stock exchange; these have a small turnover as yet and a small shift in demand or supply can cause a large shift in price, so that selling stock in an emergency may result in a low price for the seller.

Table 18 shows the structure of the assets of the commercial banks in Ghana in 1960, 1962 and 1964. The composition of the liquid assets changed considerably during this period to include a much greater proportion of treasury bills; the total of liquid assets also fell, but still amounted to 38 per cent of all assets in 1964. The proportion of liquid assets held in cash remained fairly stable at about 10 per cent.

The commercial banks thus have a limited power to create money through making loans, by some multiple of the cash or other liquid assets held by them. In Britain, the large joint stock banks, with branches throughout the country, regard 8 per cent as the conventional minimum of cash to total assets; that is, the banks can make loans (and thus create deposits) up to a total of about twelve times their holdings of cash. In the United States, banks are generally smaller and more localised, and they are legally required to retain in the form of cash 4 per cent of their savings deposits, and either 12 or $16\frac{1}{2}$ per cent (depending on the type of bank) of their current

TABLE 18. *Structure of assets in commercial banks, Ghana*

Asset	1960 £G.m.	%	1962 £G.m.	%	1964 £G.m.	%
Cash	4·7	11	7·2	11	8·7	10
Balances with other banks	11·6	28	2·1	3	2·0	2
Ghana treasury bills	4·2	10	17·3	27	18·8	21
Other bills	1·6	4	0·6	1	4·6	5
Total liquid assets	22·1	53	27·2	42	34·3	38
Ghana Government securities	0·2	—	1·1	2	12·6	14
Other loans and advances	13·5	33	24·5	38	33·4	37
Other assets	5·6	14	10·9	17	11·5	13
Total assets	41·4	100	63·7	100	91·2	100

SOURCE. A. J. Killick, 'The Performance of Ghana's Economy: 1963 and After', *Economic Bulletin of Ghana*, IX (1965), 38.

deposits. In Ghana, Nigeria and some other African countries, commercial banks work, not on a cash ratio, but on the ratio of liquid assets (as given in table 18), to total liabilities. For example, banks in Nigeria must legally maintain a minimum liquidity ratio of 25 per cent.

The ability of the commercial banks to make loans can thus be controlled either by regulating the minimum ratio of cash to deposits, or of liquid assets to deposits, or by altering the actual cash or liquid assets held. If the central bank made available to the commercial banks £10 m. in cash, and the legal cash ratio was 10 per cent, deposits could be expanded by £100 m. over the previous level, while a reduction in the cash ratio from 10 to 8 per cent would also free resources for an increase in loans. As we shall see later, altering the liquidity ratio and directly changing the amount of cash available to the commercial banks are important methods whereby the central bank tries to control the supply of money within its territory.

THE QUANTITY THEORY OF MONEY

It was pointed out on p. 162 that one essential quality of the commodity used as money is that its supply should not vary much in short periods of time, since rapid changes in the supply of money affect the general level of prices, that is, the amount of money given in exchange for other commodities. In any given unit of time, such as a year, there is a certain volume of transactions carried out in the economy for which money is used, in one or other of its forms; the total quantity of money required for the volume of transactions depends partly on the actual supply of units of money, and partly on the *velocity of circulation*, the number of times each unit is used on the average in the course of the year. We have therefore four quantities each of which is partly influenced by the others, the supply of money (M), and the velocity of circulation (V), the number of transactions in a year (T) and the average price level (P). We can express changes in these quantities by the identity $M.V. = P.T.$ If the velocity of circulation of the money and the number of transactions remains unchanged in any period, then any change in the supply of money must cause the same proportionate change in the average price level.

The velocity of circulation is normally controlled by institutional factors, such as the frequency with which wage earners are paid— whether monthly or weekly or daily; how often farmers go to market to buy or to sell; whether savings are lent to a bank or buried until required. The number of transactions again depends partly on the relative size of the monetary and subsistence economies. In African countries we can expect a steady rise in the number of transactions over time, partly because more farmers exchange more of their production against money, and partly because of the growth in population. In a static economy without sudden changes in expectations, therefore, the velocity of circulation and the total value of transactions may be relatively stable quantities. In these circumstances, the general level of prices is likely to vary approximately with the quantity of money, but over a period of time, allowance would have to be made for the growth in the volume of transactions and possibly for the effect of changing institutions upon the velocity of circulation.

However, changes in M can cause changes in both V and T, as well as in P. If consumers and business men come to expect that prices will rise sharply in the near future, they may alter their spending habits and thus the velocity of circulation of money; they may rush to buy whatever they think they will need in the next week or month, spending all their reserves of money and all their earnings as soon as they are received. This happened in China after the second world war, and in other countries where a rapid increase in the supply of money produced a rise in the velocity of circulation and a further rise in prices—the state known as *hyper-inflation*, where money can become almost worthless as a medium of exchange and as a store of value over time. Again, if people expect that prices will fall sharply, some transactions may be postponed until goods are cheaper, reserves of income may accumulate in bank deposits or in hoards, and the velocity of circulation may fall. The velocity of circulation can therefore be changed quite substantially by expectations of a change in the general level of prices.

There are also circumstances where an increase in the quantity of money can affect only part of an economy. We might suppose that farmers receiving an exceptionally high price for one season's crop might decide to save most of the excess income over their usual amount, and lend it to savings banks for future use; meanwhile, the general level of prices will not be affected, but there may be a fall in the rates of interest, since there are now more funds available for would-be borrowers.

The general level of prices is thus influenced by more things than by the quantity of money in existence at any time, but it remains true that changes in the quantity of money over short periods of time can have a powerful influence through prices on the economy as a whole.[1] Changes in the general level of prices are therefore matters of concern to governments trying to promote the development of their countries. We must now look more closely at the monetary policy of governments, and in particular at the types of monetary control which have been available for governments of African countries.

CURRENCY BOARDS

Before independence, the currency of most African countries was controlled by currency boards, instituted by the controlling governments. These boards dealt with regions rather than with individual territories; the West African Currency Board originally covered the Gold Coast, the Gambia, Nigeria and Sierra Leone, and the East African Board the territories of Aden, Kenya, British Somaliland,

---

[1] A change in the general level of prices is in fact made up of varying changes in different prices, some of which react more quickly and to a greater extent than other prices and costs; see Appendix to chap. 11, p. 198.

Uganda and what is now Tanzania, then Tanganyika and Zanzibar. These boards had no control over the quantity of bank deposits, but they were required to issue local currency in exchange for sterling, on demand. Every note or coin issued in West or East Africa, therefore, had behind it a similar quantity of some asset which had a value in sterling. The boards thus had no discretion over the quantity of currency in their territories; at any time, this quantity reflected mainly the volume of the crops sold from the territories for export in terms of sterling, and the volume of investment from overseas.

From 1954, the powers of the currency boards were enlarged, so that they could issue notes in excess of the sterling assets they held, up to 20 per cent of the total. The boards thus acquired a *fiduciary issue* of this proportion; the term 'fiduciary' implies that the notes were based on faith in their acceptability and not on the same quantity of sterling at the control of the boards. The boards could thus exercise some discretion over the quantity of currency in their territories after 1954, and they then acquired one of the characteristics of central banks.

There were two great advantages of this system of currency boards closely tied to the monetary system of the United Kingdom. Because local currencies were freely convertible into sterling, people had confidence in the stability of their value; farmers were willing to sell their crops for money and eventually to expand their production to make such sales, and investors from the United Kingdom were willing to develop business and trade with the African territories. Secondly, the mechanism of currency boards was cheap to administer, and this was an important point for relatively poor countries; central banks have generally had higher costs of administration.

The disadvantage of the system was that it did not assist the development of local markets for money and capital. The quantity of currency was determined mainly by the volume of exports, but the gradual growth of domestic trade and production, of the volume of goods exchanged against money, of the population itself, could not exercise an appropriate influence on the volume of currency. Reserves in excess of current needs were invested in the London money market, where they were quickly available to meet emergencies but they were consequently not available for loan to the local banks in the territories concerned. The currency boards were not bankers to the local governments, nor did they exercise any direct controls over the quantity of bank deposits, other than the indirect influence exerted by the quantity of currency issued.[1]

Shortly before independence, the currency boards began to invest their reserves locally, and thus to develop the local money markets. In June 1963, the East African Currency Board had invested £10¾ m. in local loans out of total reserves of around £76 m.; it also made small issues of treasury bills, which earned the banks some interest. However, these efforts were modest, compared with the development of the local money markets by the central banks in Nigeria and in Ghana, after these new organisations had taken over the issue of currency from the West African Currency Board.

CENTRAL BANKS

Central banks were established in African countries in association with the attainment of independence, and they were charged with the general functions of controlling the supply of money within their territories, and of advising their governments upon the financial side of economic policies. More specifically, central banks have four main duties:

1. To issue and redeem currency within the national boundaries and to undertake the general administration of the currency;

2. To maintain the external value of the currency, and to undertake the administration of any measures of control in the markets for foreign exchange;

3. To administer the government's policy for the volume of credit and for the conduct of banking within its territory;

4. To act as banker to the government itself, and to advise the government on all matters within its sphere of responsibility—the tax system, or *fiscal policy*, the balance of payments, the issue of government loans, the financial aspects of economic development, and so on.

Although a central bank must work in close co-operation with its government, it may at times find that its functions as controller of

---

[1] A second criticism sometimes made was that the currency board system had a de-stabilising influence on African economies. The supply of money would tend to grow when there was an expansion in exports, and thus encourage a general expansion in demand unchecked by any counter-action on the volume of bank deposits. Conversely, when exports fell and there was likely to be a fall in incomes, the fall in the supply of money would intensify the situation. In fact, this de-stabilising force does not seem to have occurred.

the value of its currency conflict with the desire of politicians to enlarge the expenditure of the State; consequently, central banks are usually given a constitution which renders them formally independent of governments, though the director and possibly a board of governors must be appointed by the government for definite terms of office.

For management of the currency, central banks have generally been given greater scope for discretion than was allowed to the former currency boards. From its institution in 1958, the Central Bank of Nigeria, for instance, was allowed a fiduciary issue amounting to 40 per cent of the total volume of currency in circulation, and in 1962, this limit was raised to 60 per cent; only 40 per cent of the currency after this date had therefore to be covered by reserves of gold or of sterling assets held by the central bank.

For reasons which are explained later,[1] almost all African countries have found it necessary to impose measures of exchange control since independence; nationals of their countries can no longer exchange local currency freely for foreign currency, but such transactions are confined to purposes approved by the central bank, on directions from the government. All central banks have been much concerned with the administration of these controls, and with the negotiations between governments for international loans and the consequent overseas payments of interest, and repayments of capital.

The third and fourth functions of central banks are closely connected with each other, for both involve the development of a local market for government loans, whether for short or for long terms. Table 19 shows how this market was developed in Nigeria between 1964 and 1966; during this period the amount of the development loans taken up by local institutions and persons (other than the central bank itself) increased from about £40 m. to nearly £60 m.

What has been the source of these funds, now lent to the government in Nigeria? As line 8 of table 19 shows, about one-quarter of the development stocks was held in 1966 by the central bank itself, which has thus lent its own funds to the government. This process leads to a direct increase in the volume of money in circulation; the loans to the government are spent by various Ministries, and the recipients of this expenditure acquire deposits with the commercial banks. In effect, new money is created in order to lend it to the government, and, as we shall see later, this is one method of inducing

[1] See chap. 14, p. 240.

TABLE 19. *Holdings of Nigerian development loans*

31 Dec. £000	1964 a	1964 b	1965 a	1965 b	1966 a	1966 b
1 Commercial banks	542·0	—	547·0	—	2,438·5	—
2 Individuals	224·6	6·5	267·5	4·5	281·8	1·0
3 Savings institutions	28,205·1	666·0	34,987·6	704·5	42,838·8	802·6
4 Statutory boards and corporations	7,035·5	—	7,489·2	42·0	5,717·7	46·0
5 Other corporations	672·1	—	596·3	—	729·2	—
6 Local and regional governments	2,097·5	—	4,072·7	—	5,363·6	—
7 Insurance companies	569·0	77·0	1,092·0	82·0	1,416·0	52·0
8 Central bank	13,731·3	—	19,027·9	—	21,272·8	—
9 Central bank sales (not yet classified)	128·4	—	41·8	—	—	—
Total	53,205·5	749·5	68,122·0	833·0	80,053·4	901·6

SOURCE. Central Bank of Nigeria, *Annual Reports*, (1965, 1966).
a: domestic; *b*: foreign.

inflation. But the great bulk of these long-term loans have been taken up by savings institutions who have thus made available to the government the deposits of savers and the banks' own reserves. The central bank has encouraged this growing demand, by itself taking up most of the government loans, as they have been issued, and then finding buyers over a period of time. In 1966, for example, the central bank took up all but £700,000 of a £9 m. loan, which it then gradually sold to other institutions and persons. Some of these funds represent past savings transferred from overseas, and future contributions from Nigerians will have to come from current savings only.

Apart from these long-term loans for development, the Nigerian Government also required, like all other governments, short-term loans to bridge the gaps between expenditure, which continues fairly evenly throughout each year, and the receipts from taxes, which tend to accumulate round two or three dates in each year; short-term loans may also be needed to continue expenditure on development projects between the longer-term loans. Like other borrowers, a government can obtain overdrafts from its bankers, but the normal method of raising short-term loans is by the issue of treasury bills, which usually run for 90 days. The lenders to the

TABLE 20. *Holdings of Nigerian treasury bills*

£ 000	Central bank	Call moneya fund	Commercial banks	Federal and regional governments	Others	Total
1960 June	526	—	4,533	—	3,941	9,000
Dec.	1,365	—	1,874	—	5,788	9,000
1961 June	53	—	6,648	—	3,299	10,000
Dec.	6,660	—	2,971	—	7,369	17,000
1962 June	3,106	—	8,870	—	9,029	21,000
Dec.	4,683	3,410	3,370	—	12,537	24,000
1963 June	2,370	3,080	5,342	2,396	9,812	23,000
Dec.	15,684	3,475	1,191	1,605	8,045	30,000
1964 June	4,107	1,270	9,196	4,566	8,861	28,000
Dec.	6,582	4,855	5,364	6,501	10,699	34,000
1965 June	4,690	5,210	6,326	5,172	10,602	32,000
Dec.	12,467	3,255	6,453	6,329	11,496	40,000
1966 June	8,490	625	13,235	4,982	15,668	43,000
Dec.	28,987	3,360	11,229	6,501	13,923	64,000

SOURCE. Central Bank of Nigeria, *Economic and Financial Reviews.*
a Funds for making loans which are repayable on demand without notice.

government buy treasury bills at a discount below the nominal value—a bill worth £1,000 at maturity may be bought for £998, for instance—collecting both capital and interest when the bill is paid at the full value.

Table 20 gives an analysis of the holdings of treasury bills issued in Nigeria between 1960 and 1966. As with long-term loans, the total amount of government debt grew enormously over this period; the central bank had to take up an increasing amount of government stock itself, but it did succeed in selling the greater proportion of the total debts. The seasonal nature of the trade of the commercial banks is shown by their holdings of treasury bills; their credit is fully extended in the harvesting season when traders are buying the main crops, but in mid-year, during the planting and growing season, the banks have unused reserves which they have recently invested in treasury bills, timed to mature when the banks require credit to lend to the ordinary trade.

This growth of a market for government loans of all types has occurred in most African countries since independence, and shows that central banks have been successful in channelling local savings into the service of their respective governments.

CONTROL OF CREDIT BY CENTRAL BANKS

In implementing the economic policies of their governments, central banks may need to control both the total amount of loans and credit outstanding at any one time, and also the use made of them. In the first place, central banks can influence the volume or the type of lending through direct instructions to the commercial banks. In April 1966, for example, the Central Bank of Nigeria requested the commercial banks to limit total advances to 13 per cent, and advances for consumption purposes to 4 per cent, above the level of the previous year. This has in fact been the principal method by which the central banks in African countries have so far tried to control the volume of credit.

Secondly, central banks can alter the volume of lending by the commercial banks through changes in their liquidity ratio—the proportion of cash and liquid assets to deposits. If banks have already lent up to the full amount allowed by the legal or conventional liquidity ratio, then raising or lowering it directly affects the volume of lending. But if banks have a considerable margin in hand between their holdings of currency and their maximum deposits, altering the ratio may have little immediate effect on the volume of credit outstanding. Again in Nigeria in 1966, the central bank directed that assets held abroad should not count towards the liquidity ratio of the commercial banks; this direction might have put pressure on the volume of lending, but was in fact aimed at compelling the banks to invest more of their reserves in local treasury bills, rather than in sterling treasury bills held in London.

Thirdly, central banks can directly change the amount of deposits in the commercial banks through *open market operations* by changing the volume of government loans held by them. If the central bank wishes to expand credit, it buys government loans from the commercial banks, paying the sums into their deposits with itself. Since these deposits count as cash for the purpose of the liquidity ratio, the commercial banks can then expand their ordinary loans by some multiple of the increase in their deposits with the central bank. In the opposite direction, if a greater volume of government bonds is sold, the deposits of the commercial banks with the central bank fall by the increased purchases, and the liquidity ratio is reduced. So far, however, central banks in African countries have encouraged commercial institutions to invest in government loans, and thus to build up a money market for loans of all types and lengths; open market operations have been of relatively little importance, compared with their frequent use in the industrialised countries.

Fourthly, central banks in countries with developed money markets can influence the range of interest rates through the *bank rate*, the rate charged on loans by the central bank to the commercial banks who might at times borrow in order to increase their holdings of cash. Changes in the bank rate usually alter the rate of interest on treasury bills, on deposits and other savings accounts with commercial banks and on loans made by them. Other interest rates, such as those charged on hire-purchase agreements, may also move in sympathy with the bank rate. In African countries, however, bank rate has hardly been used for this purpose. The central banks of Nigeria and of Ghana kept their bank rates unchanged from their establishment until the Bank of Ghana raised its rate in 1966 from $4\frac{1}{2}$ per cent to 7 per cent, and instructed the commercial banks to charge correspondingly increased rates on new loans to the less important sectors of the economy. Until this event, commercial banks and other institutions tended to follow the pattern of interest rates in Britain, partly because they were usually off-shoots of British companies.

At any one time, there will be a variety of interest rates charged in various sectors of an economy, according to the circumstances of each loan. In the first place, borrowers with a good record for prompt payment of interest and repayment are likely to obtain lower rates of interest than borrowers with poor records in this respect, or whose character is unknown; the lender will vary the interest charged to allow for such personal risks. Secondly, some trades are generally more risky than others, and a trade with fluctuating profits and a high risk of bankruptcies may again find that it can only borrow at correspondingly high rates of interest. Thirdly, it costs a bank more to lend £50,000 in ten loans of £5,000 each than it does to invest the lot in one purchase of treasury bills; small borrowers therefore generally pay higher interest rates than large borrowers. Fourthly, the lender may wish to consider the liquidity of his loan, his ability to obtain repayment of the capital on demand, in any emergency; at the same rate of interest, a bank may prefer to buy treasury bills which can be sold to the central bank at any time to a loan to a business which may not be able to repay on call. The lender's preference for treasury bills therefore may have to be overcome by the offer of a higher rate of interest by commercial borrowers. Finally, many loans are made between members of the same family with little regard for the market rate of interest, but in order to promote the advancement of the family generally, and the exchange of benefits between its members at different times. Such non-commercial loans are therefore outside the control of the banking system.

SAVINGS, INVESTMENT AND THE MULTIPLIER

Central Banks are charged with the function of controlling the supply of money, whether money in the form of currency or in the form of bank deposits. These controls are exercised almost entirely through the market for capital and credit, that is, through the market for loans between those with resources to spare, and those with opportunities for investment, whether in the short or long period. In what ways does this market for capital and credit affect the level of production and of prices?

To answer this question, we must return to the ideas set out in the diagram on p. 9, showing the two flows which make up an economy, the flow of goods and services passing through various stages of production into consumption or investment, and the flow of money incomes which results from this buying and selling. Ignoring for the moment any foreign trade, let us consider the relations between consumption, savings, income and investment.

What determines the amount which people in general are willing to save, that is, not to spend on immediate consumption? Institutional factors such as the existence of savings banks, and the habit of life insurance, are obviously important here, but the dominant influences are the level of income, and the economic status of the family—whether it derives its income from paid employment, or from farming, or from running a small business or trade.

As a general rule, the proportion of income saved in a group of families will increase with a rise in income, so that wealthier families tend to save more than poor families, both absolutely and as a proportion of income. The fact that certain families, or individuals in those families, may be spend-thrifts at all levels of income does not obscure this general tendency for the level of savings to rise with income. The studies of household budgets taken from families living in Nigerian towns and described by Prof. Oluwasanmi[1] show

---

[1] H. A. Oluwasanmi, 'Agriculture in a Developing Economy', in *Readings*, vol. I.

that the poorest families habitually spent more than they received, even though they spent very little; they could be described as negative savers, since they lived partly on loans made from other families. The families in the middle range of incomes about balanced their expenditure and their incomes, while the richer families, with cash incomes of over 600*s*. per month, spent on the average only 450–500*s*. per month, and therefore had a considerable margin for savings.

Secondly, there is reason to believe that farmers and families running their own businesses may generally save a higher proportion of any given income than those families in paid employment. The evidence is fragmentary, but a recent survey of agriculture in south-western Nigeria, for instance, indicated that farming families, with total incomes of £130–£200 per family per year, tended to save for investment in their farms about one third of their incomes, and that they might save about half of any increase in income.[1] This is probably a higher proportion than would be saved by most families of wage earners, who do not have the same opportunities for profitable investment in a business under family control.

There has been much discussion about the effect of rates of interest on the willingness of persons, and of institutions, to save. It has been argued that high rates of interest will encourage savings, since there is a high reward in the form of income from lending in the money market. On the other hand, those who save in order to accumulate a particular sum, whether for buying land or a business or for their old age, may save less with a high interest rate than with a low one, since a smaller initial sum will, over time, accumulate to a higher total of both capital and interest. It seems probable that changes in interest rates have little influence on the amounts saved from any given level of income, but much influence on the use made of savings. Conversely, the supply of savings available to any one borrower may be influenced by changes in the relative rates of interest offered, while the total supply of savings is unresponsive to such changes.

Let us assume that families with an income of 100*s*. a month usually save 5*s*. a month, thus spending 95 per cent of income and saving 5 per cent. Let us further suppose that the income of such families rises to 110*s*. a month, and that on the average the families

---

[1] M. Upton, *Agriculture in South-Western Nigeria*, Development Studies no. 3, (University of Reading, 1967), p. iii; J. Tinbergen, *Econometrics* (London, 1961), p. 98.

now save 7s. a month, an extra 2s. out of the increase of 10s. The rate of saving from the marginal income is thus 20 per cent, 2s. out of 10s. and the average rate of saving has risen from 5 per cent to about 6⅓ per cent. Briefly, we can say that at this level of income of 100s. a month, the *marginal propensity to save* for any increase in income is 20 per cent, and the *marginal propensity to consume* is therefore 80 per cent of any increase in income; for any one unit of income, these ratios may be described as 0·2 and 0·8.

With such propensities, a rise in incomes, for whatever reason, will increase the volume of savings looking for investment. What will happen in an economy if the volume of investment does not increase to correspond with a rise in incomes and in savings, or if the volume of investment changes without a corresponding change in the volume of savings?

To find the answers to these two questions, it will be helpful if we attach imaginary values to the quantities in the diagram of the flow of money. Let us assume that an economy with a national income and expenditure of 1,000 units produces and consumes 800 units of consumption goods, and saves 200 units for investment in capital goods. For some reason, the community now decides to save, not 20 per cent, but 25 per cent of its existing income, so that expenditure on consumption goods falls from 800 units to 750 units. Now if our community consists of farmers who invest their savings in buying new tools for their farms there will only be a switch from one type of production to another. After an initial disturbance in the markets, some of the producers of consumption goods, faced with a falling demand, will have switched their resources to producing tools for the farmers. But what happens if the increased volume of savings is not invested but hoarded?

The fall in the demand for consumption goods causes traders and business men to cut back production, and to pay out smaller incomes by way of wages and profits. If prices remain unchanged, the total of incomes paid in the community therefore falls by the amount of the increase in savings, as shown in stage B:

	A	B	C	D
National income	1,000	950	913	800
Expenditure on consumption	750	713	685	600
Savings	250	237	228	200
Investment	200	200	200	200

This fall has been divided in the proportions of 75 : 25 between expenditure on consumption and on savings. By stage C, the fall in expenditure on consumption between A and B (750−713 = 37) has reduced national income by a further 37 units, divided as before in the proportions of 75–25 between consumption and savings. This process will continue until the community reaches stage D, where the national income has fallen to the level which equates the proportion saved, 25 per cent of 800 units, to the unchanged volume of investment.

Of course both the marginal propensity to save and investment plans may alter with changes in incomes. At lower incomes people may save a smaller proportion of their income as well as a smaller amount in total; then the position of equilibrium, where intended savings equal investment, will be reached at a higher level of national income than D. On the other hand, if falling incomes also lower investment plans, income may well have to fall below position D for equilibrium to be reached.

Consider now the opposite position, where there are unemployed resources, and business men or the government decide to increase investment from 200 units to 250 units. Increased incomes accrue to the resources newly taken into employment. Let us suppose that the marginal propensity to save from these increased incomes remains at 0·2, so that 0·8 of any unit of marginal income will be spent on consumption goods, in addition to the existing demand. This rise in demand of 50 units will lead to some increase in production in various industries. These industries in turn will pay out extra incomes to the newly employed resources and the national income and the national output of goods and services will continue to rise, assuming resources are available, to stage D, where savings from the higher income once more equal the level of investment:

	A	B	C	D
National income	1,000	1,050	1,090	1,250
Expenditure on consumption	800	840	872	1,000
Savings	200	210	218	250
Investment	250	250	250	250

The way in which equilibrium is restored in the economy will, in fact, be more complicated than is shown above. Each rise in the national income, resulting from a rise in the volume of investment at the previous stage, will be smaller than the last, since 20 per cent of any increase is absorbed by savings. The rapid increase in incomes may, at first, lead to a further rise in investment, but as the rise in incomes slows down, the incentive to invest in further plant gradually diminishes. Secondly, the demand for loans from the commercial banks to finance this investment may push up the rates of interest, thus raising the costs of investment, whether in buildings, in plant, or in holding stocks of materials. Thirdly, the rise in the rate of interest may lower the value of existing fixed-interest stocks on the stock exchange, and this will diminish the nominal wealth of their holders. All these trends taken together will, after a time, tend to reduce the excess investment to the level of savings which the community wishes to make.

The effects of any change in the level of investment are thus magnified throughout the economy roughly in proportion to the propensity to consume from any increase in income. If all increases in income were saved, then an initial increase in investment would be matched by a flow of savings, and income would rise only by the value of the investment. If the marginal propensity to save remains at 0.2, then any increase in investment above the current level of savings would, other things being equal, increase the national income by five times the initial change in investment $(1 \div 0.2 = 5)$. The higher the marginal propensity to save, therefore, the smaller becomes the multiplying effect of a change in the level of investment; if the marginal propensity to save rose to 0.5, the *multiplier* would fall to 2 $(1 \div 0.5)$.

This concept of the multiplier plays an important part in the framing of economic policy. For if the volume of savings in any community tends to exceed the volume of investment, the result may be a period of falling prices, profits and output, rising unemployment and great hardship to many families, which may only end when the community is too poor to save much. Obviously a government faced with such circumstances should take up the excess savings and use them to improve the productive resources of the country, thus maintaining the flow of incomes and the flow of demand which will eventually again stimulate investment. This is the basic argument for positive investment by the state, whenever a cycle of falling investment, prices, profits and incomes threatens the economy.

INFLATION OR STABILITY

On the other hand, an initial excess of investment over savings can create a rise in incomes, which equally can become self-perpetuating for some considerable period. This rise in incomes is composed of two parts—a rise in output, as the business men and the government expand output to meet the greater demand, and a rise in prices. The double trend often runs together, since it is the rise in prices and in the expectations of profits which together encourage the employment of more resources, and this in turn eventually leads to greater output, which may somewhat check the rise in prices of consumption goods. But as resources become fully employed, as government, business men and farmers begin to bid up wages and other prices, so the rise in output slows down and the rise in prices intensifies. Here we have the state of affairs known as *inflation*.

Inflation can be described as a consistent rise in the general level of demand and of prices within an economy. It may cover a wide range of situations, from a small rise in prices persisting over several years to a violent surge in prices which destroys confidence in the value of the currency, and which leads to a complete breakdown in the monetary sector, so that the economy reverts largely to barter. Inflation may arise from unplanned increases in costs, such as an increase in the prices of imported goods or a shortage of local foods, which reduces the real value of money incomes and leads to pressure for higher incomes. More frequently, inflation is a consequence of an increase in the level of demand, caused by optimistic investment by business men and by government in excess of local savings, or by a transference of demand on to the home market when imports have been sharply reduced for any reason. In Ghana, the imposition of import controls in 1961, coupled with expenditure by the government on unprofitable investments, stimulated inflation, which was shown especially by the rise in the prices of foods on which much of the increase in money incomes was spent. Undeveloped countries are particularly prone to inflation from this cause, because much of any increase in money incomes is spent upon locally-grown foods whose supply may be inelastic in the short period to a rise in prices, owing to the scarcity of certain resources such as farm labour or transport.[1] An increase in demand may then show itself in an *inflationary gap*, with an increase in prices rather than an increase in output, even though there may be substantial numbers of unemployed unskilled workers.

The degree and duration of inflation which may follow any initial stimulus depends on the relative bargaining power of different

[1] See A. J. Killick, 'Inflation and Growth', in *Readings*, vol. II; H. A. Oluwasanmi, 'Agriculture in a Developing Economy', and R. M. Lawson, 'The Markets for Foods in Ghana', in *Readings*, vol. I.

sectors of the economy, and on the degree to which it is possible to expand output. Paid employees in the service of governments and of public corporations may be able to ensure that their wages keep pace with the rise in the prices of consumer goods. Business men may be able to push up their prices a little in advance of costs, and thus obtain higher incomes to offset the rising prices of the things they buy. But the faster these groups adjust their incomes, the faster becomes the prices/incomes spiral and the annual rate of inflation, while other groups, such as producers of export crops, suffer a continuing fall in real incomes. It is the earners of such falling real incomes who pay the price of inflation which may cause a sudden redistribution of consumption between social classes.

The usual method of checking inflation is for the government to try to increase the volume of savings by propaganda among its citizens, or to reduce the volume of money in circulation by raising taxes and reducing its debt to the central bank. If the initial stimulus to inflation came from a sudden rise in the prices received for export crops, working back through larger incomes for farmers, then again taxation may be the answer, combined perhaps with some scheme for averaging surplus receipts this year with probable low prices for exports at some later year. If imports have had to be cut, then again it may be necessary to raise taxes to reduce incomes temporarily, as well as taking special measures to hasten the production of alternative commodities. In addition, the central bank can raise the rates of interest, thus raising the costs of borrowing for investment; it can also operate directly on the liquidity ratio of the commercial banks, so that they have to cut down the volume of their lending.

There has been much argument over the relative advantages and disadvantages of a general price level which is stable, slowly falling or slowly rising; there is no argument over the overwhelming disadvantages of any sudden and large change in price levels which upsets rational planning and the customary differentials in incomes and rewards. Governments and central banks are sometimes advised to aim at a stable general level of prices, allowing individual prices to go up or down, according to the state of supply and demand in their individual markets. Incomes would then reflect the balance of costs and of profits in particular industries and occupations; there would be fewer opportunities than under inflation for the large-scale speculation in commodities and in financial assets which so often leads to sudden fortunes and conspicuous consumption for the few.

A slowly falling price level has been advocated as a method of ensuring that those groups in the community with weak bargaining power obtain their share in the greater output of goods and services, through a gradual rise in the purchasing power of their fixed incomes. This is an important point in societies where the average expectation of life has risen, where a high proportion of the population can expect to live for many years beyond retirement, drawing incomes from past savings and from pensions. But such a policy, even if achievable, has little relevance to conditions in most African countries.

Moderate inflation has been advocated as a necessary part of the policy for economic development for a number of reasons. The pressure of demand upon prices and upon production is likely to spur business men to expand output quickly, and to overcome small blockages to production. Business men, like farmers, probably have a high marginal propensity to invest extra income in their own businesses; a rising level of prices thus puts income into the hands of those who will save and invest more than the wage-earners and holders of government debts. The fact that many incomes are rising gives people a feeling of getting richer and thus encourages them to take an optimistic view of development, even though the rise in prices may leave the majority of citizens with no more purchasing power, and some of them may definitely be poorer. On the other hand, rising costs afflict governments as well as the private sectors of the economy, and it may become politically difficult for the government either to tax the increased incomes sufficiently, or to raise the prices of the services provided, such as schools, railways, or electricity. Indeed, governments may be under strong pressure from the urban wage earners to control the prices of foods and basic necessities such as house rents which take up a large part of the budget of the poorer families. Then governments become committed either to costly subsidies for certain prices, or to low prices for foods which, in turn, quickly react on supply, thus causing genuine scarcity and greater hardship.

MONETARY POLICY

Over the last twenty years, the general level of prices in every country has tended to rise, though in varying degrees.[1] The rise in prices has generally been larger in the industrialised countries, and less conspicuous for those African countries whose exports consist mainly of agricultural crops and raw materials; prices of industrial goods have generally risen faster and further than prices of agricultural products and of raw materials, such as oil, timber and minerals. In a few countries, inflation has gone so far and so fast than their currencies have lost much of their former value, whether for internal use or in exchange against the currencies of other countries; almost all countries have, at some time in the last twenty years, *devalued* or reduced the value of their currency in terms of gold, or of the American dollar which is based on gold. Since all countries are linked together by the network of international trade, and by the structure of prices in international markets, monetary and fiscal policy has generally taken the form of allowing some measure of inflation in prices, partly to keep in step with other countries, and partly to assist in the process of mobilising resources for increasing output.

Whatever the price level attempted, central banks and governments should ideally combine their controls, whether over the money market or over taxes, into a single coherent policy. Generally speaking, the controls operated by central banks over the market for loans are more direct and more immediate in their effect than changes in taxes, but in many African countries the market for loans is as yet poorly developed, and much investment and saving goes on outside the commercial and saving banks. Moreover, monetary policy, even with a developed money market, can more easily check inflation, by raising interest rates and reducing loans, than it can coax an economy out of a fit of depression; business men will not borrow to invest, even at low rates of interest, if they do not expect to make a profit out of expanding their production. Governments may here have to step in with more positive measures of encouraging the expansion of output.

The two main problems of monetary policy arise, firstly from the activities of governments which promote development at the cost of severe inflation, and secondly, from the pervasive influence of

[1] See table 22, p. 196.

foreign trade upon prices, incomes and production. And we must now look briefly at these two aspects of economic policy, the financing of governments, and the flow of international trade.

APPENDIX: NATIONAL INCOME, SAVINGS AND INVESTMENT

The relation between national income, the propensity to save and the level of investment can be demonstrated geometrically, as in graph 23. Here expenditure is measured along the vertical axis, and income along the

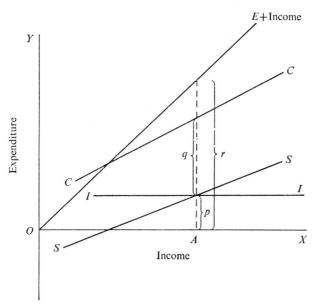

Graph 23. National income, savings and investments

horizontal axis; it is assumed that investment is a constant proportion of total income.

Through the origin *O*, the line *OE* represents the equality of total income and total expenditure, drawn at an angle of 45° to the axes. The line *SS* represents the propensity to save, which rises with income but which for low levels of income may be negative, that is, people will dis-save at low levels of income in order to maintain certain minimum levels of consumption. The line *CC* is drawn to represent the value of total consumption; since consumption plus savings equal total income, the vertical distances from the income line at any point of *SS* and *CC* add up to the vertical distance from the same point to OE; thus p plus q equals r, at point A.

The line II represents the volume of investment for different levels of income. For stability in the national income, savings must equal investment, since the value of consumption goods is the same both for expenditure and for income. OA is therefore the equilibrium value of the national income, with the given propensity to save and the given relation between income and investment. At any lower levels of national income, investment exceeds savings, and income will therefore rise; at any higher levels of income, savings exceed investment, and income will fall.

11. Public finance and fiscal policy .

INTRODUCTION

Public finance is concerned with the effect on an economy of government expenditure and taxes; fiscal policy refers to the detailed administration of taxes and loans. The scope of public finance thus reflects the general philosophy adopted in each country about the relative importance of private business and collective affairs. In centrally planned economies, almost every activity could be included under the heading of public finance, since governments concern themselves with the planning of production, investment, savings and incomes all through the economy. In European countries and in America, the scope of government action has gradually been extended, partly as a result of wars, partly because of growing dissatisfaction with the results of leaving much of the economy to private enterprise. Because the scope of government activities varies so much, it is always dangerous to make comparisons of public finance between countries with widely differing political systems; nevertheless, much can be learnt from the experience of different countries dealing with the same problems of tax collection, control of government administration, subsidies and development grants, the financing of state enterprises and the like.

TAXES, THE STATE AND THE INDIVIDUAL

Given the fact that a government wishes to spend some fraction of the gross domestic product (G.D.P.) of its country, whether this be 10, 20 or 30 per cent, how should it raise the necessary funds from its citizens?

From the point of view of the individual citizen, or company, taxation should fulfil three qualifications. Firstly, there should be certainty, so that people know what taxes they will be called upon to pay and when they must pay, so that they can plan their economic affairs accordingly. Taxes should not therefore be made retrospective in their incidence, nor framed in such vague terms that local collectors can alter them at will. Secondly, taxation should impose a rough equality of sacrifice on citizens, who may all be regarded as benefiting roughly to the same degree from the major policies of the state. Citizens in equal circumstances with approximately the same incomes should therefore pay approximately the same level of taxation; the proportion of income taken in taxes should generally rise with income—the tax system should be progressive with income, since it is assumed that the marginal utility of the last increments of a large income is less than the marginal utility of smaller incomes.[1] Thirdly, taxes should not discourage the production of goods and services, the earning of incomes by the citizens and the normal types of economic activity. Taxes should not, for example, absorb all of some increment of income, so that there is no inducement to earn more; savings should not be confiscated so that thrifty citizens are discouraged from accumulating funds for future investment; companies engaged in risky enterprises should be allowed to offset their losses against profits before profits are taxed, and so on.

From the point of view of the government levying taxes, the problems of taxation are rather different. Easy and cheap administration is highly important, with as little opportunity as possible for evasion by the taxpayers and dishonesty by the tax collectors. Taxes whose yields rise with rising incomes both in times of inflation and during the process of economic development are to be preferred to taxes whose yield remains constant; otherwise, the costs of government may rise but not its revenue. Speaking generally, direct taxes on incomes of individuals are costly to administer, especially in Africa where many taxpayers are illiterate, keep no accounts and engage in many types of petty trading; taxes on the sale of commodities, indirect taxation, are generally cheaper to collect and less easily evaded.

Most African countries impose income taxes upon civil servants, paid workers in industry, limited liability companies and the larger traders. Those not liable to income tax usually pay a poll tax, levied upon all adult males, or upon all adults, which ensures that all citizens pay something towards the cost of local and national governments. In addition, levies upon the export of agricultural products tax farmers' incomes in proportion to their production of these crops, leaving untaxed the incomes derived from the local sale of these and other products. Some countries also levy a tax upon every adult head of cattle that can be counted. Indirect taxes come

[1] See p. 157.

TABLE 21. *Revenue in Kenya, Ghana and Nigeria*

	Kenya 1965/6		Ghana 1966		Nigeria[a] 1965	
	£ m.	%	n.c.m.	%	£ m.	%
Income tax	15·9	27·6	48·0	20·8	13·5	7·0
Export duties	0·7	1·2	16·2	7·0	15·8	8·2
Import duties	17·2	29·8	75·4	32·7	84·6	44·0
Excise and other sales taxes	7·5	13·1	60·8	26·3	16·5	8·6
Other revenue	16·3	28·3	30·5	13·2	61 8	32·2
Total revenue	57·6	100·0	230·9	100·0	192·2	100·0

SOURCE. Adapted from *Ghana Economic Survey* (1966); *Kenya Economic Survey* (1968); Central Bank of Nigeria, *Annual Report*, (1966).

[a] Consolidated accounts for federal and regional governments.

largely from duties upon imports, upon certain home manufactures regarded as luxuries, such as beer and cigarettes, and upon certain activities which are visible and linked to high incomes, such as owning a car, or a house. Many local authorities raise a substantial part of their revenue through taxes on houses, on built-up land within their boundaries and on trading activities in local markets.

Taxes upon incomes of course restrict the purchasing power of the taxpayers, whether individuals or companies, and thus alter their demand for goods and services bought in the markets. If a company has to pay a third of its profits in taxes, it has so much less to pay out as dividends to its shareholders, or for extending its plant; some of the taxes thus collected undoubtedly reduce the volume of private saving and investment in the economy. Indirect taxes upon the sale of commodities change the level of demand, of prices and of production, and their effects are therefore difficult to trace. If at any level of price, demand for a commodity is highly elastic to a further rise in price, then imposing a tax might so reduce demand and production that there would be little revenue. From the point of view of the government, therefore, indirect taxes should be levied upon commodities whose demands have a low price-elasticity, so that sales are not much affected by a rise in price. Table 21 shows the revenue from the principal taxes levied in recent years in Kenya, Ghana and Nigeria.

TAXES AND SUBSIDIES

In previous chapters, we looked at some of the reasons why a multitude of businesses conducted primarily for the profit of their organisers might not lead to the most economic use of the national resources, and why the distribution of incomes which results from free markets might also be regarded as in need of amendment. It is now generally agreed that governments should use their powers of taxes and of subsidies to promote a greater efficiency in the use of resources and a more equal distribution of incomes among its citizens.

The damage inflicted by heavy lorries upon roads, for instance, is usually regarded as an adequate reason for imposing annual taxes upon their use, as well, possibly, as import duties. The congestion of large towns, and the external economies and costs which draw firms to their suburbs may be countered by providing facilities in other regions, by building new railway lines to the interior, by giving a road to an inland centre an all-weather surface in advance of the growth of traffic which will make it pay. The risks of starting new industries, in the face of competition from imports, can be reduced by the imposition of import duties, putting the costs of establishing the new industry upon the present buyers of that product; or by giving new firms subsidies for some years, thus spreading the burden over the whole body of taxpayers. Since it is difficult to charge farmers for the work of agricultural advisers and veterinary assistants, such services can legitimately be financed by taxing the incomes arising from export crops.

More difficult problems arise with the policy to be adopted for the financing of government services to the taxpayers. It is possible to charge the users of a new bridge, by stationing toll collectors at one end, and in America the use of some motorways is similarly subject to the payment of tolls, entry being restricted to specified places. But generally, it is not administratively possible to charge citizens as they use the services of roads, the police, civil servants and the like; such services are provided free to the users, and financed by taxes from the general funds of the government.

There are two services where the argument between free use and taxation, or paying as you use, remains unsolved, education and medical services. From one point of view, education is a consumer good, to be bought by parents for their children just as they buy clothes for them.[1] From another, education can be regarded as an investment for a family, since the educated member may earn a high salary, from which he could repay loans and help his relatives. Again, in so far as education encourages people to become more efficient producers and citizens, the state could regard education as an activity which ought to be encouraged by subsidies, providing it below cost or even without charge to all who take advantage of it. Alternatively, education can be regarded as designed to train people for specific posts within an expanding economy—so many clerks, so many scientists, so many mechanics and craftsmen; schools and colleges must then be organised to provide the required numbers in the required subjects. Finally, education at any one time is ultimately limited by the number and quality of the teachers who are themselves the product of the educational system of the recent past; the expansion of education in the near future is therefore already conditioned by the numbers now at various stages of education.

In the same way, medical services can be regarded as something to be bought in the market in the normal way by those who are prepared and able to pay for them. Alternatively, the care, and if possible the cure, of sick people can also be regarded as part of the humanitarian function of the state who must therefore provide medical and hospital services for all who need them. In addition, there are the infectious diseases—cholera, smallpox, plague, malaria —whose prevention requires measures on such a large scale that only governments and international organisations can provide them. There is therefore no principle which clearly demarcates the parts to be played in providing these services by private enterprise through the market, or by government enterprise financed by taxation. All countries rely on both, though to different degrees, for reasons more of history than of economics.

A second field for state intervention concerns the distribution of incomes between its citizens. The distribution of incomes under a system of free markets can diverge widely from the usual concepts of just reward for effort, skill or responsibility; the existence of monopolies and of imperfect competition in many trades and in-

---

[1] P. Williams, 'The Cost and Finance of Education', in *Readings*, vol. II; *Interim Report on Education in a Rural Area of Western Nigeria*, International Labour Office Pilot Project (Geneva, 1967); *Report of the Conference on the Review of the Educational System in Eastern Nigeria*, no. 25 (Enugu, 1964); P. Kilby, *Technical Education in Nigeria*, Bulletin, Oxford Institute of Economics and Statistics, vol. 26, no. 2 (1964).

dustries implies that many incomes may remain for long periods of time above the level which would induce competition and a return to a 'normal' level. Moreover, large incomes accumulate as capital, itself a scarce resource in many African countries; capital not only earns large incomes for its owners but also gives economic and political power. In countries where the vast majority of citizens are still desperately poor, such accumulations of capital and large incomes lead naturally to claims that the state should take countervailing action through taxation, both on large incomes and upon capital wealth.

Industrialised countries have developed in recent decades the practice of compulsory levelling of incomes over time for individual citizens, through the payment of pensions for the old and the chronic sick; unemployment and sickness benefit for those temporarily unable to earn; allowances for large families, fatherless children, widows and university students. An enormous volume of taxation is now levied in the United Kingdom in order to pay such benefits to those in need. These *transfer payments* represent not an increase in demand, but a transfer of claims upon resources from those earning incomes at any one time to those who are not then earning; in a sense, the only costs involved are the salaries of the officials who carry out the transfers and investigate the claims to benefits. On the other hand, the working citizen pays these taxes along with the others, and it is the total burden of taxation upon his income which may impede his incentive to earn more by producing more.

LOANS AND TAXES

In the previous chapter, we looked at the part played in the money market by the various kinds of government debts, such as treasury bills and development loans. At any one time, a government must have some policy concerning the proportion of its expenditure which should be covered by taxes and the proportion which can be raised by internal loans or by grants or loans from overseas. Taxes and internal loans represent a transfer of claims to resources from the taxpayers to the government, but these transfers take place in different circumstances and for different reasons. Taxes are usually a compulsory transfer, for which the individual citizen may or may not obtain compensating benefits, while loans are a voluntary transfer, for which the citizen expects some return in the form of interest at stated intervals, as well as the return of the sum lent, either directly from the government, or through the money market. Consider the case of a new railway being built by the government. Here there is a huge volume of capital expenditure to be incurred over a period of perhaps five years; then there will be another period of years before there is sufficient traffic to cover the costs of transport; finally the railway may be expected to make a profit. How should such an enterprise be financed?

In the nineteenth century, railways were built in many countries by private companies operating with loans raised on the London money market, through the offer of a share in the profits, if any, which might eventually accrue. Capital therefore only flowed into the building of railways if the surplus over costs seemed likely to provide as good a return, allowing for risks and uncertainties, as might be earned in other investments. If the railway proved unprofitable, as many did, the providers of capital earned little income, and their share capital became of little value.

Raising capital in this way has two great advantages. In the first place, the initial expenditure does not involve a sudden increase in taxation; it is provided voluntarily by those with resources to spare at that moment. Secondly, if the railway should prove unprofitable, the company running it does not have to continue paying interest on capital which is now worth very little. For it is one peculiarity of capital, that, once invested, it may become obsolete, unprofitable and useless through cheaper forms of production or through changes in demand. The investors in such enterprises take a risk in providing capital in the hope of an appropriate return; they may obtain high dividends and a rise in the value of their capital, but they may also face a loss both of interest and of capital.

For similar reasons, such large enterprises can suitably be financed through loans, rather than through taxation; the state raising such loans has the advantage of being able to offer the security of taxes for the payment of interest and eventual repayment of capital, if the enterprise should prove unprofitable. However, few African countries can as yet mobilise sufficient local savings on a voluntary basis to finance large enterprises of this sort, and in recent years African governments have drawn heavily on foreign loans, and on loans from international agencies. Nevertheless, as local money markets develop, it should be possible to raise more loans from citizens for investment of this nature.

In deciding whether to raise taxes or loans, the government must pay attention to the existing volume of both. For loans, the government has two possibilities open to it. It can offer to borrow money with no fixed date for repayment, relying on the local stock exchange to provide a market for those citizens who wish to get back their capital by finding a buyer for their security. Alternatively, it can offer a dated loan, promising to repay the stated sum on a specified date to the then holders of the security. At the specified date, the government must therefore repay the sum borrowed, or, which is more common, must again borrow the same sum to repay those holders of the security who do not wish to continue lending their capital in this way. Consequently, it is important that government loans should not be bunched together for repayment; the government must spread out its loans so that there is a regular flow, year by year, waiting for repayment.

This regular flow of loans for repayment is important both for the government, which has to pay them off, or borrow again, and also for the commercial institutions which are concerned with the problem of liquidity, the ability to get back quickly the resources invested in interest-earning loans. How much a government can borrow this year depends very much upon the amount it borrowed in previous years, and how much of the former debt is now held by different institutions with varying needs for liquidity. If the commercial banks simultaneously sell their securities in order to increase their cash reserves, then the price of government loans may fall sharply, since there will be few buyers; a new loan can then only be raised by tempting new buyers, either by offering very high rates of interest, or by offering the loan below *par*, taking £98 or £95 as equivalent to £100 when calculating the interest due and the sum to be repaid eventually. Both these devices of course raise the cost of borrowing for the government.

In all cases, the interest paid year by year on government loans represents a transfer payment, from the taxpayers to the holders of the loans, who may well be taxpayers themselves. In a sense, therefore, the payment of interest represents no cost to the community as a whole; it is merely a transfer of claims from one group of people to another, partly overlapping, group. Here again, however, the government must consider the total burden of taxation both on the flow of incomes within the community and upon the incentives for individuals to increase output; if payment of interest upon outstanding loans already takes a sizeable fraction of the annual budget, it may be highly undesirable for the government to add to that burden by trying to launch another loan.

THE INFLATIONARY GAP

In this discussion upon public finance, we have so far assumed that, in levying taxes and asking for loans, governments wish to transfer resources from the taxpayers and lenders to government agencies. There may be occasions, however, when such a transfer is undertaken with the objective of not using resources—for instance a government may consider that there is excess demand in the economy, and that the resulting inflation requires corrective measures.

There are various ways in which an inflationary gap may be closed. The government may cut its own expenditure upon investment, while leaving its revenue unchanged. This directly reduces the level of demand by setting the multiplier to work in a downward direction; the surplus funds accruing to the government can be used to pay off maturing loans held by the central bank which can then cancel some of its fiduciary issue of notes. Alternatively, the government can raise taxes, while leaving its own expenditure unchanged; the fall in demand is then concentrated upon the citizens and companies paying the extra taxes. A government must remember that an increase in direct taxes will usually reduce savings as well as consumption; a reduction of, say, £10 m. in excess demand might require an increase of £12½ m. in the total yield of taxes, if the propensity to save is reckoned at 0·2. An increase in indirect taxes might lead some individuals to maintain their rate of saving and to accept that their expenditure upon consumption goods will now buy less than before; but some reduction in savings is more probable as citizens attempt to maintain their customary consumption.

Thirdly, the central bank can cause the commercial banks to reduce the level of their advances. Finally, measures may be taken to ease the scarcity of whatever resource is currently holding up the expansion in output; alternative supplies may be obtained through imports, either of materials or of skilled workers, or of particular machines. Before these measures are applied, however, a government needs firstly the facts about the present flow of money and of supplies through the economy, so that the current situation can be correctly analysed; secondly, a policy about inflation and invest-

TABLE 22. *Changes in consumer prices in selected countries*

1958 = 100	1962	1963	1964	1965	1966
Ghana	120	126	139	174	185
% change over previous year	9·4	5·0	10·3	25·3	6·3
Nigeria	122	122	124	130	144
% change over previous year	4·2	—	1·6	4·8	10·7
Kenya	107	109	107	113	117
% change over previous year	2·8	1·9	−1·9	5·6	3·5
Tanzania	100	97	98	105	110
% change over previous year	—	−3·0	1·0	7·2	4·7
Uganda	95	97	105	123	117
% change over previous year	−13·7	2·1	8·2	17·1	−4·9
Zambia	105	104	108	116	128
% change over previous year	1·0	−1·0	3·8	7·4	10·3

SOURCE. International Monetary Fund, *International Financial Statistics* (Dec. 1967).

ment and the price level; and thirdly, an electorate that will respond to the government's measures in the required fashion.

Since independence, most African countries have undergone varying degrees of inflation, ranging from acute in Ghana to very moderate in Tanzania. Much of the general tendency towards inflation has come from the industrialised countries, whose inflation has been transmitted through international trade to virtually all other countries. But the Nkrumah government in Ghana used inflation to centralise, in the hands of members of the government, an increasing share in national resources, some of which were invested in huge enterprises which provided virtually no output. Between 1956–7 and 1963–4, the amount of public debt in Ghana increased from about £25 m. to nearly £240 m.; the total value of the reserves in the Consolidated Fund, Development Fund, Contingencies Fund and Special Fund fell from nearly £64 m. to about £7 m. over this period.[1] Some of this debt represented only a change in the form of assets, as marketing boards and other lenders transferred from British Government securities to Ghana securities; but government borrowing from the central and commercial banks increased by some £33 m., and this created a rise in the total supply of money which undoubtedly helped in the inflationary rise in prices which took place from 1963, and

[1] A. J. Killick, 'The Monetary Effects of Recent Budgets in Ghana', in *Readings*, vol. II.

which was intensified by the scarcity of imports and of some home-grown foods.

The theory of the multiplier, as it relates to public finance and monetary policy, was originally developed to cope with the problems of *deflation*, or economic depression, which was peculiarly a feature of the twenty years between the wars. Here the multiplier worked in a downward direction. An initial slackening in the rate of expenditure upon new investment, whether by private enterprise or by governments, reduced the incomes of those engaged in the industries producing capital goods; this fall in incomes reduced the prices and profits of the trades supplying consumer goods, which in turn restricted output, cut wages and dismissed workers, thus intensifying both the lack of demand and the unemployment. The process continued in America and in Europe between 1929 and 1933 until national incomes had fallen by ten or twenty per cent, unemployment had risen to a quarter or more of the industrial labour force, new investment was at a standstill, and most banks and financial institutions were technically bankrupt, since every one wanted money and no one could pay their debts. It was indeed this experience which produced for the first time a clear analysis of the process of deflation and inflation, expounded by Maynard Keynes (later Lord Keynes) in his *General Theory of Employment, Interest and Money*. Since his theories became generally accepted by economists and governments, the early signs of a general deflation can, it is recognised, be countered by appropriate measures, stepping up the expenditure upon investment out of government funds, reducing taxation and interest rates. Once the resulting flow of new demand begins to be felt in the markets, private business men will begin to take a more hopeful view of their future output and profits, and normal investment can be expected to reappear.

But for the last twenty years, governments have been trying not to prevent depressions but to control inflationary gaps. Practice has shown the difficulty of the task. In the first place, few governments have adequate information about the current flows of money and the current intentions about investment and what information they possess is often several months or even years out of date before it becomes available. Lack of information is especially serious for the governments in Africa. Secondly, government expenditure cannot be reduced at short notice without grave inefficiencies in the process of capital formation, in which governments are now so heavily engaged. Not to add the roof to a building because expenditure in the current year must be cut below estimates implies that the capital already invested in the building yields no output and will rapidly cease to have any value at all. Governments are often over-optimistic about the cost of their larger investments, whether the capital cost of construction or the running cost of the eventual output, so that total expenditures on any project tend to exceed estimates. On the other hand, delays in planning, in government administration and in construction often delay expenditure far beyond the original time limits, so that the flow of government expenditure is, in many economies, both unplanned and also incapable of fine adjustment. Thirdly, the emphasis upon development and upon expanding output encourages the general public in all countries to press for higher wages, salaries and profits, in order that each individual may enjoy the benefits. But if the total of such monetary claims continuously exceeds the rise in productivity and in total output, demand continuously exceeds the corresponding flow of goods and services. Finally, there are the problems created by the spread of inflation through the mechanism of international trade, to which we must now turn.

APPENDIX: INDEX NUMBERS

Index numbers are much used in economics to provide a summary of trends, over a period of time, in a number of related quantities—output of various industries, prices of various commodities, incomes for different groups of persons.

For the simplest case of an index number, take an imaginary price recorded on each market day for one commodity on four separate occasions:

Market day	Price per lb	% of 1st date	% of average (4·75)
1	5	100	105
2	4½	90	95
3	4	80	85
4	5½	110	116

If the first price is taken as the base figure for the series of index numbers, the other prices are expressed as a percentage of this figure; for day 2, the index number, with 5 as base, equals $(4 \cdot 5 \times 100/5) = 90$. Alternatively, if we are interested in the seasonal variations of this price series, the individual prices can be expressed as index numbers with the average price $(19/4 = 4 \cdot 75)$ as a base, as in the fourth column.

With recorded quantities of two commodities (or of any larger number), two methods are available for summarising trends. In the first method, each series is converted to index numbers, with the same date as base; the index numbers for each subsequent date are then averaged:

Market day	Beans Maize pence per lb		Beans 5 = 100	Maize 4 = 100	Average
1	5	4	100	100	100
2	4½	4½	90	113	101¼
3	4	3½	80	88	84
4	5½	4	110	100	105

For the second method, the individual items are weighted, to indicate their relative importance in the final average. Suppose that a family normally buys twice as much maize as beans, so that a change in the price of maize has more importance than the same change in the price of beans. If we wish to measure the effect on this family's expenditure of changes in prices, we take a typical 'basket' of the day's purchases, say 2 lb of maize and 1 lb of beans:

Market day	Beans	Maize	Price of maize × 2	Total expenditure	Index 1st date = 100
1	5	4	8	13	100
2	4½	4½	9	13½	104
3	4	3½	7	11	77
4	5½	4	8	13½	104

This method provides a weighted index, in which changes in the price of maize have approximately twice as much effect on the final index as changes in the price of beans. Between dates 1 and 2 the price of beans fell and the price of maize rose; the unweighted index showed a rise of only 1¼ per cent, while the weighted index rose by 4 per cent.

Remember that index numbers are only averages, and averages of figures which may themselves be only approximations to the facts. Weighted indices may also become out of date and misleading if price changes are large. In the example given above, a family is likely, over time, to reduce its consumption of foods which become relatively dearer, and to spend more on foods which have become relatively cheaper; people may even cease to buy the dear commodity and adopt some substitute which was not on the market in the base period, and therefore not included in the price records. If the income of the family changes there may again be considerable changes in the relative importance of the expenditure on the different commodities.

12. International trade

INTRODUCTION

Most of the African countries south of the Sahara are highly dependent upon international trade, with exports accounting for anything up to one-third of their gross domestic product (G.D.P.):

TABLE 23. *Exports and gross domestic products of selected countries in 1965*

U.S.A. $ at current rates of exchange	1 Exports m.	2 G.D.P. m.	3 Col. 1 as % of col. 2
Ghana	227	1,608[b]	14
Kenya	216	806[a]	27
Malawi	40	177[b]	23
Nigeria	750	3,413[a]	22
Sierra Leone	88	365[b]	24
Tanzania (Tanganyika)	193	683[a]	28

SOURCE. Adapted from *Ghana Economic Survey*, (1966); *East African Economic and Statistical Review*, (1967); International Monetary Fund, *International Statistics* (Dec. 1967).
[a] At factor cost.   [b] At market prices.

In the United Kingdom, the ratio between exports of goods and services and G.D.P. has been about 25 per cent in recent years, while continental countries like the United States and Russia have a lower ratio of exports to G.D.P. A further peculiarity of the trade of African countries is their high dependence upon the exports of a few products only, while their imports consist of a huge variety of manufactured goods. Mauritius depends upon sugar for about 94 per cent of total exports; cocoa provides about two-thirds of the exports of Ghana; cocoa, groundnuts and palm oil and kernels provide two-thirds of the exports of Nigeria.[1]

[1] Food and Agriculture Organisation, *Agricultural Commodity Trade and Development*, F.A.O. Commodity Policy Studies Programme no. 2 (Rome, 1964) p. 5; the ratios given above refer to the average of the years 1958–60. *Economic Bulletin for Africa*, vol. VI, no. 1 (1966), chaps. 1 and 2, contain a review of recent trends in the trade of African countries.

COMPARATIVE ADVANTAGES AND INTERNATIONAL TRADE

The function of international trade is to increase the wealth of the participating countries by enabling them to exchange among themselves the specialised productions of each. As a general rule, countries will import commodities which are cheaper at their ports than the corresponding home production, and they will export commodities whose prices are lower at home than in the importing countries. In dealing with this question of relative cheapness of imports and exports, we must distinguish the three elements which make up the cost of an imported commodity—the cost at the point of export, described as free on board (f.o.b.); the costs of transport including insurance and dock charges, so that commodities upon import are priced at cost with insurance and freight (c.i.f.); and the conversion of one currency into another required to pay for this trade, the cost of foreign exchange. In many cases there is also a fourth item, the cost of import duties or export taxes levied by governments on goods passing across their frontiers.

To consider the basic elements of international trade, let us take two adjacent countries using the same currency, but initially without trade (table 24). Suppose that one man-year in country A produces either 6 bags of rice or 2 bags of maize, and that total production of these commodities is 6,000 bags and 2,000 bags respectively. In country B, one man-year of labour produces two bags of either crop and total production is 2,000 bags of each. Without any exchange of products, the total production in the two countries combined is thus 8,000 bags of rice and 4,000 bags of maize. Let us make the further assumption that prices reflect the inputs of labour and nothing else, so that in country A the price of one bag of rice will be one-third the price of a bag of maize, while in country B the two commodities will exchange for equal quantities.

If the frontier is then opened to international trade in commodities (but not to resources such as labour and capital), country A will be able to export rice which is cheaper than rice grown in country B; this inflow of cheaper rice will discourage some farmers in country B from growing rice and they will turn to the alternative crop, maize, some of which can now be sold in the new export market, since some farmers in country A have switched from maize to rice. A new balance in production will be struck, where marginal costs for each

TABLE 24. *Comparative costs and international trade*

	Output in bags		Employment in man-years	
	Rice	Maize	Rice	Maize
A. *Before international trade*				
Country A	6,000	2,000	1,000	1,000
B	2,000	2,000	1,000	1,000
Total	8,000	4,000	2,000	2,000
B. *After international trade*				
Country A	9,000	1,000	1,500	500
B	1,000	3,000	500	1,500
Total	10,000	4,000	2,000	2,000
C. *Complete specialisation*				
Country A	12,000	—	2,000	—
B	—	4,000	—	2,000
Total	12,000	4,000	2,000	2,000

crop equal marginal revenue or price; the new pattern may take the form shown in section B, or, assuming constant costs in our production functions, changes may continue until there is complete specialisation between the countries, as shown in section C. Each country employs the same quantity of man-years, but there is a greater production of rice, as country A begins to specialise on the product for which it has a comparative advantage, compared, that is, with its trading partner, while country B specialises on the trade in which it has the least disadvantage.

Specialisation in production between countries is thus only another example of the benefits of specialised production between different people in the same village, or between farmers in different areas of the same country. A skilled goldsmith or trader may give his full time to his specialised work, using the money so earned to buy food and clothing, because his total command over goods and services is thus larger than it would be if he had to spend several days each week growing his own food. Cocoa farmers in Ghana may plant all their land with cocoa, and buy the greater part of their food; the Fulani in West Africa and the Masai in East Africa exchange the

milk and manure of their herds for grain, rather than spend their
time in cultivating land for grain production. University professors
may employ typists and gardeners, rather than waste their time
typing their own correspondence and weeding their own flower-
beds; other people specialise upon typing and gardening, and
become proficient at these particular jobs.

Wherever such specialisation occurs, the standard of consumption
of individuals, and of countries, depends upon two things, their
output, and the relative prices of the things sold and the things
bought, what we may call the *terms of trade*. One of the risks of
specialised production is that the increased output made possible
by greater efficiency may at some time have to be sold at relatively
low prices, so that the quantity of goods which can be bought by
the specialist is also low. In the extreme case, the highly specialised
man may find no one who will buy his output or his skill. Cocoa
farmers whose trees are destroyed by swollen shoot, or whose output
can only be sold at prices which barely cover the cost of harvesting,
are probably worse off than the local farmers growing a variety of
crops, but on the whole, the bulk of cocoa farmers have probably
earned more from their specialisation, over the years, than the crop
growers.

For individual countries, foreign trade enables them to escape
from the limitations of the local markets, one of the principal
constraints upon production. No African country could profitably
utilise all the output of crops produced by its farmers in recent
decades; palm oil, cocoa, coffee, sisal, cotton, tea, as well as mineral
ores and oil itself, have been developed for overseas markets, and
the resulting income has financed the imports not only of consumption goods but also of the capital goods required for major works of
development. Governments have also relied greatly upon export
taxes of various sorts for their revenues, both in East and in West
Africa.[1]

Returning to table 24, it is important to note that as a result of
international trade both countries in our example are better off
than they were in isolation. They can each enjoy the same quantity
of maize but the output of rice has increased by one-half of its
former output in both countries combined, from 8,000 tons to
12,000 tons in the situation of section C. As a result, rice will have

---

[1] G. K. Helleiner, 'The Fiscal Role of the Marketing Boards in Nigerian
Economic Development 1947–61', in *Readings*, vol. II.

become relatively much cheaper than it was in country B in isolation, and a little cheaper than it was in country A in isolation. (The reader is referred to the Appendix (p. 219) for the geometric explanation of these changes in price ratios and in the production possibility boundaries.)

COMPARATIVE ADVANTAGES AND THE STRUCTURE OF COSTS

The theory of comparative advantages just outlined gives one answer to the question, what are the advantages to be gained from international trade between countries which have different production functions in their economies. The specialisation of production in the countries which have a comparative advantage increases the efficiency of the factors of production, which we assume cannot cross the frontiers; the increase in the total volume of production leads to lower prices and higher real incomes for consumers in the countries concerned. This increase in production, resulting from specialisation, implies that trade should flow freely between countries, bringing about adjustments in relative prices between commodities and between countries, so as to encourage production to expand where it is cheapest and to shrink where it costs the most. The fact that almost every country impedes the flow of international trade through various forms of import barriers shows us that the real world is more complicated than is indicated by the simplified example given above, which does, nevertheless, contain an important fact. To understand these complications, let us look briefly at revenue duties, at the relationship between production costs and foreign trade, and finally at the influence of foreign trade upon the volume of employment and the level of incomes. In the next section we shall take up the question of the markets in foreign exchange.

In the first place, most countries tax some imports in order to raise revenue for their governments. The effect of such import duties is like that of any other tax upon the sale of a commodity—the price will rise by some proportion, depending upon the relative elasticities of demand and of supply, both at home and in the other markets in which this commodity is sold. A duty imposed to raise revenue should be levied on commodities for which the demand is relatively inelastic to a change in price, so that the volume imported is not changed much by a rise in the c.i.f. price. If demand is highly elastic to a change in price, then imports may fall sharply and the revenue will be small; it will also fall in total as the import duty is increased.

Secondly, our simplified example assumed the existence of constant costs in our production of the two commodities, both before and after foreign trade; it was also assumed that prices reflected only the relative costs of labour needed to produce each commodity. Neither of these assumptions corresponds to the facts in many industries concerned today in international trade.

If most of the resources within a country are already fully employed, the expansion of output in one industry, to meet an expanded demand from international trade, is likely to meet with increasing costs. This is particularly the case with certain agricultural commodities, where output may be conditioned by certain limiting factors of soil, climate or altitude, and where expansion implies using land less favourable for any one product. But in industry also, we may expect increasing costs to any sudden expansion in demand, as the business men compete with themselves and with other users for the scarce resources, whether of labour or capital or management. Hence we often find that countries both import and produce at home similar commodities, both imports and home production expanding until their marginal costs are equal, allowing for differences in quality and in transport costs. Thus the United Kingdom imports some wheat and sugar, but also grows these crops at home; the various government measures protecting British agriculture against imports alter the proportions in which the supply is obtained, but probably do not alter the fact that, even under free trade, some of each product would be home-grown and some imported.

In the long period, however, we can expect that some industries will obtain decreasing costs to an expansion in output. Moreover, these industries are those with large capital structures where the variable costs associated with production may be a small proportion of total costs. If excess capacity exists, then a new demand in a foreign country can be supplied at the low prices dictated by the variable costs of the extra output, which may be much below the average cost of the factory and also below the average costs of smaller factories which may exist in the importing country. Consequently, whatever firms have been long established on a large scale are likely to have lower costs than competitors, starting up on a small scale. The international location of industries is then a matter of economic history—of which countries possessed enterprising managers when economies of large scale production became possible for the first time.

Again, established industries may enjoy external economies from their environment which give them comparatively low costs, as against new firms starting up in poor countries with small industrial centres, few public services and high overhead costs falling on individual enterprises as a result. For many types of manufacture, therefore, the current costs which determine the flows of international trade are themselves determined, not by fundamental differences in natural environments, but by historical events in the fairly recent past. And the existence both of economies of scale and of external economies implies that comparative costs, at any one time, are likely to favour the established industries and manufacturing regions, as against new industries starting up in non-industrialised regions.[1] This balance of advantage in favour of past economic growth applies, of course, as much between countries within Africa, as between America and Europe, or Europe and Africa. The large towns in the south of West Africa attract new trades more easily than the inland countries; the established industrial centre round Nairobi attracts new industries more easily than the smaller towns farther from the ports in Uganda, Malawi and Zambia.

The existence of the economies of large scale production and of external economies leads to the general practice of giving tariff protection to new or 'infant industries' against their well-established competitors in other countries. Clearly, however, such infant industries cannot be economically established just anywhere, on the theory that size of plant is the only influence upon costs. Industries with economies of scale require a certain minimum market before these economies can be obtained; since an infant industry is unlikely to be able to compete in the export market, firms must be placed where they can reach the required market with the lowest total of transport costs. Moreover, small countries may never be

[1] Among the various theories which attempt to explain the main trends in international trade may be mentioned that advanced by Professors Heckscher and Ohlin which states that a country normally exports those commodities which use intensively the factors of production which are most abundant within it, and it normally imports those commodities which use intensively the factors of production which are most scarce in the importing country. This theory and criticisms of it are summarised in J. Bhagwati, *The Pure Theory of International Trade; A Survey, in Surveys of Economic Theory*, vol. II, published by the American Association and the Royal Economic Society (London, 1965).

able to provide a minimum market for some types of plant. There are in Africa today about twenty countries with populations not exceeding $2\frac{1}{2}$ millions,[1] and most of these populations are still so poor that little is bought in the way of industrial goods. Hydroelectric power, iron and steel plants, assembly plants for vehicles, chemical manufacture, oil refining are some of the trades which would require regional markets larger than those at present existing in these small countries; the establishment of such industries therefore requires some form of agreement between the governments of adjacent countries. This question of trade agreements and customs unions is briefly discussed in a later section.

FOREIGN TRADE, THE MULTIPLIER AND THE NATIONAL INCOME

The theory of fluctuations in the national income set out in chapter 10 assumed a closed society without foreign trade. This assumption is of course unrealistic, especially for African countries, and we must now consider the effect of foreign trade upon the national income of any one country.

National income (Y) of any country may be defined as a quantity determined by expenditure on private consumption (C); the level of investment (I); and the expenditure of government (G). The level of national income would be in equilibrium when intended savings were equal to intended investment ($S = I$)[2]. When we introduce the possibility of foreign trade, the equation determining the equilibrium level of national income must be amended to $Y = C+I+G+E$, where E stands for the difference between the value of exports and the value of imports—*the balance of trade*.

If there is a rise in the value of exports, the incomes of the exporters increase, and hence their demands for goods and services. An increase in exports, therefore, has the same expansionary effect upon the economy as a rise in government expenditure, or of an increase in investment. Given a marginal propensity to save (and to import) of, say, 0·25, an initial increase of £50 m. in the value of exports will therefore lead eventually to a rise of £200 m. in the total demand.

[1] United Nations, Committee on Trade and Agricultural Development (UNCTAD), *Trade Expansion and Economic Integration among Developing Countries* (New York, 1967), p. 16.
[2] See pp. 176–80 and 185–6.

Conversely, an increase in imports has a deflationary effect on the national income, like an increase in savings. When incomes are spent upon imported goods, only the incomes of foreigners are affected. Let us assume that a given country has a marginal propensity to save of 0·25 and a marginal propensity to import of 0·25, that is, of every increase of £1 in the national income, one quarter will be saved and another quarter will be spent upon imported goods and services. Then of any increase in national income, only one-half will increase the demand for locally produced goods and services; the multiplier (which is the inverse of the marginal propensity to consume) will then have a value of 2, twice the original increase in income. It is important to remember, then, that any curtailment of imports (for example by the imposition of import controls), will, in the absence of counteracting fiscal measures, tend to create an inflationary gap by increasing the multiplier.

FOREIGN TRADE AND EMPLOYMENT

Changes in imports and exports which may thus affect the level of national incomes through the multiplier are determined primarily by the relative level of prices in the countries concerned; these relative prices reflect partly the differences in natural resources, partly the recent history of individual industries in different countries, and partly the level of transport costs. But, on the other hand, prices and costs may also themselves be greatly influenced by international trade in many countries—the 'open-ended' economies importing and exporting a high proportion of their G.D.P.

Table 24 showed how the opening up of two countries to foreign trade might affect the relative prices within them. In that example, the flow of rice into country B brought down the price of that commodity, pushed its rice growers out of that trade into the production of maize, whose price might then fall enabling them to export to country A, and to develop an export trade. In this example, it was assumed that producers could move easily from one trade to another within each country, that as prices and profits of rice-growing fell below the normal level in country B, the farmers would shift their production at once to the next most profitable use, that of growing maize for export. Given such mobility in resources, international trade therefore tends to equalise the prices of the traded commodities in the countries concerned. Trade flows out of areas where prices are low and into areas where prices are high until the prices of traded commodities are approximately equal, allowing for transport costs and other expenses.

However, in both countries the opening up of international trade may be opposed by those producers whose prices and profits will be reduced. The maize growers in one country and the rice growers in the other may not be able to find alternative employments in the foreseeable future; the resources formerly used in one trade may become unemployed through foreign competition, while the new production develops in some other region, with resources hitherto unemployed. Towns or villages dependent upon one trade for their income may become centres of depression rather than of economic growth, as the mining and shipbuilding towns of the United Kingdom fell into acute poverty between the wars, with the decline in these industries. Here, the costs of the transition period may be localised on small sections of the community, arousing opposition, while the benefits which each country obtains—greater consumption at lower prices and a possible expansion of exports—are more widely spread, less easily calculated and partly deferred until the transition has been made to the new position of equilibrium. If this transition period and the resulting unemployment is prolonged, the inhabitants of country B may collectively be worse off than before the change. And since governments, in particular, plan mainly for the short period, it is not surprising that tariffs have often been imposed in order to protect particular groups and industries, and their incomes, from the effects of foreign competition.

The desire to temper the effects of foreign competition is especially strong if there is already considerable unemployment in the countries faced with larger imports which compete with domestic industries. During the economic depression which dominated the years between the wars, almost all the industrialised countries greatly increased their tariff barriers, and often imposed import quotas as well, as unemployment mounted in each country and the flow of imports was seen as yet another threat to the falling volume of employment and the level of incomes. Taken together, such measures largely defeated their objects, since reducing other countries' exports led to further retaliation in a continuous circle. But economic depression is essentially an event in the short period, in which the shortest of views prevail.

One result of such protection for employment-producing industries has been the maintenance, in the industrialised countries, of the industries processing the raw materials exported from African countries. This division of labour may have been the most economic use of different resources in the early decades of the present century, but there is no reason to think that it represents a permanent 'comparative advantage' of Europe and America. The refining of vegetable oils, the processing of cocoa, cotton and coffee, might reasonably be developed where the crops are grown, in order to economise on transport to the final markets. But African countries trying to process their raw materials find that many countries, which admit the raw materials free of duty, impose heavy tariffs on even the slightly manufactured product, in order to protect the established industries within their own boundaries from the painful process of foreign competition. This is a subject which again and again comes up for discussion under G.A.T.T, the General Agreement upon Trade and Tariffs promoted by the United Nations.

FOREIGN EXCHANGE AND RELATIVE PRICE LEVELS

We must now look at the working of the markets in foreign exchange, in order to understand how the flow of international trade affects the monetary systems and relative price levels in the participating countries.

We assume that we have a number of countries each with a separate currency administered by separate central banks; these currencies are exchanged against each other at prices which are generally declared by the central banks and which are not usually changed. The markets for foreign exchange are therefore rather unusual, in that prices are fixed, and, under the present system, demand and supply have to adjust to each other by a different mechanism.

Consider an importer in one country who is buying a product of another country. The manufacturer will require to be paid in his own currency. The importer must therefore go to a bank, or trader in foreign exchange, and buy with his own currency the necessary sum of the foreign currency, allowing for the price of the product, and for any costs of transport or insurance to be paid to foreign firms. The bank now holds a quantity of local currency which is available for any exporter who has sold for foreign currency and who wishes to convert it into currency for domestic use.

In any short period, there is no reason why such demands and supplies should exactly balance. For most African countries, there is a strong seasonal variation in the flow of receipts from export crops which are sold for foreign currency, while the volume of imports continues fairly steadily throughout the year; the volume and value of exported crops also change from year to year. In addition, there are interruptions to trade through dock strikes, interruptions to the flow of export crops to the ports, delays in shipping and so on. Clearly, all central banks need to keep substantial reserves of foreign currencies, or of some commodity which can quickly be converted into foreign currency, if the demand from importers for foreign currencies temporarily exceeds the supply arising from the exports from domestic production.

The two commodities commonly used by African countries to fill this requirement are claims on sterling (or on the French banks) and the metal gold. The sterling commercial bill became an international currency in the nineteenth century, when the merchant houses, the discount houses and the banks of London financed a large proportion of the international trade, whether or not the trade ever reached London. Currency boards which formerly existed in East and West Africa, and their successors, the central banks in Africa, continue to keep their reserves largely in claims to sterling which can quickly be converted into most other currencies through the international money markets. Alternatively, reserves can be kept in gold, the currency of the central banks, but holding gold involves considerable costs by way of measures against theft and it earns no interest. In the modern world, gold is held largely by a few central banks who occasionally ship it to each other; they also provide gold bars for industrial use and for the hoarders who doubt the stability of the major currencies.

With fixed rates of exchange between the currencies of the major countries, how do the supply of and demand for each eventually balance? If one country habitually imports more than it exports, what happens? For a short period, the central bank can draw upon reserves to meet the excess demand for foreign currencies, but no reserves are inexhaustible, not even the vaults of Fort Knox, where the United States stores its monetary reserves of gold.

In the first place, let us note that the existence of international currencies—sterling, the American dollar, Swiss and French francs— enables countries to balance their trade accounts as a whole, and not with individual partners. If Kenya sells more to Uganda than Uganda sells to Kenya, Uganda can pay the Kenyan exporters with the proceeds of the cotton crop sold in London, in Hamburg or in Tokyo. What concerns a central bank is a continuing excess of demand for foreign currency over the actual and prospective supply, arising from a continuing excess of imports, from all countries, over the proceeds of exports, to all countries.

Secondly, the central bank can draw upon the reserves held either in its own vaults or in those of the commercial banks; it can sell these assets for foreign currencies. Alternatively it can borrow from other central banks, thus postponing the day when the balance of trade must balance, and also reducing the future flow of imports by the amount of exports which must be sold to pay the interest on the loan and to provide the eventual repayment of capital.

Thirdly, the central bank, or the government, can reduce imports by direct measures. Imports may be made subject to licence, and licences only issued for the import of certain classes of imports, judged necessary or desirable. Banks can be rationed in the amount of foreign exchange allowed them, both for the purchase of goods and for tourists, with the purposes for which that exchange can be used left to their discretion. Import duties may be imposed, or increased, not to raise revenue but to reduce the total expenditure upon foreign exchange. Alternatively, exports may be encouraged by various methods, but the stimulation of more exports is usually a slow process; countries with an imbalance of trade usually try to reduce imports immediately, while waiting for other measures to take effect.

Fourthly, the central bank and the government can tackle the difficulty at its roots. Exports must be stimulated by reducing costs, so that more can be sold overseas at lower prices; imports can be reduced by reducing the level of incomes which enables people to buy the excess volume of imports. Such a policy implies that government expenditure on capital account must be cut; taxation and the volume of savings must be increased; interest rates must be raised so as to reduce the level of new investment; and the multiplier set to work in a downward direction, until costs have been reduced, imports lessened, and exports increased.

Now this is an uncomfortable process. It means creating unemployment, while efficiency is being raised and costs are being reduced; cuts in government expenditure put civil servants and direct employees out of work; the fall in imports leads to queues in shops, unfair distribution, rising prices and political unrest. In limited doses, most countries have adopted this unpopular measure and made it work, but it works slowly and it creates political dangers.

As an alternative measure, the government of the day can devalue its currency—it changes the fixed rate at which its own currency is exchanged against other currencies, especially the two major international currencies, the dollar and sterling. When the Ghanaian Government devalued the cedi in 1967, the result was that importers wishing to buy foreign currency had to pay so much more in Ghanaian currency for a given quantity of some other currency; in effect, imports became so much dearer, and these higher prices, in the new currency, automatically reduced the demand for imports. At the same time, a ton of cocoa, sold on the London market for, say, £100 sterling, was now worth more in cedis; farmers could therefore be paid more in cedis for their cocoa, and so production and export of cocoa was encouraged. These changes in imports and exports increased the pressure of internal demand, because of the mechanisms outlined on p. 182. To check this inflationary gap and in order to eliminate the gross inflation created by the Nkrumah government in previous years, the new government also adopted the measures outlined above. Taken altogether, these measures should, given time, bring about a new balance between imports and exports, though, in this case, the government has still to cope with the huge volume of overseas debts also incurred by the previous regime.

But it must be emphasised that devaluation is only one method of achieving the necessary reduction in real incomes in a country where the level of prices and of costs has got out of line with those of the rest of the world. A country with a persistent surplus of imports is like a household with a persistent level of expenditure in excess of its income; sooner or later, it must reduce its expenditure and repay its debts. For any one country, this implies reducing imports or increasing exports or both, thus reducing the present volume of goods and services available for consumption. The adjustment can be brought about either by deflation, or by devaluation, and both have often been necessary.

CUSTOMS UNIONS AND FREE TRADE AREAS[1]

Until the mid-1950s, large areas of Africa were linked together by common currencies, either the pound sterling or the French franc; within each of the major groupings, there were few barriers to trade or to migration. Since independence was gained, countries have instituted their own currencies and trade policies, and trade between African countries has been hindered by customs duties as well as by formalities over the exchange of currencies. Such trade has always been a small part of the foreign trade of African countries; in recent decades, inter-African trade has amounted to less than 10 per cent of total external trade, and most of this small proportion consists of trade within East Africa, and between South Africa and the adjoining states.

Recently, a number of attempts have been made to rebuild free trade areas and to negotiate customs unions for adjacent groups of countries, though not all these attempts have been successful. Trade agreements between Ghana and Upper Volta, and between Ghana and Niger were promoted by the Nkrumah government in Ghana, but neither lasted for more than a year or so; a regional agreement between Guinea, Ivory Coast, Liberia and Sierra Leone was also shortlived. In 1966, Congo (Brazzaville), Cameroon, Gabon, Chad and the Central African Republic formed the Central African Customs and Economic Union, including about 10 million people; the objects are to institute a common external tariff, a central bank controlling a common currency, and agreed sharing in the customs revenue collected at the frontiers. The West African Customs Union was set up in 1959 between Dahomey, Ivory Coast, Mali, Mauretania, Niger, Senegal and Upper Volta; a smaller union, excluding Mali, Mauretania and Senegal, now exists. Meanwhile, the East African Common Market, which became effective in the mid 1920s, has recently become less effective, with the three countries concerned setting up separate currencies.

[1] UNCTAD, *Trade Expansion and Economic Integration among Developing Countries*, and *Report of the Committee of Experts* (New York, 1966); B. F. Massell, *The Distribution of Gains in a Common Market: The East African Case*, (California, 1964); N. G. Plessez, *The African Common Market: Myths and Realities* (University of Virginia, 1962); R. G. Lipsey, 'The Theory of Customs Unions: A General Survey', *Economic Journal*, vol. LXX (1960); A. Hazelwood, *East African Common Market, Importance and Effects*, Bulletin of Institute of Economics and Statistics, Oxford University (Feb. 1966).

There are various arguments in favour of customs agreements between adjacent countries. Most of the arguments are basically derived from the advantages either of specialisation, where there are differences in natural resources, or of the economies of scale from large plants, producing industrial goods under decreasing costs. Given two small adjacent countries A and B, they are likely to obtain their hydro-electric power and their iron and steel more cheaply with one large plant for each product serving both markets than if both countries set up smaller plants for both products. Moreover, the impediments to trade encourage local monopolies both in manufacture and in distribution; the opening of frontiers to competition may reduce prices and improve efficiency in a number of trades, at the cost of creating a certain amount of unemployment and loss of capital in the process of adjustment.

Further, the smaller the unit covered by a separate currency, the greater is likely to be the volume of international trade, relative to the G.D.P., for the same level of economic development. Hence small countries will meet proportionately greater fluctuations in their balance of payments, and will require proportionately larger reserves in their monetary system. The larger the area covered by a single currency system, the more chance there is of fluctuations in a single trade being counterbalanced by other changes in other trades, so that a smaller proportion of monetary reserves will suffice for a given volume of external trade.

On the other hand, gains from the integration of adjacent countries into one customs union and one currency system are not easy to allocate. If both countries have much the same structure, then freer competition for their industries may indeed break down monopolies and improve efficiency. But if there are large economies of scale for some of these industries, and if one partner has a better developed industrial base than the other, then competing trades may finish up as monopolies concentrated in the already flourishing urban centre, where external economies are the greatest. One of the difficulties of the East African Common Market was the relatively greater attraction for new industries offered by the existing industrial centre at Nairobi, compared with the less developed external economies offered by either Uganda or by Tanzania.

Secondly, a customs union may divert trade from cheaper sources to dearer sources, and thus reduce consumption and welfare of the inhabitants of one of the partners. Country A for instance may habitually import one commodity from the cheapest source, taking revenue from a small customs duty upon its import. If it then has to buy this product from country B, which produces this commodity under high protection, country A is definitely the loser, unless the addition of the market in A will enable the industry in B to obtain equivalent economies of scale. In any case, there must be some agreement about the distribution of the new customs revenue between the partners; at first some division based upon previous consumption or previous revenue may suffice, but such a base becomes increasingly irrelevant as the economies change over time.

Perhaps the greatest difficulty over such trading agreements stems from the aspirations of each partner for a high rate of increase in the national output of goods and services for all its population. When such an increase does not materialise, the partners are apt to blame each other for grabbing an undue share of the benefits of growth, without realising that aspirations differ from actuality. A country may show a slower rate of increase in its G.D.P. than its neighbour, and yet be getting richer faster than it would have done in isolation, with limited markets and high internal costs. As so often in economies, comparisons have to be made, not between two situations that actually exist, or that did exist within the recent past, but between the current situation and some hypothetical situation that would have existed if history had been different.

THE BALANCE OF PAYMENTS

The transactions which occur in a year between one country and the rest of the world can be conveniently summarised in a statement of the *balance of payments*. Such statements are usually divided into a current account, giving for one year or a series of years the payments and receipts for goods and services imported and exported; and a capital account, giving the payments and receipts which occurred in the same period of time for loans and other monetary transactions. A balance of payments must, by definition, balance, so that any deficit or credit in one part of the statement (for example, an excess of imports over exports) must be balanced by an opposite item in some other part (for example, an inflow of foreign capital or a reduction in reserves of foreign exchange).

Table 25 summarises the balance of payments for six African countries for the year 1966, with the national currencies converted

	Ghana	Kenya	Malawi	Nigeria	Sierra Leone	Tanzania (Tanganyika)
Current account						
1. Exports (f.o.b.)	321	219	39	742	83	199
2. Imports (f.o.b.)	-437	-273	-57	-749	-94	-194
3. Balance of trade (1 - 2)	-116	-54	-18	-7	-11	5
4. Balance on service and private transfers	-107	37	-8	-270	-27	-6
5. Balance on current account	-223	-17	-26	-277	-38	-1
Capital account balances on:—						
6. Private capital flows	86	2	4	173	26	-2
7. Central government flows of capital and aid	54	40	30	60	8	22
8. Other short term capital flows; errors and omissions	10	-22	4	58	1	-14
9. Changes in reserves (increase —; decrease +)	73	-3	-12	-14	3	-5

SOURCE. International Monetary Fund, *Annual Report*, (1967).

NOTE. The balance of trade (item 3) refers to the balance between the payments made in a period for transactions in goods; payments for imports are entered as negative and for exports as positive. It should be noted that payments may fall into different accounting periods from the actual transit of goods, and that payments may change either because the quantities traded change or because their prices change. Imports, which are valued at c.i.f. for the ordinary trade statistics, are valued f.o.b. for the balance of payments; the cost of transport and insurance is included under services (item 4).

Item 4 includes payments for insurance and freight, for banking services, tourist transfers, and 'factor payments'—interest on loans; all these are sometimes described as '*invisibles*', since no goods are seen to pass the frontiers. A tourist visiting East Africa buys East African currency with his foreign exchange, and therefore provides foreign exchange to East Africa as though he were buying East African exports; payment to a Greek shipowner for shipping goods to Kenya is a debit in the balance of payments, equivalent to a payment for imports.

The capital account shows how the balance of payments on current account was financed, and also includes transactions in loans, grants, and other transfers of claims. Borrowing from overseas enables a country to purchase imports in excess of the value of exports, and therefore the transfer of the loan counts as a positive item in the balance of payments, as an export of goods. Statistics for payments for services and movements of capital are still unreliable in all countries; the entry 'errors and omissions' warns readers that such figures are estimates made from the available evidence which is often far from complete.

TABLE 26. *Nigerian balance of payments 1954–1964 (£ million)*

	1954	1955	1956	1957	1958	1959	1960	1961	1962	1963	1964
Current account											
1. Balance of trade (net)	33·9	−18·5	−27·8	−38·9	−33·9	−18·1	−55·4	−53·5	−33·6	−14·6	−34·7
2. Services	−5·5	−5·6	−5·6	−7·6	−8·5	−12·2	−13·3	−10·7	−11·1	−20·2	−26·2
(a) transport	−1·1	−0·3	−0·1	—	—	−1·8	−1·4	0·8	4·8	3·9	3·5
(b) travel	−2·9	−3·5	−3·3	−4·2	−4·1	−4·0	−5·7	−6·9	−10·9	−10·3	−12·6
(c) other	−1·5	−1·8	−2·2	−3·4	−4·4	−6·3	−6·2	−4·6	−5·0	−13·8	−17·1
3. Net factor income transfer	−1·4	−0·6	0·9	4·2	0·7	−3·0	−4·8	−3·9	−3·9	−17·0	−20·3
4. Net transfers											
(a) to persons	−0·7	−0·6	−0·5	−2·1	−3·2	−5·2	−5·7	−6·4	−3·2	−5·2	−6·4
(b) to governments	3·2	3·9	2·6	3·4	3·9	3·5	4·9	2·0	9·8	2·5	6·6
5. Balance on current account	−29·5	−21·4	−30·4	−41·0	−41·0	−35·0	−74·3	−72·5	−42·0	−54·5	−81·0
Capital account											
6. Private investment	18·7	24·3	28·9	31·4	16·8	24·0	19·0	23·0	10·4	37·9	43·3
7. Official loans	−4·3	0·5	−0·1	−0·3	2·9	4·3	8·1	9·0	4·3	−5·3	10·6
8. Errors and omissions	−23·7	8·9	4·4	3·2	2·9	3·5	2·5	25·1	−0·8	−8·3	10·0
9. Changes in reserves (increase −; decrease +)	−20·2	−12·3	5·8	6·7	18·4	3·2	44·7	15·4	28·1	30·2	17·1
10. Total 6–9	−29·5	21·4	30·4	41·0	41·0	35·0	74·3	72·5	42·0	54·5	81·0

SOURCE. Nigerian Federal Office of Statistics.

at current rates of exchange into the American dollar, for purposes of comparison between them. All countries imported more goods and services than they exported and ran a deficit on their current accounts. In four countries, Kenya, Malawi, Nigeria and Tanzania, the deficit was covered by the inflows of private capital, of foreign grants and foreign loans; the two other countries ran down their reserves of foreign exchange.

Table 26 gives the balance of payments for Nigeria, from 1954 to 1964. The current account showed a surplus of exports over imports (a positive balance of trade) only in the first of these years; from 1955 there was a deficit, and from 1956 onwards, the country reduced its official reserves of foreign exchange.

The deterioration in the balance of payments was partly due to a fall in the terms of trade, a fall in the average price of Nigerian exports compared with the average price of imports. The prices of cocoa, groundnuts and palm oil—the principal exports of Nigeria before the commercial exploitation of the reserves of mineral oil— were relatively high in the early and mid 1950s; at the end of the 1950s and during the early 1960s, there was a sharp fall in the price of cocoa and a smaller decline in the prices of the other exports. As a result, by 1962 a given quantity of Nigerian exports would only purchase 93 per cent of the volume of imports obtainable in 1953, and 70 per cent of the volume obtainable in 1954.

In addition, government investment on capital projects during the later 1950s and in the 1960s involved imports which exceeded the value of foreign loans, causing some reduction of the reserves of foreign exchange; in addition, there was the increasing debit item of interest payments on these foreign loans. The increase in the item 'factor income' in 1963, however, was caused mainly by the repatriation of profits of the oil companies whose activities made possible a favourable balance of payments in 1965, when there were large exports of oil.

APPENDIX: COMPARATIVE ADVANTAGES AND THE PRODUCTION POSSIBILITY BOUNDARY

From table 24 (p. 202), country A, with 2,000 man-years of labour available, can produce either 12,000 bags of rice or 4,000 bags of maize, indicated by line *A* on graph 24; in isolation, the relative prices determine production at 6,000 bags of rice and 2,000 bags of maize. Similarly, line *B* shows the production possibility boundary for country B, with 4,000 bags of either crop; relative prices determine production at 2,000 of each. After trade has begun, the production possibility boundary for both countries combined becomes operative. To obtain this, however, we must assume that the available labour moves freely between countries into the most profitable use; that maize growers from country B could, as rice farmers in country A, be as efficient as the existing rice farmers. With 4,000 man-years of labour to be devoted to either crop, the production possibility boundary then becomes 24,000 tons of rice (the available labour multiplied by the yield in country A, 4,000 × 6 tons), or 8,000 tons of maize, as shown by line *AB*:

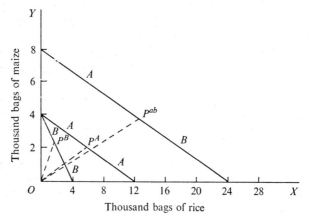

Graph 24. Comparative advantages and the production possibility boundary

With the assumption of constant costs, the situation shown in section B of table 24 is not one of equilibrium since it lies within the production possibility boundary and not upon it; it could be reached temporarily during a transition period, or it could reflect long-period equilibrium if the production of either commodity was subject to increasing costs in the country specializing upon it. The situation of section C of table 24 is shown by the relative price line OP^{ab}, determining production at 4,000 bags of maize and 12,000 bags of rice in the two countries combined. OP^A and OP^B are the original relative price lines in the two countries.

PART 5

Economic development

13. Breaking out of the stationary state

INTRODUCTION

The preceding chapters will have shown the great complexity of a nation's economy, and the dependence of each part of it upon other sectors, as well as upon the flow of money and upon foreign trade in goods, capital and knowledge. The poverty of many countries is partly due to this complexity and dependence, since poverty itself, combined with resistance to change, acts as a constraint upon the spirit of enterprise. Low incomes mean small markets for industrial goods, low savings for investment and lack of education and health. Small markets give little scope for business enterprise and for economies of scale in industries whose technology now demands large units of production. Low savings out of low incomes restrict investment in productive capital and also the yield of loans from which governments can finance the provision of public services such as transport and education. Poor transport and education in turn imply limited markets and scarcity of the many skills required for the growth of industries and services, including the skill of teaching. An almost stationary level of poverty has therefore been the common feature of most of the human population in Africa.

Breaking out of this equilibrium requires firstly the technical inventions in agriculture, transport and industry which can raise output per man; secondly, the human skills required to operate the new enterprises and to achieve the rising output made possible by technology; thirdly, the willingness of men and women to accept the continuous hard work and the risks of social and economic changes on a huge scale; fourthly, the willingness to make, from the existing low incomes, the investment in productive capacity whose output may mature five, ten or twenty years in the future.

These are conditions necessary for an appreciable and enduring increase in output which raises a substantial proportion of a population out of primary poverty. But neither economists nor economic historians have as yet been able to explain fully why such increasing

[223]

output occurred in the past in certain areas and at certain times, and not elsewhere and at other periods; nor can they propel an economy into rapid growth according to exact plans. But it is worth looking briefly at the main types of economic models which have been devised to explain the processes of growth.

ECONOMIC MODELS

Governments wishing to hasten the process of economic growth must have some 'model' in mind of the relationships within the economy they wish to influence. All economic thinking postulates some model, some set of relationships between the factors considered. The traditional analysis of the effect of a change in price upon the quantity demanded of a commodity (chapter 7) provided a model of an economy in which only two things change, changes in one of them (demand) entirely dependent upon the other (price). In discussing the effect of a change in wage rates upon the profits and output of one firm, (chapter 5) the model assumed that such an initial change in wages had no appreciable influence upon any other part of the economy than one firm—that the rise in incomes did not appreciably affect the demand for the output of the firm, for instance. But in discussing external economies (chapter 9), our model had to be enlarged to include indirect results of the growth of one firm upon the costs of other firms, and upon the flow of incomes within one area which might enlarge the markets for other products.

In Part 4, dealing with macro-economics, we took as our model one economy under the control of one government, and we assumed certain relationships between, for instance, changes in the level of investment and subsequent changes in the total of incomes and the flow of demand through the markets. Certain influences arising from outside such an economy—a change in the terms of trade, or in the flow of foreign loans—might impinge upon the model, which would react in certain ways, according to our assumptions about the effect which changes in incomes of exporters exerted upon current prices and current outputs, or changes in the flow of imports affected the patterns of demand by consumers. We noted that, on certain assumptions, an economy might be propelled into changes which became self-perpetuating. An inflation might get completely out of hand. An increase in export prices might generate a flow of incomes which in turn led to a continuing increase in the flow of new investment in a variety of industries and services, which in turn stimulated further development. Here, our model leads us into the problems of economic growth, where the relationships originally assumed between the various parts of the economy themselves undergo drastic changes.

It must be realised that the concept of economic growth is itself difficult to define. The aggregate output of a community may be increasing at the same rate as the population; this type of growth obviously does not substantially increase real incomes for the majority, and it may perhaps be described as economic stagnation. Secondly, aggregate output may be increasing faster than the population, and yet the increase may accrue only to a small section of the community, whose consumption may increase rapidly while that of the majority may be stationary or even falling. Technically, such a situation may be called one of economic growth; indeed, it describes some of the early development in Africa, when mines and plantations, managed and financed by expatriates, provided paid employment and some amenities for a few Africans, but were otherwise hardly connected with the local economies. Again, during the early stages of growth, a high level of investment in capital may imply no increase in consumption, in spite of the larger total output of consumption goods and capital goods taken together.

Another difficulty is the changing composition of the output of a growing economy, with the production of new commodities, the increasing output of others, and possibly the declining production of *inferior goods*, for which better substitutes become available. The only method of measuring such a changing total is that of aggregated values, adjusted roughly to allow for changes in the general level of prices. But when price levels, individual prices and the composition of the total are all changing, an index number of output can only provide the roughest measure of trends over time.[1] Growth may also be smooth and continuous, or fluctuating, with periods of slower growth, stability or even reversion. Finally, statistics inevitably ignore the non-monetary aspects which play so large a part in human happiness. Nevertheless, economic growth is normally defined as occurring when the statistical measure of the output of goods and services is rising faster than the population of a territory.

[1] See Appendix, pp. 198–9.

THE MALTHUSIAN MODEL

The first economic models were devised in the early part of the nineteenth century by British economists studying agricultural improvements and the first stages of industrialisation. It was a period when the British population was increasing rapidly, and there were many fears about the supply of food and of raw materials, such as wool, leather and timber. The Reverend Thomas Malthus, in his 'Essay on Population', pointed out that the human population in any territory was likely to increase faster than the food supply, and was normally kept in check only by periodic famines and by epidemics, often following war. As population increased, it obtained diminishing returns from the fixed area of land, and these diminishing returns were only temporarily evaded by improvements in agriculture which enabled the more fertile farms to produce more at lower costs. For an increase in output of this type, which resulted in lower prices for foods, enabled the families of wage earners eventually to bring up more children from their wages, so that the population increased more rapidly; the rising demand for food eventually raised its price, and reduced the real level of wages which were also affected by the competition of more wage earners seeking employment. Wages would then fall again to subsistence level, the improvement in output would fade away under the influence of diminishing returns, and a series of poor harvests would create famine by which the increase in population was kept down to the level of food supplies. The remedy proposed by Malthus for this periodic misery was the voluntary limitation of births, so that the human population in any territory increased less rapidly than its supply of food.

We can represent this model as in graph 25, where $P'P'$ and P^2P^2 represent the pattern of average output per head before and after an improvement in agriculture.[1] The line AA represents the output per head corresponding to subsistence level for a stationary population working a fixed area of land. An improvement in techniques increases output per head, but the resulting increase in population, under conditions of diminishing returns, brings the average output per head back to its former level, so that there is a larger population at the same subsistence level, after a period of comparative comfort. But if the population could be held stationary, then the agricultural

[1] See H. Leibenstein, *Economic Backwardness and Economic Growth* (New York, 1957), p. 21.

improvements could maintain it above subsistence level for an indefinite period. The Malthusian model is thus one of a stationary state, rather than of economic growth. It does explain, quite realistically, the constraints upon economic growth in an agricultural country with simple techniques, crowded land, and a population tending to expand faster than its food supply.

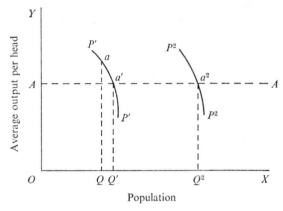

Graph 25. Population and production of food. (NOTE. The curves $P'P'$, P^2P^2 represent possible levels of average output per head at two levels of resources; AA represents the subsistence level, or the average output per head which keeps the population stationary. If average output per head is higher than the subsistence level, as at a, then population will increase from Q to Q'; any further increase in population then reduces average output per head below subsistence level, the mortality rate rises and population is eventually reduced to Q'. If a technical improvement increases production from the fixed area of land, then P^2P^2 represents the new relation between average output per head and the size of the population, but the subsistence level has not changed, though the equilibrium level of population is greater than before.)

Put into modern forms of expression, the effect of rising demand upon a more slowly rising supply in such conditions is to turn the terms of trade in favour of farmers; prices of foods tend to rise faster than other prices, thus making possible some further expansion in agricultural output but at rising costs, while imports of food will also increase, putting a strain upon the balance of payments. Within agriculture and industry, the growing numbers of those who seek paid employment because they have no rights to occupy land find their real incomes declining, through lower earnings and rising prices of food, while higher profits and rents accrue to those who occupy the scarce factor of land.

One way out of this constraint, of course, lies in the transformation of the technical and social structure of agriculture in order to procure a faster rate of growth in its output. An alternative or supplementary cure lies in the path adopted by Britain in the nineteenth century, of developing exports of industrial goods (and of capital) in return for imports of food and raw materials from countries where they could be grown more cheaply than in Britain; Britain also exported population to create the new farms in other continents from which food and raw materials were exported to Britain and to other markets.

CONCEPTS USED IN MODERN THEORIES OF GROWTH

Modern models of economic growth concentrate attention on five main factors: (1) population; (2) the propensity to save; (3) the capital/output ratio; (4) productivity, the labour/output ratio and (5) income-elasticities. Let us look briefly at each of these five important matters.

1. The early theories of economic growth regarded the rate of increase of population as a function of the food supply in each territory, since they assumed that imports of food would never be significant, a reasonable assumption in the days of sailing ships and land transport by horse. Although a substantial fraction of the population of Europe in the eighteenth and nineteenth centuries enjoyed comfort well above the subsistence level, a large number of wage earners were entirely dependent for their support on the food they bought with their wages; any lack of employment, therefore, or any large rise in food prices such as occurred after bad harvests, did bring a rise in the death rate and especially affected the death rate of young children. There was therefore some reason for regarding the growth of population as depending primarily on the supplies of food.

Over most of Africa, however, land is still available for most families in their area of origin, and food of a sort can be grown fairly easily. It is doubtful therefore if the food supply is itself a determinant of the growth of population, except in some semi-arid regions where periodic droughts cause famines affecting both herds of cattle and their human companions. The elimination of the major killing diseases like plague, cholera, malaria, sleeping sickness, has probably been the greatest single influence in bringing about a falling death rate in Africa, and this influence is only partly derived from economic growth within Africa. The factors affecting the birth rate are still beyond measurement, and modern theories of economic growth therefore tend to regard an increase in population of 2–3 per cent a year as one of the basic facts affecting the rate of growth in the national income, but hardly affected by it; the growth of population then becomes an independent *parameter* to be included in all calculations and plans for development, affecting both demand and also the number of persons seeking employment. It should be noted that the proportion of the population economically active depends partly on the recent pattern of population growth (which affects the age distribution), and partly on customs about education and paid employment for women.

2. The propensity to save has already been discussed in chapter 10. Here we are concerned more particularly with the marginal propensity to save, the amount which will be saved out of any increase in incomes. For if the whole of any increase in incomes is spent on consumption, the proportion of income saved will fall with rising income, and the rate of increase will slow down in future periods of time. If the rate of saving is to be raised from the 5–8 per cent customary in a traditional society to the 10–15 per cent required for sustained growth, clearly there must be a high marginal propensity to save for investment in productive capital, possibly of the order of 25 per cent or higher.

The dependence of economic growth upon a high marginal propensity to save has often been put forward as the main argument for high taxation and for government operation of profitable businesses, so that much of any increase in incomes arising from early development can be controlled by the government and used for further investment. The marketing boards in West Africa have thus been used as collectors of taxes on the incomes accruing to farmers from sales of export crops. However, recent reports on the use of such funds in both Nigeria and in Ghana make it doubtful if governments do invest in productive capital, as distinct from prestige buildings, as much of these resources as farmers might have done if they had been given the use of their earnings from export markets; it was argued that the production of oil palms in Eastern Nigeria in particular was limited by the low prices paid by the marketing board after deduction of taxes.[1] One of the difficulties of planners is the

---

[1] See pp. 138–44 above, and G. K. Helleiner, 'The Fiscal Role of the Marketing Boards in Nigerian Economic Development', in *Readings*, vol. II.

lack of statistical measurement of new investment by farmers in their farms, and as a result this source of increased income is often left out of the national accounting.

In any case, it will be easier to save a rising proportion of the national income when that income is itself increasing than if it is stationary or declining. People are more inclined to save when they expect a higher income than when they actually experience a fall in income, when they may, indeed, dis-save by borrowing in order to maintain current standards. To this extent, the marginal propensity to save is itself a function of the change in incomes and is likely, therefore, to change in the course of development. If, as is sometimes argued, saving is discouraged by lack of profitable opportunities, the process of economic growth may remove this particular constraint, as farmers and business men find new markets and therefore need investment for extending their outputs.[1]

3. The *capital/output ratio* attempts to measure the amount of capital, usually expressed as a percentage of the national output in any one year, which must be invested in order to add one per cent to that output. A capital/output ratio of 4 implies therefore that 4 per cent of the national income must be invested in order to add one per cent to output in the subsequent period of time. This ratio has been calculated for a number of countries; it appears to lie between 3 and 4 for the industrialised economies, but varies between 2 and 5 for undeveloped countries,[2] so far as it can be measured from the inadequate statistics.

There are obvious reasons why the capital/output ratio may vary between countries, and between periods in the same country. The larger pieces of investment may take several years to build and yet more years before they are properly run in; during this period, their output may be low. Again, plants may be running at less than capacity for long periods, during which the addition to output is less than expected; later, when run to capacity, the addition to output is made with very little addition to the existing capital. One reason for such failure to work to capacity is the lack of complementary resources, such as raw materials, transport or the necessary skilled workers, both technical and managerial; markets may have been over-estimated when the plant was designed. Fluctuations in the

---

[1] S. P. Schatz, 'The Capital Shortage Illusion' in *Readings*, vol. I.
[2] United Nations, *Programming Techniques for Economic Development*, ECAFE, (Bangkok, 1960).

weather may also have a marked effect on output from the agricultural sector over a short run of years, and these effects may mask opposite trends elsewhere in the economy. Finally, the capital/output ratios vary with different types of investment which may fall into different periods of time; investment in roads and hydroelectric schemes may yield a relatively low output from much capital for many years, while investment in clearing land for vegetable farms gives a high ratio of output to capital from the start.

The difficulties of measuring the capital/output ratio for industries and for countries are considerable, and the margin of error attached to existing ratios must be borne in mind. Nevertheless, the concept has been much used in plans for economic development together with the concept of a capital/employment ratio—the amount of capital required to provide employment for one man. This concept is obviously important for countries with chronic unemployment tending to increase with the rapid growth in population; like the concept of the capital/output ratio, the capital/employment ratio is difficult to calculate and obviously varies with the type of employment offered, as shown in tables 11 and 12 (p. 83).

4. The concept of *productivity*, of output per man, brings us back to the basic problem of poverty—the result of a low output per man over wide sections of agriculture, industries and commerce. The previous concepts—growth in population, propensity to save and capital/output ratio—are attempts to break down the concept of productivity into simpler elements which can be more closely studied, in order to understand the constraints upon the growth of productivity, and how these constraints can be eased.

A rapidly increasing population based on a limited area of land may be subject to diminishing returns only partially alleviated by improvements in techniques; low productivity is then a function of population growth. Improvements in techniques may be available but require capital for their introduction; low productivity, low incomes and a low propensity to save may then combine to keep productivity low. Capital, when invested, may yield a low output because supporting resources were not available, or because the growth in demand was over-estimated so that the capital remains largely unused, or because costs were under-estimated at the planning stage. Or productivity is low because available resources have been invested in high-cost, rather than minimum-cost, combinations.

5. The concept of *income-elasticity of demand* is useful in explain-

ing the changes in demand which occur during the course of development. For as incomes rise, people do not spend the increase in the same proportions as they spent their previous incomes; demand for some commodities rises rapidly, for other commodities demand rises only slowly, and for some commodities (the inferior goods), demand may even fall as incomes rise. And it is these changes in demand, working through the markets, which influence relative prices, relative incomes of producers and therefore finally the pattern of production.

The *income-elasticity of demand* may be defined as the percentage change in the expenditure on a commodity by an individual, or by a group of constant size and composition, divided by the percentage change in income which caused that change in expenditure, other things remaining unchanged, including prices. Thus we may assume that a family has an income of 50*s.* a week, of which half, or 25*s.*, a week is spent on food. If the income rises by 10 per cent, from 50*s.* to 55*s.*, and the expenditure on food rises also by 10 per cent, from 25*s.* to 27½*s.*, the income-elasticity for food is one, since the two percentage changes are the same. If the amount of the increased income spent on food had risen by only 1*s.* or by 4 per cent, then the income-elasticity would be 0·4 (4% ÷ 10%).

The measurement of income-elasticity, like the measurement of price-elasticity, is not easy. The flow of income accruing to a group of families in one week or year often cannot be accurately measured, and total expenditure, which may be more easily counted, need not closely follow changes in income. Allowance must always be made for changes in the size of families, since a change in income per head can be caused by a change in the number of earners in a family, or in the number of dependents. Again, a change in the expenditure on any one commodity may involve buying a greater or smaller quantity, or only a dearer or cheaper quality; a wealthy man may smoke more than a poor one but he may also choose to smoke the same number of a more expensive brand of cigarette. In the real world, moreover, prices are usually changing as well as incomes, and these obscure the changes in expenditure caused by changes in income. Finally, it is not often that the same families can be observed before and after a change in incomes; families of the same size at different income levels can be observed, the different patterns of expenditure noted, and it is then assumed that the poorer families would adopt the pattern of expenditure of the richer families, if their incomes were increased to the same level. Where the population being observed is fairly uniform, this assumption may be reasonable, but where income levels also correspond with ethnic differences, similar incomes may not lead to similar patterns of expenditure. Nevertheless, a comparison of patterns of expenditure between different income groups may give useful indications of the probable change in demand, if incomes change during the process of economic growth.

The propensity to save and the propensity to import are two types of income-elasticity which have already been discussed. Income-elasticity of demand for food is a concept also of great importance, since it measures the effect of changes in income upon the changes in demand for agricultural products. In the nineteenth century, Engels observed that expenditure upon food, as a proportion of the total expenditure of a family, fell with rising incomes; in modern phrasing, the income-elasticity of demand for food is high—0·7 or 0·8—when incomes are low, but falls with rising income. Studies of household budgets for town-dwellers in Africa bear out this general conclusion, and also show that different types of food have differing income-elasticities.[1] Income-elasticities are lowest for the bulky foods supplying the main sources of carbohydrates; a rise in income from low levels causes the expenditure on these foods to increase a little more slowly than the rise in income, so there was not much change in the proportion of total expenditure upon food devoted to these products. On the other hand, income-elasticities for foods containing animal protein were generally high, exceeding 1; expenditure on these foods took a rising proportion of the total expenditure upon foods, as incomes rose.

[1] H. A. Oluwasanmi, 'Agriculture in a Developing Economy', in *Readings*, I, 207, 209.

14. Economic planning

INTRODUCTION

With the attainment of independence, African governments took up the task of economic planning with enthusiasm. Their main objective was to speed up the economic growth of their countries above the current trend by encouraging or undertaking investment in public services, in large industrial units and, to a lesser extent, in agriculture. Further, the governments required official plans as a basis for their negotiations for foreign loans and the services of foreign experts.

TYPES OF PLANNING

Economic plans published by African countries vary greatly in scope and complexity.[1] One type of planning consists of a collection of projects requiring foreign loans or technical assistance, put together with some indications of the probable course of government revenue and expenditure, assuming current trends to continue in other parts of the economy. It is then assumed that the collective result of these projects will stimulate the rest of the economy into greater output through the multiplier and that the demand of these projects for raw materials and the incomes earned in them will provide *linkage effects* on other industries and on the output of consumer goods (including houses) on which the wages will be spent.

Alternatively, economic planning may consist of a series of targets for the outputs of specified parts of the economy set above the current trends, accompanied by information about the actions intended in order to achieve these targets. Targets may be set for the construction of schools, for the exports of agricultural products which are to provide foreign exchange for imports, for import-saving through new industries, and these targets may be combined with one or two complex structures such as hydro-electric schemes or an extension to a railway. Inducements offered to stimulate the attainment of these targets might take the form of grants to local

[1] See R. H. Green, 'Four African Development Plans', in *Readings*, vol. II.

authorities for education, subsidies on fertilisers or improved palm trees, tax concessions for pioneering firms, government loans at low rates of interests for land settlements, more technical advisors and teachers, and so on. In addition, there must again be detailed accounts for the financing of the extra expenditure which will fall upon government funds, including both expenses at home as well as the extra costs of imports and of servicing and eventual repayment of foreign loans. Such accounts depend upon some estimates of future trends in wages, in costs of imports, in local prices and incomes, all of which affect both costs to be incurred and receipts from taxes.

Finally, the centralised economies bring into their planning almost every major activity, since they exercise direct controls over the flow of raw materials and of labour upon which outputs are based. In African countries, such controls are more limited, but the output of certain materials such as cement, or the use of imported materials, can be controlled by licences to give priority to government demands; the construction industry may be almost entirely controlled in this way. But the output of agriculture and the levels of wages and of prices have proved to be outside direct controls, and here the African governments have had to work upon current trends and indirect influences, as indeed have most other governments.

GATHERING THE DATA

All governments engaged in any form of planning find that they largely lack knowledge of the basic facts and of the relationships between the varied activities making up the economy they are trying to control. Some African governments do not know even the number of people in their territories; their information may be a partial census taken ten years earlier. So schools must be planned without knowing the number of children who are to be taught; houses, water and sewerage schemes devised for towns whose population is unknown but is clearly growing faster than the public services. Again, there are hardly any studies of income-elasticities of the rural population, and only a few of the urban population, so that only the roughest of estimates can be made of the future demand for imports or for different types of foods, and of the marginal propensity to save.

The first requirement for a coherent plan is a table setting out the composition of the existing gross national product, by the major sources, subsistence agriculture, commercial farming, manufacturing, mines, distribution, transport, public services, private services, imports and exports. As noted in chapter 2, such a table is based on estimates of the quantities of output from each of these sectors, multiplied by the prices at which that output is sold, minus the quantities of inputs which each sector buys from the other sectors. A second requirement, therefore, is an input-output table, such as table 3 on p. 15, showing the flow of commodities and of services between the sectors.

The usefulness of such tables depends upon the number of sectors for which information is provided, as well as upon the accuracy of the estimates, at all stages. The effects of a projected investment, for instance, might need to be studied under a number of headings— the requirement of imports both for the capital structure and for replacements and maintenance, the extra demand for specific resources such as cement, steel, transport, fuel and electricity; the effects of a corresponding expansion in these outputs would again need to be studied. It might be misleading to assume that an increase in the output of one industry would increase all inputs by the same proportion, since an increase in cocoa exports, for example, might well require a large increase in imports of sprays or of lorries for transport, but hardly any increase in the use of labour.

Apart from the flow of materials and services between sectors of the economy, there is the problem of the human resources required for certain specific work such as teaching, administering, managing large firms; on the other hand, there may be a problem of unemployed men looking for employment. 'Manpower budgets' for scarce skills have been attempted in a number of countries, where such scarcities may form the main constraints upon the general processes of development,[1] but here again, the lack of statistics is itself a constraint upon central planning of these scarce resources.

The purpose of these calculations, in the scheme of economic planning, is to ensure that the resources which will be required for a particular stage of development are likely to be available, and available in the right form and place and time. At any one time, the lack of two or three resources in the right form, or place, may be holding back the rising level of output, and statistical analysis of the resources available should indicate what these constraints are, and what sectors of the economy are particularly affected by them. Let us take two

[1] R. H. Green, 'Four African Development Plans', in *Readings*, vol. II.

examples of the kind of constraint which may develop during a phase of rapid growth. The construction of a large cement works, to supply more cement in the later years of a development plan, may itself take so much cement and structural steel that the Ministry of Public Works and the building industry have to be rationed in their use of cement for two or three years to a level below that current in the past two or three years. Can such a constraint be removed by imports, and if so, at what cost? Can exports be expanded to meet this cost, or can other imports be cut without affecting the planned expansion? Secondly, the increased flow of children into schools requires not only more schools and equipment, but more teachers at all levels. If a higher proportion of the leavers from secondary schools are to become teachers, what about the supply of administrators, clerks and technicians? Should teachers' salaries be geared to the European level, in the hope of attracting more teachers to the schools at high cost; or should they correspond to the level of other incomes in each country, thereby reducing the cost of education, but possibly restricting the supply of teachers?[1]

CONSISTENCY AND THE INFLATIONARY GAP

Finally, there is the planning of the financial side of economic development, the flows of the money incomes within a country, and between it and the rest of the world with which it exchanges goods and services. Three aspects of these money flows are of especial importance to the planners—the flow of savings compared with investment, the flow of government revenues compared with government expenditure, and the flows which indicate an inflationary gap.

In Part 4, we saw the influence of the level of investment upon the level of income and the level of prices. Raising the rate of investment from an average of 8–10 per cent to 15 or 20 per cent is commonly regarded as the first step in securing an acceleration in the growth of the national income in most African countries. One of the principal difficulties, however, is to secure that resources are released for use in planned investment. The resources devoted to the construction of capital, which will increase output in the future, must be matched by a corresponding diversion of incomes from consumption goods and services into various types of savings.

[1] P. Williams, 'The Cost and Finance of Education', in *Readings*, vol. II; see also chap. 11, above.

If capital investment is to rise sharply, the marginal propensity to save must rise even more sharply, in order to lift the average proportion of savings to income above its previous level. To some extent, the amount saved out of incomes can be influenced by propaganda, by the provision of proper facilies such as life assurance, savings banks and post office savings accounts, and by taxation. But ultimately, the level of savings is the result of innumerable decisions by individuals and families, reacting to varying prospects and disappointments, rising incomes and rising taxes, family needs and aspirations. The proportion of private incomes, or of the expected increase in private incomes, put into savings may have to be regarded, in the short period of a five or seven year development plan, as something largely outside the control of the planning authorities.

This uncertainty over the level of savings throws importance upon the national budget, which is more directly under the control of the government. If more can be collected in taxes than is required by current expenditure on goods and services, then the surplus can be devoted to investment whether in public services designed to induce external economies, or directly in productive forms such as industries under government control. The larger the surplus between resources taken by taxes and current expenditure, the larger the investment which can be undertaken by government without creating an inflationary gap. Hence development plans pay particular attention to the 'capital budget' proposed by the planning authority.[1]

Here, the question of timing assumes great importance. The flow of revenues and the flow of expenditure by governments are both affected by the timing of capital investment, but in different ways and to different degrees. Investment in a large factory, or in a dam, or in schools and hospitals, involves a series of outlays in a pattern which varies with each project. There are the preliminary expenses of drawing up the specifications and putting the different parts of the project out to tender, either to home or to foreign firms. Once a tender is accepted, there is the purchase of land or other rights in the area affected, the preparation of the site, possibly with special roads or water supplies, and the actual buildings. Machinery and equipment must be purchased, transported to the site, installed and run in; spare parts must be provided, as well as the working capital represented by raw materials, the cost of wages and transport and marketing, before the final output begins to flow into consumption,

[1] Green, 'Four African Development Plans', in *Readings*, vol. II.

and to bring back a flow of income. There may then be a period of several years before the new project earns sufficient to pay its running costs and to provide interest and amortisation on its capital. When a government, or large firm, has a number of such large projects under consideration, the balance between revenue and expenditure at all stages needs careful calculation. A buyer of machinery or a building may of course be able to secure credit from the seller, so that payments can be deferred in part for some period of time, but such credits must usually be paid for by extra interest charges which raise the total cost. Moreover, almost all large projects cost more than was originally expected, so that allowance must be made for what are commonly known as 'contingencies'. Thus four hydro-electric schemes begun in Scotland between 1944 and 1954 were costed at £19–20 m.; the final cost upon completion amounted to £45–46 m., more than double the original estimates.[1] The matching of revenue with expenditure upon large projects of capital investment is by no means easy, and governments, as well as business men, farmers and individuals, have often found themselves with an uncomfortable gap between their incomes and the expenditure to which they are committed by past decisions.

We have looked at the different types of taxation which can be imposed by governments, and we have noted that all types carry some dis-incentives and disadvantages to the taxpayers, who benefit in different degrees from the results of government expenditure. One of the chief handicaps for African governments is undoubtedly the difficulty of collecting taxes in economies where many incomes never flow through a bank or other point of record and where there is an acute lack of experienced and honest officials. Much can be done to improve the collection of the existing taxes,[2] but no government can indefinitely raise the general level of taxes upon its citizens beyond what is currently regarded as 'reasonable', having regard to past experience and to present prospects. Government revenue is always likely to prove less adjustable upwards than government expenditure, and the yield of taxes is another constraint upon investment out of the government budget.

[1] A. J. Youngson, *Overhead Capital* (Edinburgh, 1967), p. 64.
[2] J. F. Due, 'The Reform of East African Taxation', in *Readings*, vol. II; G. Oka-Orewa, *Taxation in Western Nigeria*, Nigerian Institute for Social and Economic Research (Ibadan, 1962), chap. 2.

Finally, there is 'the inflationary gap', the flow of rising prices and rising incomes which indicates the existence of some bottleneck in the economic structure, setting a constraint upon further expansion in output. This term has been used to describe a variety of situations. There is firstly the inflationary gap which exists when planned investment in the economy as a whole exceeds the expected level of savings over the same period. Secondly, the term may be used of the difference between planned expenditure by governments and expected receipts from taxes over a period. This gap may, of course, be filled by further taxation, by borrowing from the commercial banks, or from the public. Thirdly, the national plan may reveal a gap between the value of planned imports over a period and the expected value of exports, a gap which it is hoped to bridge by foreign loans and international aid.

It has been argued that an inflationary gap, in all three senses, is unavoidable for a poor country which wishes to raise sharply its level of savings, investment and of output. Some degree of profit inflation and of general expectations of rising prices is thought to encourage enterprise, and to reduce the risks of starting new businesses. The sweeping away of former constraints upon output, and the adoption of new techniques and social customs may be stimulated by the hopeful atmosphere of rising prices and profits, even if costs also rise. As long as prices and profits rise ahead of costs, there is a transference of income to the enterprising business men, at the expense of those whose fixed incomes buy less as prices rise. After incomes have risen and output has begun to increase, then it may be possible to increase taxation upon the new increments of income in a variety of ways. A moderate degree of inflation has thus been considered by some economists to be an essential part of the breaking out of the stationary state into a phase of rapid economic growth, which will become self-sustaining.

Those who hold such a theory argue, therefore, that an undeveloped country should plan for a small inflationary gap, and allow for a rise in prices and in costs during the period of the plan. On the other hand, the deliberate creation of such gaps involves serious risks. Inflation contributes to the growth of output first because prices and profits do rise ahead of costs and of many incomes, and secondly, because people do not generally expect such a rise in prices in the immediate future that they lose confidence in the purchasing power of the currency. Unfortunately, a rise in prices, however begun, may often be followed by a rise in wages paid by governments and by large firms under semi-government authority, which employ a high proportion of the wage earners in many African countries. Costs may therefore rise equally with, or even ahead of, prices, so that a planned inflation leads quickly to a further, cost-propelled, inflation, as governments increase their expenditure to maintain their investment plans at the higher level of costs. Nor is it easy to collect a sufficiently large slice of the increments of income from thousands of business men and migratory workers to offset, through increased receipts, such increased costs. And if rising prices and costs become a regular feature of the economy, then people may begin to spend their savings, and to increase the velocity of circulation of money until inflation gets out of hand.

IMPORTS AND THE COST OF FOREIGN LOANS

Moreover, in the open economies of Africa (as in the open economy of Britain), a rise in incomes immediately affects the balance of trade. The income-elasticity of demand for imports is high, partly through the markets for the variety of consumer goods not produced at home, including foods; partly because of the volume of imports required for investment in new factories and machinery;[1] partly because of the high import content of the continuing demand for replacement and renewals of existing capital equipment, and for the flow of raw materials. Moreover, a cost-propelled inflation with wages rising as fast as prices may also impede the increased flow of exports, thereby aggravating the inflationary gap in the balance of payments.

In these circumstances, an obvious first step is to restrict 'unessential imports' by direct licensing, thus reducing the expenditure upon consumer goods. Such measures do immediately reduce the inflationary gap in the balance of trade, but they also intensify the inflation on the home market, where the purchasing power, formerly devoted to imported goods, spills over into other markets. Moreover, the direct licensing of imports puts a further burden on the administrative staff both in government offices and in the offices of the firms requiring imports; it is an obvious opportunity for the

---

[1] According to J. F. Due, in 'Import Substitution and Export Promotion' (in *Readings*, II, 151) about one half of the new investment in East Africa in 1961 consisted of imported goods.

growth of corruption and collusion between those who administer the licences and those who can make above normal profits by selling a reduced quantity of goods at higher prices.[1]

FOREIGN LOANS

Many countries have recently turned to foreign loans and to international aid, in order to bridge the inflationary gap in their balance of payments. Shortly after the second world war, the British Government took two enormous loans from the United States, the Anglo-American loan of 1945 and the loans under the Marshall Plan in 1947, in order to bridge the gap in the balance of payments while British export trades were revived after the destruction and dislocation of the war. The decade of the 1960s, which saw so many African countries attain independence, led to similar feelings of emergency over the need for economic development, and in the last twenty years a variety of agencies have been concerned with the flow of loans and of international aid to the poorer countries, struggling with imbalance on their foreign trade.

Accumulated experience has shown that, even at low rates of interest, the cost of loans can add severely to the future burden of payments of a country, a burden which can eventually only be discharged by creating a surplus of exports over imports. Take for instance a loan of 100 units, for ten years at 5 per cent, the loan to be repaid by ten equal instalments, one at the end of each year. By the end of the ten years, the debtor will have repaid the original loan of 100 units, plus $27\frac{1}{2}$ units by way of interest. If therefore exports would have to be increased once by 100 units to allow for the import of a piece of machinery, a foreign credit for this amount at 5 per cent with repayment spread over ten years implies that the rise in exports can be slower but must be greater in total by these $27\frac{1}{2}$ units. The use of foreign loans to bridge a gap in the balance of payments is thus an expensive method of financing development; interest and repayments can quickly mount up until a fifth or a quarter of current exports is required simply to service existing debts, and is therefore not available to pay for current imports. Further, imported machinery requires spare parts and renewals which usually must also be imported.

---

[1] R. Wraith and E. Simpkins, *Corruption in Developing Countries* (London, 1963).

These difficulties with the balance of payments in the early stage of development have been intensified for African countries in the 1960s by the adverse price trends in international markets. Inflation in the industrialised countries has led to generally rising prices for the industrial goods they export, while the prices of the agricultural products they import have fluctuated round a stable level. More exports from African countries have thus been required, year by year, to buy the same quantity of imports, and this in itself has put a heavy strain upon the balance of payments of the exporting countries, apart from the deliberate creation of inflationary gaps, under official plans for more rapid development.[1]

Inflation in the industrialised countries since the second world war appears to have arisen from the high level of investment both by business firms and by governments, in an attempt to maintain full employment. In turn, full employment has implied rising wage levels and rising incomes which have outstripped the rise in productivity occurring from technical improvements of many types; rising incomes in turn have maintained a high level of monetary demand pushing up prices and costs. As noted above, the result in Britain has been a continuing pressure on the balance of payments, since the value of total imports has continually tended to outstrip the value of exports. Moreover, the expenditure overseas on political commitments and upon aid for developing countries has intensified the pressure upon the balance of payments, both for Britain and for the United States. These difficulties with the balance of payments in the industrialised countries, and their rising prices for industrial goods and services have reduced the purchasing power of the underdeveloped countries in international markets; the inflationary gaps in their balance of payments may be a continuing constraint upon their development plans.

PLANNING WITH MODELS

Let us take a highly simplified 'model' of an economy in order to show the use of the concepts employed in economic planning.

We have a population p increasing at a steady rate dp each year; we have a labour force n also increasing at a steady rate dn which may be slower or faster than the increase in the population. We

[1] G. Blau, 'Commodity Export Earnings and Economic Growth', in *Readings*, vol. II.

have a national income Y, and the community has a voluntary propensity to save a fixed proportion, s, of this income. We have a stock of capital K which can be increased by investment out of savings, and a gross domestic product, G.D.P., at factor cost made up out of consumption goods C and investment goods I. We assume that the capital-output ratio is 4, and that there is no foreign trade. We then have the following situations in years 1, 2, 3:

	Year 1	Year 2	Year 3
1. Population	p	$p+dp$	$p+dp+d(p+dp)$
2. Labour force	n	$n+dn$	$n+dn+d(n+dn)$
3. Capital	K	$K+sY^1$	$K+sY^1+sY^2$
4. G.D.P.	$C+I$	$C+I+\dfrac{sY^1}{4}$	$C+I+\dfrac{(sY^1+sY^2)}{4}$
5. National income	Y^1	Y^2	Y^3
6. Consumption per head	$\dfrac{C^1}{p}$	$\dfrac{C^2}{p+dp}$	$\dfrac{C^3}{p+dp+d(p+dp)}$

In the course of the first year both the population and the labour force have increased; savings have been invested and have increased the capital, and in the second and third years there is a corresponding increase in G.D.P. What will have happened to the national income and to the volume of employment?

Given the assumptions of a fixed capital/output ratio and a fixed propensity to save, the increase in G.D.P. shown in years 2 and 3 represents the maximum value obtainable assuming that all savings find investment, and that the labour force is adequate to man the increase in capital. But if there is a scarcity of labour, either in total or in particular types and places, then the increase in G.D.P. may fall short of the growth warranted by the investment of capital. In that case, the increase in incomes generated by the increase in K will cause some rise in prices with a rise in output smaller than the warranted maximum. Alternatively, if n is increasing faster than K, the G.D.P. may increase at the maximum warranted rate of growth, but there will be unemployed labour, or, more accurately, an increase in the number of persons either unemployed or engaged in subsistence farming outside the monetary economy. The increasing pressure of these unemployed persons should then be tending to lower wages and incomes of wage-earners, but imperfect competition may keep wage rates above the level which would enable all the unemployed to be absorbed. But this highly simplified model does not tell us which of these alternatives is occurring, nor does it tell us how the new output is distributed between consumption and investment goods, so that without further data we do not know whether there has been a rise in the average level of consumption (line 6).

Our model only provides the answers which correspond to the assumptions made in the equations, and it may not indicate which of the possible answers is the most probable. By enlarging the number of variables included, and by finding values for such relationships as *s*, we narrow the range of answers which satisfy the equations, but at the risk of obtaining inaccurate answers because of inaccurate estimations of the values. Nevertheless, we could not make much progress with such a model unless we included the propensity to import, the income-elasticities for the basic foods and some idea of the supply-elasticities of such foods and of exports. For among the assumptions that lie behind such models is that available resources will flow smoothly through the market mechanism into the new patterns of employment required by accelerated investment and faster expansion in G.D.P.

Let us summarise, in the light of our previous model, the statistics of the development plan for Kenya, for the years 1964–70, given by R. H. Green.[1] Here it was assumed that private investment over the six years would amount to £188 m., compared with a G.D.P. of £243 m. in 1962 and of £364 m. (at constant prices) in 1970; this level of investment implies that savings would amount roughly to 11 per cent of G.D.P. In addition another £129 m. was to be invested from public funds, including at least £34½ m. from foreign loans and grants, and an uncovered sum of £4½ m. Total investment of £317 m. over these years was therefore roughly equivalent to 15 per cent of G.D.P., while the planned expansion of G.D.P. amounted to 5·2 per cent a year, a capital/output ratio of about 3. The output of agriculture was expected to increase by 4·9 per cent a year, in order both to satisfy the expected increase in home demand and to supply a greater volume of exports. The plan assumed that an expansion of this magnitude in output would expand the volume of employment by about 2·8 per cent a year, of which half would necessarily occur in agriculture; since the population is thought to be increasing at about the same rate, there would be little chance of reducing the existing level of unemployment and under-employment. Shortage of capital, shortage of imports and shortage of skilled manpower together restrict the growth of employment for the large numbers of unskilled and partly literate workers in the labour force.

[1] Green, 'Four African Development Plans', in *Readings*, vol. II.

15. The development of agriculture and industry

INTRODUCTION

One main objective of economic development is rising productivity, so that a greater output from each man enables the majority of the people to possess more goods, whether by their own labour or by exchanging the output of that labour with other families. On the other hand, a farm or factory may have a high productivity, as measured by the total output divided by the number of persons employed, and yet it may be running at a loss, because an extravagant amount of capital is being used to produce commodities which buyers do not value at their cost. Nevertheless, rising productivity is one useful measure of rising prosperity, and we may consider the results of a rising level of productivity in African agriculture.

PRODUCTIVITY IN AGRICULTURE

Let us assume that an improved hand hoe enables a group of farmers to produce more food for themselves and also more of an export crop such as cotton, with no extra expense; better organisation of harvesting, we may also assume, enables the extra output to be picked and taken to market by the same number of men. We have therefore a higher output per man, with very little extra expense. Who benefits from this innovation?

If the farmers employ only their families, then those families obtain an increase both in their food supply and in income from selling the increased surplus of food and cotton; the country also benefits from the increase in exports which has been achieved without any increase in imports. But if all farmers begin to adopt this desirable innovation, the increase in output may begin to depress the price of foods on the local market, as the sellers compete to sell more. The farmers will still gain a higher income so long as the demand for their products has a price-elasticity greater than one; consumers then also gain, by being able to buy more at a slightly lower price.

There is economic progress all round. But if demand has a low price-elasticity, then the increase in output on the local market may cause such a fall in price that farmers obtain a smaller total of receipts for the larger quantity; to maintain their income, they will have to shift part of their production to some other commodities where the demand has a higher price-elasticity. Provided their patterns of production are flexible, everyone may still gain from the extra output, but if some of the original farmers can only produce one or two commodities, a general rise in productivity may mean for them a lower income, or at least not much increase in income.

Consider now the case of farmers employing hired men, whose output has been increased by the new tool, and by better management. If the men need no extra effort, the greater output may be sold by the farmers with little or no increase in costs. But if the men are aware of this, or if the new hoe involves greater effort and there is a scarcity of labour, then the men may demand a rise in wages, so that some of the benefits of higher productivity accrue to them. But this rise in costs, and the possible fall in local prices, restricts the increase in farmers' profits; they may plan to dismiss some of their men and produce only a small increase over the old amount. The benefits of higher productivity will then have been spread between the buyers of the output, the farmers with a slight rise in profits, and those men who remain in employment at higher wages and who can buy the product at slightly lower prices. The men pushed out of employment lose, by the difference between their existing wages and those they can earn in the next most profitable employment. Finally, if the hired men insist on their wages increasing equally with the rise in productivity, the same output may be produced at the same cost but by fewer men; there is then only the higher wages of the men in employment to set off against the loss inflicted on those who must change their job, and who became unemployed for a shorter or longer spell. Alternatively, the farmers may decide that there will be no advantage to them from making any change.

The purpose of this analysis is to show that the benefits of rising productivity will be differently distributed among groups of the population in different circumstances; the two most important factors here are the price-elasticity for the final output, and the bargaining strength of different groups of workers. There have been many cases in industrialised countries where groups of workers have refused to operate labour-saving machinery which would both give high productivity (and higher wages) to those who remained employed, and also put some men out of work. Again, a strong trade union can at times insist on such a rise in wages accompanying an innovation that there is no advantage to the employers from installing new tools; but if there is sufficient competition in the market for the final output to bring down costs all round the employers can insist on higher productivity at lower costs, in order to prevent a factory from closing down through loss of profits.

INCOME-ELASTICITY OF DEMAND AND INCOMES OF FARMERS

In the short period, the effect of increasing output upon the incomes of farmers depends on the price-elasticities of the commodities farmers sell. In the long period, income-elasticities are also important, as indicating the probable increase in the volume of demand for different commodities which is likely from increases in incomes.

The limited amount of information about income-elasticities for agricultural products in African countries confirms the general pattern shown by other countries, though with special features arising from the customary diets of different areas.[1] With a rise in incomes, the poorest families may buy a little more of the staple food, whether maize or millet or yams, on which they already spend a high proportion of their income. But beyond the very poor families, a rise in income leads to a rapid increase in expenditure on the more palatable foods such as meat, fresh vegetables and fruit, on processed foods such as bread and biscuits, and on imported foods such as tinned milks and meats. And with an increased consumption of these proteins, consumption of the basic starchy food usually falls so that richer families may buy less per head than the poor families. A further trend is the shift in the qualities bought, so that richer families not only buy more meat and vegetables, but they buy the dearer and better qualities, since they can afford the pleasures of eating good foods. Briefly, therefore, income-elasticities are still positive for the starchy foods, though they become low for the

[1] See H. A. Oluwasanmi, 'Agriculture in a Developing Economy', in *Readings*, vol. I; H. Kaneda and B. Johnston, 'Urban Food Expenditure Patterns in Tropical Africa', *Food Research Institute Studies*, vol. II, no. 3 (Stanford, California, 1961); T. T. Poleman, *Food Economies of Urban Middle Africa, the Case of Ghana* (Stanford, California, 1961); Food and Agriculture Organisation, *State of Food and Agriculture* (Rome, 1959), pp. 93–131.

higher incomes; for other foods, income-elasticities are generally high at all incomes, though they gradually fall for the higher incomes, as the richer families spend more of a rising income on clothes, furniture and other consumption goods.

A government planning economic development must therefore allow for a substantial fraction of any rise in income to be spent on the products of home agriculture as well as upon imports of processed foods. The pattern of this increase in demand will vary partly with local diets and partly with the distribution of the increased income among different classes of income. If the unemployed in towns are found employment and wages, much of the increase in income will be spent on the basic food, with some further expenditure upon protein foods and clothes; if the increase in income accrues to a small section of skilled workers, the rise in expenditure may affect only a few foods and may be spent largely on the output of industries and upon imports.

Further, the volume of food purchases also reflects the proportion of the population which at any time is working in towns and must buy its food. The majority of families in rural districts and in villages will grow the bulk of their diet (though they may buy a few luxury foods which they cannot grow), so that families moving from the country into towns will increase the volume of expenditure upon food, even though they may not be consuming more themselves. Hence any measure of the probable increase in expenditure upon foods during the process of development must take account firstly of the numbers of families in urban areas, secondly of the distribution of the increase in incomes among the population, and thirdly, of the income-elasticities of the different income groups for the different types of food.

Let us now assume that we start with a position of equilibrium, in which the prices for agricultural commodities provide normal profits for farmers, so that supply just balances demand. Assume further that a foreign loan enables work to be started on a multi-purpose dam which will, some years later, provide both hydro-electric power and also water for irrigating farm land. The wages offered to the construction workers must be high enough to attract them to unfamiliar work in a rural area, while there will be some families of foreign experts buying local foods. What will happen to the prices and supply of those foods?

As the first wages are spent, demand will rise in local markets by varying amounts; some of this increase in demand may only represent a transference from the other areas from which some families have moved, but there will be a net increase in expenditure from the higher earnings. The present stock of foods in the markets may obtain higher prices, and this will encourage farmers in the area to plan for higher production, in subsequent seasons. The elasticity of supply in response to this rise in price will vary with the technical factors associated with local conditions, with the investment in new capital and also with the absence or existence of unused resources of land and labour.

Let us consider two examples, out of the many possible results, to illustrate this type of price change. In graph 26(*a*), *SS* represents a supply curve of foods grown by farmers in a country or area, $D'D'$ the demand curve for those foods at time T', and P' the equilibrium price at that time. Because of the growth of incomes and of the urban food-buyers, demand increases first to D^2D^2 and then to D^3D^3. Farmers' prices rise slowly, and we may assume that a considerable part of their increased incomes is devoted to investment in clearing more land and in technical improvements, so that *SS* is elastic to a rise in price throughout this length of time. The required increase in food production is then secured with only slowly rising prices and incomes in the agricultural sector, and at little extra cost to the food buyers.

Consider now circumstances such as those depicted in graph 26(*b*), where the original supply curve $S'S'$ has a low price elasticity. We may assume that there is little unused land or labour in this area, and that poor transport raises the costs of bringing food into it; we may assume further that when water is made available, farmers should be able greatly to increase the local output, but only after considerable investment in irrigation channels, in new tools and in learning new techniques. The supply curve will therefore shift outwards and to the right, represented at, say, five-year intervals by the curves $S'S'$, S^2S^2 and S^3S^3.

With the increase in demand from $D'D'$ to D^2D^2, prices will therefore rise sharply from P' to P^2; after a time lag, the increase in production will tend to lower them again to P^3. But the continuing rise in demand represented by D^3D^3 will again raise prices to P^4 on the supply curve S^2S^2; after a further time lag, prices will again tend to fall to P^5 on S^3S^3. In these circumstances therefore we can expect a rising demand to cause sharp increases in food prices only slowly

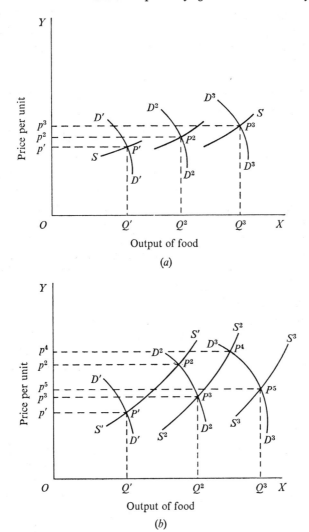

Graph 26. Food prices under development

alleviated by increases in production which depend partly on the re-investment of profits made in the first period of time.

Two further complications may here be mentioned. An initial rise in food prices will reduce the real incomes of food buyers who, being concentrated in towns, are better placed than farmers to bring political pressure to bear on governments, probably in favour of price control. But price control not only creates problems in distribution, discussed on p. 115; it may restrict future increases in output required to meet the growing demand, and thus intensify the shortage of supply. Secondly, the increase in the supply of food may also depend on the existence of hired labour willing to work on farms. If large construction works succeed in attracting men by the offer of relatively high wages, then the costs of increasing output from the farms will rise correspondingly, unless farmers invest in labour-saving devices as well as in new methods of increasing output. These two complications can, unfortunately, easily combine to produce a spiral of rising prices, rising wages to offset the rising cost of food to the buyers, rising costs on the farms, an inadequate increase in output and so a further rise in prices. Some such mechanism seems to have been operating in many African countries in recent years. Farmers need time to adopt new methods and to invest in more intensive farming, and they may also need more hired labour at certain seasons of the year, for clearing land or for harvesting. But demand has been increasing rapidly, partly because of the high income-elasticities for many foods and partly because of the rapid increase in the number and the incomes of wage-earners and of the urban population. As a result, the local prices of many foods have risen sharply, accentuated possibly by a run of poor harvests at a crucial time.

FOOD AS A SOURCE OF CAPITAL

It has been argued that countries which possess a surplus of labour on farms or in towns can use that labour in the creation of capital at a low real cost. The unemployed or partially employed consume food provided by their families; when employed, a high proportion of their earnings will also be spent on the same food, so that the only extra cost of their employment consists of the small amount of non-food consumption, plus the costs of the supporting resources used in production. All that is required to mobilise this surplus labour for productive investment is that their families should market the food which the newly employed would otherwise have eaten; relieved of their unemployed members, the farm families must not consume more of their own output.

This argument, put forward by Dr Ragnar Nurske in his book

Problems of Capital Formation in Under-developed Areas, gave rise to much discussion. In the first place, the existence of surplus labour on farms was questioned, especially in the continent of Africa. Underemployment was common in many countries, because of the seasonal peaks in work, especially in areas dependent upon one rainy season; but if workers were not available for the weeding, or for the harvesting, production might be seriously affected, unless new techniques were adopted at the same time. Whether surplus labour did exist required detailed study of many types of farming, and in most cases the knowledge did not exist. Secondly, it was argued that if surplus labour did exist and was attracted into the construction of capital by the offer of regular wages, there would be far more changes than a simple transference of food consumption. Attracting men to work at unfamiliar tasks in strange surroundings required wages considerably higher than the subsistence which they tolerated at home. Further, families which had been kept at subsistence level by the existence of diminishing returns to excessive numbers would surely consume more of their own output when relieved of some of that burden, so that the marketed surplus of food might not increase appreciably for a time, before the families began to invest some of their better incomes in new tools and more efficient production. Taking together the earned incomes of the newly employed, and the larger consumption of farm families relieved of their unemployed youths, the marginal propensity to save might be very low, and demand for food and for other consumption goods might rise sharply, against an almost static supply.

One result of these arguments has been the realisation of the importance of increased supplies of food in the early stages of economic development, when the incomes of more wage-earners are added to the normal demand and might easily create an inflationary rise in food prices. From this realisation has stemmed the flow of food imports as part of the international aid towards the development of the poorer countries. Secondly, some African countries have attempted to expand quickly the output of agricultural products by the creation of new types of farming enterprise, mechanised farms, land settlements and the like.

CAPITALIST FARMING AND
LAND SETTLEMENTS

Two attempts were made by the British Government shortly after the second world war to introduce large mechanised farms into Africa, in order to break out of the existing structure of small dispersed plots cultivated by families with low productivity and low incomes. The mechanised groundnut farming at Kongwa in Tanganyika (Tanzania) and the mechanised grain production at Mokwa in Nigeria both failed in their purposes.[1] Machinery which was originally unsuitable for tropical conditions, excessive costs of upkeep, repair and renewal, land cleared which either could not be planted, or, when planted, could not be kept weeded, crop yields below those obtained by ordinary farmers in spite of far higher expenditure, the unwillingness of local families to take up paid employment and their hostility to the introduction of strangers into their territory, all combined in varying degrees to keep the output much below the value of the inputs.

In the parts of Uganda and of Northern Nigeria free of tsetse fly, agricultural officers introduced work-oxen with simple implements such as ploughs, harrows and seed drills. Several thousands of farmers managed to buy this equipment, and have become cultivators of twenty to thirty acres of land; some of them earned part of the purchase price by ploughing for their poorer neighbours who had consolidated plots. From this beginning, departments of agriculture in these two countries developed a tractor hiring service. In Uganda, the service has been widely used by the larger farmers, but the charges have never covered the costs, so that the general taxpayer has been subsidising this service. Costs have been high, partly because the tractors have not been used enough to justify their purchase price and depreciation, partly because of the expense of travelling between widely scattered farms, and partly because the plots of land were too small for tractors to operate efficiently.[2] In Northern Nigeria, the tractor hiring units also could not cover their costs and were gradually abandoned; there has been however a successful scheme for mechanised cultivation of fadama (river

[1] A. Wood, *The Groundnut Affair* (London, 1950); S. H. Frankel, *The Economic Impact on Under-developed Societies*, (Cambridge, U.S.A., 1953); pp. 141–53. K. D. S. Baldwin, *The Niger Agricultural Project* (Oxford, 1957).
[2] *Report of the Committee of Enquiry into the Cotton Industry* (Kampala, 1966).

soils) for rice production in the Jere Bowl, near Maiduguri, where the charges nearly covered the costs and there was a marked increase in output, from land which had previously been little used.[1]

More ambitious schemes were developed in the late 1950s in the Eastern and Western Regions of Nigeria, for training the new generation of school leavers in improved techniques on a big scale. Villages were asked to provide large blocks of land, on which the youths were to create their own consolidated farms, under the direction of technical officers of the Ministry of Agriculture; the farms were to combine various tree crops with food crops on approved rotations and either poultry or cattle. The new farmers were to hold their land as tenants either of the Ministry or of the settlement, on terms which bound them to approved rotations and allowed for eviction in certain circumstances; they were also to repay over many years the capital costs of establishing their crops, of their own maintenance for the first few seasons and of the machinery, water supplies and other amenities.

A report made by Food and Agriculture Organisation[2] some years after the first settlements had been established recommended that further sites should not be attempted, and that the existing farms needed closer supervision and a higher output if they were to support families at a level which would enable them even to begin to repay their debts. Costs were higher, output lower and the pace of development slower than had been expected, as has so often proved the case with large schemes for rapid development; the F.A.O. investigators were doubtful if the eventual incomes to the farmers would allow for any repayment of capital or for any return by way of interest. The technical staff had been over-burdened in trying simultaneously to establish a large and mechanised enterprise under centralised control, and to train young men both in unfamiliar techniques and in the virtues of hard work, self-reliance and decision-making; the concentration of advisory staff on these settlements had also deprived farmers in other areas of the same help.

[1] J. C. Wells, 'Appraising an Agricultural Project in Northern Nigeria', *Nigerian Journal of Economic and Social Studies*, vol. v (1963).
[2] F.A.O., *Agricultural Development in Nigeria 1965–1980* (Rome, 1966) chap. XXI; C. Davis Fogg, 'Economic and Social Factors Affecting the Development of Small Holder Agriculture in Eastern Nigeria', in *Readings*, vol. I; E. H. Whetham, *Co-operation, Land Reform and Land Settlements*, Plunkett Foundation for Co-operative Studies (London, 1968).

In Uganda, and also in Eastern and Western Nigeria, farmers are themselves beginning to experiment with new forms of cultivation, with lower capital cost and risks than these state-sponsored settlements. Groups of farmers, all known to each other, are taking leases of land either from local occupiers who do not need it or from District Land Boards; with the help of the government tractor service, these lands are being cleared, planted either to tree crops or to cotton and food crops, and run as individual farms, using co-operative societies for the hire of machinery, the sale of crops and the original lease. In Eastern Nigeria, also, a subsidy for the planting of improved oil palms invoked a good response, after several years of very low prices paid through the Marketing Board had reduced the output and the rate of new plantings. This type of improvement brings into use resources of capital, labour and land lying idle in the community; the funds of the taxpayers, combined with technical advice, can, if wisely used, start off a substantial increase in output by these informal means and at comparatively low costs.

In Kenya, about one million acres of land formerly owned by European families in the highlands were bought by the Kenyan Government with the aid of foreign loans, mainly from the United Kingdom, West Germany and the International Bank; these were broken up into small farms of varying sizes for purchase over a term of years by men from the same or adjacent areas. The new farmers were required to follow approved patterns of cropping and stocking appropriate to each area for three reasons. Many of the new farmers had previously only worked subsistence plots or grazed cattle, and it was feared that they might continue their previous patterns of shifting cultivation and over-grazing and destroy the fertility of their new farms. Secondly, the towns needed food and the country needed the exports of agricultural products previously provided by the European farmers. Thirdly, the farmers could only repay their debts if they quickly adopted systems of intensive farming designed to maintain their families, to grow crops and livestock products for sale, and to improve the capacity of their farms by further investment. The farmers were also required to form co-operative societies to carry out common functions, such as cattle dips, the supply of fertilisers and seeds, the collection and sale of the main crops and of dairy products, and to undertake the first processing of pyrethrum, coffee and similar crops. Some 33,000 small farms were established on this model within five years, absorbing a substantial part of the administrative and technical staff of local and central government. It is too early to assess the results, but preliminary surveys indicate that most of the farmers had not been able to attain the planned levels of output, income and repayment of debts, since the patterns of intensive farming require both more capital and more management than the farmers realised.[1]

In Tanganyika (Tanzania),[2] plans for rapid development included community farms to be run by villages, either with hand labour or with a tractor bought from a government loan; settlements were also organised near towns for the urban unemployed and elsewhere by the T.A.N.Y. (Youth Service), to give work to unemployed youths in rural districts. Government support included technical advice as well as free seeds and maize, to support the workers until the first harvest. There were also a number of schemes for growing cotton upon large mechanised farms, newly cleared from bush and controlled by co-operative societies or village communities. In spite of some successful enterprises, the general results seem to have been discouraging to the farmers and workers; little extra output seems to have been produced in return for the effort and expense involved. For here, as elsewhere the art of managing intricate combinations of machinery, crops and livestock can only be learnt by time and experience; the pace of agricultural development is conditioned finally by the learning process of the farmers when offered new opportunities in enterprises and income levels.

THE TERMS OF TRADE FOR AGRICULTURE

The attempts at mechanised farming or at new settlements based on unfamiliar techniques and social structures have used a lot of capital and administration but added little as yet to the national output of agricultural products. Meanwhile, farmers have showed that they will generally respond to higher prices and higher incomes by investigating in the clearance of more land or in minor improve-

[1] R. H. Clough, 'Economic Survey of Land Settlement in Kenya', *East African Economic Review*, N.S. vol. I (1965); J. D. MacArthur, 'The Evaluation of Land Reform in Kenya', Food and Agriculture Organisation, *World Land Reform Conference* (Rome, 1966); Annual Reports of the Department of Settlement, Kenya.

[2] *Development Plan for Tanganyika 1961/2–1963/4: Five Year Plan for Economic and Social Development 1964–1969*, vol. I; H. Ruthenberg, 'Agricultural Development in Tanganyika', *Afrika-Studien*, no. 2 (Berlin, 1965).

ments increasing output in inconspicuous ways.[1] Governments can assist the process by judicious subsidies for the prices of particular inputs such as water supplies, improved plants, fertilisers, and sprays; by providing technical advisers who understand the economic problems of farmers as well as the technical difficulties; and by improving roads and bridges, so that farmers can exchange more goods, at lower costs, with the industrial markets.

Improved farming requires not only larger markets for the final output but also an adequate supply of inputs derived from industry— tools, machinery, mineral fuels and oils, sprays and disinfectants and drugs for animals, building materials and fencing wire and pipes for water. Farmers' incomes then depend upon the prices and quantities purchased of such products, as well as upon the prices and quantities of the things they themselves sell. Like other manufacturers, farmers must learn to think of their own 'terms of trade', of the relative prices of the output they sell and of the inputs they buy, including the input of labour. Rising prices for foods may not add to the incomes of farmers, and therefore to their ability to finance further investment, if the prices of their inputs are rising even faster. The terms of trade between industrial products and agricultural products are bound to change in the process of economic development; political and economic danger arises when the changes are violent, so that farmers are impoverished and cannot increase output, or industrial workers are affected by high prices and the scarcity of the ordinary foods.

Within short periods of time, changes in the terms of trade, in the relative prices of the things farmers buy and sell, may indicate fairly accurately the changes in farmers' cash incomes. But in the longer period, changes in the efficiency of inputs must also be considered, in the quantities of inputs required to yield one unit of output. Productivity for instance can often be improved by better management, often with little extra investment. As noted earlier, great differences always exist between farmers in the same village in the productivity of labour, and progress depends a great deal upon the less efficient farmers learning to copy the methods and management of the more efficient men; one of the most useful tasks of the advisory service is to make known what methods the best farmers in an area have found most profitable.

[1] C. Davis Fogg, 'Economic and Social Factors Affecting the Development of Small Holder Agriculture in Eastern Nigeria', in *Readings*, vol. I.

One form of increasing productivity lies in the greater specialisation of farmers, with a correspondingly greater exchange of goods and services. In the past, farmers and their wives have spent days taking a small quantity of their output to market by headload or donkey load; or they grow maize for their own consumption although their soil is not suited for maize; or they keep a bull to get their cows in calf; or they rear their own chickens for later sale of eggs. Intensive farming often requires so much of the farmers' working time that marketing must be handed over to the manager of a co-operative society, or to a private trader; farmers may grow rice or vegetables, buy maize with the proceeds and enjoy an increase in incomes; they may pay for artificial insemination from improved bulls kept by the local veterinary station and save the cost of keeping a bull on their own farm; they may buy day-old chicks or pullets at point of lay, because they can then keep more hens and sell more eggs. During this process of specialisation, farming throws off separate industries—hatcheries, marketing, transport contractors—with people specialising in certain functions which formerly were part-time occupations of farmers. Such specialisation can be a cause of rising productivity within agriculture, and partly accounts for the falling proportion of the population recorded as engaged in farming during the process of development.

In the 1960s, most African countries required at least half of their working population in agriculture, in order to provide raw materials and food for themselves, for the non-agricultural part of the population and for export. Income-elasticities for most foods are still high, so that large increases in demand can be expected for many home-grown foods in the foreseeable future. The required increase in supply can be met partly by the investment of labour in clearing more land for cultivation by traditional methods, partly by investment in fertilisers and other industrial inputs in order to obtain higher outputs per acre, partly by better management to achieve higher productivity. The current rate of growth of population in most African countries is so high that much of the increase in numbers will inevitably remain on the land, for want of capital and industries to give other employment.[1] This pressure of workers seeking employment may keep down the levels of wages in rural areas, so that farmers are not constrained to invest in labour-saving

[1] D. M. Etherington, 'Projected Changes in Urban and Rural Population in Kenya and the Implications for Development Policy', in *Readings*, vol. II.

devices to offset rising wage costs, but the balance between rising employment and rising productivity cannot be foreseen with any accuracy.

MINING

The economic development of most African countries until the second world war took the form of the growth of exports, either of agricultural produce or of minerals, to the industrialised countries. The agricultural exports, mainly vegetable oils, rubber, cotton, cocoa, and coffee, were grown by the ordinary farmers, as the result of persuasion and inducements provided by the controlling governments and commercial firms. Such exports provided both increased incomes for the farmers themselves, from which they began to buy a variety of industrial products, and also increased incomes for the governments, through different forms of taxation. On the other hand, the development of the mining industries, as of the occasional large plantation, represented investment of foreign capital; although thousands of Africans earned wages in these enterprises, and governments drew taxes from them, the bulk of the salaries and profits were remitted overseas, to the countries which supplied the capital, the technical experts and the managers.

Partly for this reason, the mining industries had less effect than might have been expected in creating further industrial developments in their immediate areas. Their linkage effects, the effects of their demands upon subsidiary industries and upon industries supplying consumer goods for their workers, were directed as much to the overseas countries, which supplied capital equipment, spare parts and markets, as to the local farmers and traders supplying home-grown foods and drink. Nevertheless, such industries have provided opportunities for education in a number of technical functions, as well as a considerable volume of taxation for central and local governments to spend on services and further development.

IMPORT SAVING AND EXPORT PROMOTION

When governments began, after independence, to take more positive steps towards economic development, the immediate question arose —what types of industries should be encouraged? On the answer to this question depended the further questions, on how the chosen industries should be encouraged, whether by direct investment, by offering subsidised services and tax concessions to immigrant firms, by government loans to local business men, and other such devices. It has been generally agreed that the promotion of industries for export should be deferred until a later stage of development, for various reasons.[1] In the first place, competition in international markets requires expensive preliminaries in order to ascertain what markets want and to provide the necessary services. Secondly, most of the industrialised countries protect their own industries against foreign competition by a variety of devices, such as tariffs and import restrictions. Indeed, one of the major difficulties of the developing nations is the tariff protection afforded by the industrialised countries to their established processing plants for the tropical food and materials bought from Africa; cotton and groundnuts may be imported into Europe free of duties, but textiles and refined vegetable oils bear considerable duties. Thirdly, exports from one African country to another are limited at present partly by the high costs of internal transport but chiefly by the similarity of their agriculture in their present stage of development; they are more competitive with each other than complementary.

Hence, the initial steps towards further economic development have generally taken the form of import substitution, of producing at home some or all of a commodity which has commonly been imported. Provided the quality of the local product conforms to local taste (which has often been influenced by the imports) and provided costs can be kept within reasonable range of the delivered costs of imports, a market can be made available for the output, if necessary by the use of tariffs or progressive import quotas.

The most obvious types of import-saving industries are those using locally-grown raw materials—refining of vegetable oils for use in soap or in foods; cement manufacture where lime is available, or brick-making where there is suitable clay; brewing and the manufacture of soft drinks; and textiles, using local cotton or sisal. In addition, there are other industries which can be developed with imported raw materials to save the import of the final products— bread and biscuit making from imported wheat; many types of metal products which can be manufactured from imported steel and aluminium; household goods made from plastics; the assembly of

---

[1] B. van Arkede, 'Import Substitution and Export Promotion as Aids to Industrialisation in East Africa', in *Readings*, vol. II.

such things as bicycles, radios and sewing machines from imported parts. Given the existing markets for such things, and the expected increase in demand arising from the results of future growth, there is then the problem of how the chosen industries should be encouraged.

It can be assumed that, in the early stages of their growth, the costs of these industries are likely to be higher than those of the competing imports, for else local enterprise would already have moved into these trades; some type of subsidy or tariff protection may be required. Further, if new firms set up their factories in established centres, their costs may be lower than if they are required to build in a small town, which is to be developed as the centre of a different region; again there is a balance to be calculated between present costs and possible future benefits from regional development. Setting up new factories also implies a further demand for services from the construction industry, which may yet be fully employed on government work; imports of machinery and raw materials may be required, which will immediately put a further strain on the balance of payments, while the fall in imports caused by increased production at home may not occur for several years.

CAPITAL-INTENSIVE AND LABOUR-INTENSIVE INDUSTRIES

Having decided on the types of industry to be encouraged, decisions then have to be reached upon the choice of techniques to be adopted to make the chosen product. Where capital is the principal factor limiting further increases in output, and where citizens are looking for paid employment that they cannot find at the current wage rates, should the latest capital-intensive machinery be installed, imported direct from industrialised countries, or should the developing countries adopt techniques which employ more people with less capital?

The problem of increasing unemployment has recently come into prominence in parts of Africa, such as the over-crowded districts of Kenya and the southern areas of Nigeria. Where fertile land is scarce, or school leavers are unwilling to take up farm work, there is a drift to the towns which results in numbers of unemployed and half-employed young people hanging about in hope of casual work. The problem is still more acute in the densely populated countries of Asia, such as India and Pakistan, where the creation of jobs through industrialisation is one of the principal arguments in favour of a high rate of capital investment.

From the experience of existing industries in other countries, it is possible to estimate the number of people likely to be employed in factories of a certain type and size, assuming the same combination of labour and capital. But ought such combinations of labour and of capital to be transported to a different economy, where the marginal efficiencies and the prices of the various resources may be quite different? We have already seen that the lowest-cost combinations appropriate to one set of resources may be far from the lowest cost in another economy. If we transplant such a combination to an economy where the price ratios, or the marginal efficiencies, are different, the total cost of producing a given output is higher than could be achieved with some other combination, the prices to be charged for the final output may therefore be higher than is necessary and consumers must therefore make do with a smaller output.[1] It is often argued therefore that the capital/employment ratios suitable for the industrialised countries cannot be imported direct into Africa, where techniques using less capital and more labour are indicated as much by the lower price of labour and the higher costs of capital equipment, as by the existence in some areas of unemployed labour looking for paid work.

We noted in chapter 4 one example of this importation of resource combinations unsuitable for a different environment—the use of imported tractors and scarce mechanics in cultivating land, where, in areas free of tsetse fly, oxen and ox-drawn implements might be cheaper. More difficult problems arise when labour-intensive techniques prove to be more costly than the capital-intensive pattern current in industrialised countries. Thus in India, the government has encouraged the spinning and weaving of textiles as a cottage industry, in order to provide employment, although the cloth costs more and is often inferior to the output of the ordinary textile factories. There are two arguments used to justify this choice. The persons thus employed would have to be supported somehow, presumably by their relatives; the marginal social cost of this labour therefore is only the difference between earnings in cottage industries and subsistence as dependents, and this will be far less than the nominal incomes so earned. Secondly, unemployment has so

[1] See chap. 5, pp. 81–4.

disastrous an effect upon the human character that economic development should be geared to provide the greatest increase in the volume of employment, rather than the greatest increase in the volume of output at lowest cost. Employment of the existing generation of school leavers then becomes of more importance in current objectives than the greater employment that might be available in the future from investing a higher proportion of a larger output at the present time. Such a choice must essentially be made by the framers of policy rather than by the economists; the economists can only try to show the magnitude of the costs involved in the alternatives.[1]

[1] International-Labour Office, 'Economic Development, Employment and Public Works in African Countries', in *Readings*, vol. II.

Glossary of economic terms

(Terms in italics in the definition are themselves in the glossary)

asset: property owned.

average cost: total costs incurred divided by the units of output.

average output, or *average return:* total output divided by the units of the variable input.

backward-sloping supply curve: a *supply curve* showing that less will be supplied for a rise in price; a curve that slopes up from right to left, when price is measured on the vertical axis and the quantity supplied, the *dependent variable,* is measured on the horizontal axis.

balance of payments: a statement showing the annual payments crossing a country's boundaries in return for goods and services bought and sold.

balance of trade: the difference between the value of imported goods in one year and the value of exports in the same period.

bank rate: the rate of *interest* charged by a central bank on loans made by it to commercial banks and other financial institutions.

bonds: loans raised, usually by a government, at fixed rates of *interest.*

buffer stocks: stocks of a durable commodity accumulated to adjust the flow of supplies so as to reduce the fluctuations in price.

capital: (1) man-made tools used to assist the production of goods and services; see also *fixed capital, working capital;* (2) the *assets* of a person or company.

capital/output ratio: the amount of *capital* required to produce a given quantity of output. When applied to a country, both capital and output are usually expressed as a percentage of the current *national income.*

circulating capital: see *working capital.*

cobweb theorem: the effect of fluctuating prices in causing increasing or decreasing fluctuations in planned production.

commercial bill: a loan made to a trader and accepted, or guaranteed, by a bank, *discount house* or other authority.

company union: see *trade union.*

comparative advantage: an advantage for a particular type of production possessed by one country in relation to some other country.

competition, imperfect: a market where any one of a few buyers or sellers can, by altering the quantity he buys or sells in a unit of time, influence the prices he receives for his output or pays for his purchases.

competition, perfect: a market in which there are so many buyers and sellers that no individual can influence the market price by altering the amount he buys or sells in a unit of time.

competitive resource: a resource that can be used instead of another in a particular combination.

complementary resource: a resource required in combination with a stated quantity of another in the process of production.

compound interest: interest chargeable on a loan which is added to the principal of the loan each year. The formula for calculating the value of the sum (P) due in the nth year with a *rate of interest R* is $P(1 + R^n + nR + nR^2 + \ldots nR^{n-1})$.

constant costs: a farm, firm or industry produces at constant costs when changes in output leave *average costs* unchanged.

constant returns: a farm, firm or industry obtains constant returns when successive units of the variable input yield the same return in output.

constraint: a limit upon output set by a fixed quantity of some input.

consumer durables: commodities with a life of several years bought for use in households, such as radios, refrigerators, cars.

consumers' surplus: the difference between the market price at which a unit of a commodity is bought and the highest price that the buyer would be willing to pay for that unit rather than go without it.

cost-of-living index: a series of *index numbers* showing changes in retail prices of consumption goods over a period of time.

cost-benefit analysis: appraising the costs and benefits to be expected from an investment to the economy as a whole.

currency boards: the institutions controlling the supply of currency in East and West Africa before independence.

current accounts: deposits at banks which can be withdrawn without notice and which therefore earn no *interest.*

custom union: an agreement between countries to promote trade between themselves and to charge similar duties upon imports from outside the union.

debentures: loans bearing a fixed rate of *interest,* usually made to a company or public corporation.

decreasing costs: a firm or industry works under decreasing costs when average cost falls with successive increases in output.

deflation: a fall in the general level of demand and of prices.

demand curve: a line on a graph showing a relationship between price and the quantity demanded at each price, with demand as the *dependent variable.*

demand, elasticity of: see *income-elasticity, price-elasticity.*

dependent variable: the quantity in a graph or an *equation* which varies with changes in the independent variable.

deposit accounts: see *savings accounts.*

depreciation: the progressive fall in the market value of a piece of *capital* because of use, age and *obsolescence.*

derived demand: a demand for a commodity derived from expectations of future prices upon resale.

devaluation: a fall in the value of one currency in terms of gold or of another currency.

diminishing returns: a farm, firm or industry works under diminishing returns when the addition of successive units of a variable input to a fixed quantity of some other input yield a diminishing *marginal output.*

direct cost: see *variable cost.*

direct taxation: taxes assessed on incomes or on each person (*poll tax*) as distinct from taxes levied on commodities or services.

discount houses: financial institutions specialising in very short loans.

discounted cash flows: a method of appraising the present value of expected receipts.

discounted value: the present value of a sum expected in the future, allowing for the risk and uncertainty of receipt.

discriminating monopolist: a sole seller who sells at different prices to buyers with differing *price-elasticities* of demand.

dividend: annual payment out of *profits* upon *share-capital*; in co-operative societies, the dividend is paid not on share-capital but on the value of the business done by each member with the society.

dynamic analysis: the study of an economy undergoing large changes.

economic models: sets of relationships designed to show the changes in dependent variables which are likely to follow changes in the independent variables, or *parameters,* in an economy.

economies of scale: possible reductions in *average costs* associated with an increase in the scale of output of a farm, firm or industry.

elasticity of demand: see *income-elasticity; price-elasticity.*

elasticity of supply: the percentage change in the supply of a commodity divided by the percentage change in the price which caused that change in supply, all other things remaining unchanged.

enterprise: see *entrepreneurs.*

entrepreneurs: people who take the risks of managing, or of investing *capital* in, the production and marketing of goods and services, thus providing the resource called *enterprise.*

equal marginal returns: a resource with alternative uses employed so that the marginal output is equal in each use.

equation: a formula in algebra showing the equality of two expressions when certain values are given to the symbols; used for calculating the value of an unknown quantity.

exchange ratio: the ratio at which a specified quantity of one commodity will exchange in a market for a quantity of another.

excise tax: a tax levied on the production of a commodity.

external economies of scale: economies of scale derived from increased output in an industry as a whole and which reduce costs to the individual firms composing that industry.

factor cost: output valued at market prices less any taxes or *subsidies* upon the market price.

factors of production: resources of land, labour, *capital* and *enterprise*, or management.

fiduciary issue: currency notes issued in excess of the value of gold and international currencies held by the issuing authority, usually a central bank.

fiscal policy: the policy of a Government over the extent and nature of its taxes and loans.

fixed capital: the buildings and *plant* of a business.

fixed costs: costs, usually associated with capital equipment, which are incurred by a business irrespective of small changes in the scale of output.

free trade area: groupings of countries which aim at eliminating import restrictions between themselves.

freehold: the sole and unrestricted ownership of land.

general unions: see *trade unions.*

gilt-edged securities, or gilts: loans to the government and other borrowers regarded as certain to pay the specified interest—loans without risk.

gross domestic product: the estimated output for final use of goods and services of a country within one year, including the output of goods and services used in the maintenance of the existing *capital.*

holding company: a company which does not trade or manufacture but which holds *shares* in other companies.

hyper-inflation: a degree of *inflation* which produces a continuing and rapid rise in the general level of prices and a corresponding fall in the *value of money.*

identity: an *equation* in algebra which is true for all values of the quantities.

income: the flow of money accruing to a person or firm in a specified period of time, usually one year.

income-effect: the effect of a change in the price of a commodity upon the *real income* of the purchasers.

income-elasticity of demand: the percentage change in the demand for a commodity divided by the percentage change in the income of consumers causing that change in demand, all other things remaining unchanged, including prices.

increasing costs: a farm, firm or industry works under increasing costs when *average cost* rises for successive increases in output.

increasing returns: a farm, firm or industry works under increasing returns when the addition of successive units of a variable input to a fixed quantity of some other input yields an increasing *marginal output.*

index numbers: a series of quantities expressed as percentages of some number taken as 100.

indifference curve: a line on a graph joining all the points which indicate equal satisfaction from various combinations of two commodities, units of which are measured along the vertical and horizontal axes.

indirect taxation: taxation levied on the import, export, production or use of goods, as distinct from *direct taxation*, levied on incomes or persons.

inferior goods: goods for which demand falls with rising incomes.

inflation: a rise in the general level of prices in any economy.

inflationary gap: the excess of demand over supply in any economy likely to cause *inflation*.

inputs: resources employed in any farm, firm or industry.

interest: payment for the use of *capital* over a period of time; the rate of interest is the equivalent payment for the use of 100 units of capital for one year.

intermediate goods: goods and services produced for further processing in production.

internal economies of scale: economies of scale associated with increases in the output of one firm.

investment: the act of buying a piece of *capital* or a financial *asset*; the *asset* so bought.

invisibles: payments made across an international boundary for services, as distinct from commodities.

isoquant: a line on a graph showing the same total quantity derived from varying combinations of two variables, units of which are measured on the vertical and horizontal axes.

joint costs: costs incurred in producing two or more commodities which cannot be allocated to any one of them.

land tenure: customs and law relating to the ownership, inheritance and use of land.

legal tender: the *medium of exchange* which in each country can legally be offered in satisfaction of a debt.

liabilities: what is owed to other persons or institutions.

linkage effect: the influence of one industry upon the economy through its purchases of inputs and through the demand created by the incomes paid to the resources employed.

liquidity: the power to sell *assets* quickly for cash.

liquidity ratio: the proportion of cash and liquid *assets* to the deposits held by a bank.

macro-economics: the economics of aggregates, such as the major sectors of an economy, or the level of prices.

margin: see *traders' margin*.

marginal cost: the addition to total cost caused by producing one more unit of output.

marginal output, or *return:* the addition to output caused by adding one more unit of a variable input to a fixed quantity of some other input.

marginal productivity: the value of the output of the marginal input.

marginal propensity: the proportion of an additional unit of *income* devoted to a particular outlay, such as consumption, savings, or imported goods.

marginal revenue: the change in total receipts caused by changing the amount sold by one unit; marginal revenue thus consists of the change in the quantity sold and the change in the average price received.

marginal utility: the usefulness to the buyer of the marginal unit bought of any commodity in a unit of time.

medium of exchange: any commodity often taken in exchange for goods and used in further exchange.

micro-economics: the economics of small units, such as firms, households.

monopoly: a market where there is only one seller (monopolist).

monopsony: a market where there is only one buyer (monopsonist).

multiplier: the reciprocal of the propensity to save. If the propensity to save is given as e.g. 0·2 (of any unit of income 0·2 or 20% will be saved), then the multiplier is 1/0·2, or 5.

national expenditure: see *national income.*

national income: the estimated value of the output of goods and services for final use in a nation in a year; the estimated total of incomes accruing in a nation in a year.

national output, or *product:* see *national income.*

net output: see *value added.*

normal profit: a *profit* just adequate to maintain a firm or industry at a constant size.

obsolescence: the loss of value in a piece of *capital* because of the development of improved equipment.

oligopoly: a market in which competition occurs between a few large firms.

open-market operations: the purchase and sale of *securities* by a central bank in order to regulate the *liquidity ratio* of the commercial banks and thus their lending policy.

opportunity cost: the *income* which might have been earned by a resource in the next most profitable use to its present employment.

output effect: the effect of a rise in the price of an input upon the cost, and therefore the output, of the final product.

overhead cost: see *fixed cost.*

par: the nominal value of a *security.*

parameter: a quantity in an equation whose constancy or change is not determined by other variables in the equation.

partial equilibrium: the *position of equilibrium* in one market, ignoring the rest of the economy.

payee: a person receiving payment.

piece-rates: wages calculated by a rate for each piece of output.

plant: the physical equipment of a business.

poll tax: tax levied on persons, irrespective of income.

position of equilibrium: a state of balance between demand, price and supply, or between costs and prices, so that a market, firm or industry has no impetus towards further change.

primary occupations: farming, fishing, forestry; mining is sometimes included in this term.

price-elasticity of demand (or supply): the percentage change in the demand (or supply) for a commodity divided by the percentage change in price which caused that change in demand (or supply), all other things remaining unchanged (including incomes).

production function: a specified relationship between inputs and outputs.

production possibility boundary or *envelope:* a line on a graph showing the maximum production possible within the constraints set by the inputs.

productivity: output per unit of input of land, labour or *capital.*

profit: the margin between total receipts and total costs, available as payment for the resource of *enterprise.* Rate of profit normally describes total profit earned in a year expressed as a percentage of the capital used in earning that profit.

progressive taxation: taxation which removes a rising proportion of the higher incomes.

propensity to consume, import, save: the proportion of *income* received in any period of time devoted to these uses.

quantity theory of money: $M.V. = P.T.$, where, for any period of time, M is the supply of money, V is the *velocity of circulation* of money, P is the average price level, and T is the number of transactions using money.

quasi-rent: a temporary surplus earned by a resource over and above the *supply price* required to keep it in its present use.

rate of interest: see *interest.*

ratio: the number of times one quantity can be divided into another quantity.

real income: the purchasing power of a given income at different periods of time, allowing for the changes in the prices of the goods and services purchased.

regressive taxation: taxation which takes a higher proportion of the smaller incomes.

rent: annual payment for the use of land or buildings. Economic rent is the difference between the earnings of a resource in its present use and its earnings in the next most profitable use. As applied to the total of land, economic rent is the surplus, over the costs of production, accruing to the owners of the land.

savings: income not used for consumption.

savings accounts: deposits at a bank which can be withdrawn only by giving the specified notice and which normally earn *interest*.

secondary occupations: all those other than *primary occupations*.

security: a financial *asset*, such as *shares* in a company.

share, or *share capital:* the equal parts of the capital of a company, supplied by *shareholders* in return for a share in the *profits*.

shareholders: the legal owners of a company who supply the risk capital in the form of *shares*.

static analysis: the study of a stationary economy.

stock: (1) a reserve of goods; (2) fixed-interest loans to companies or governments.

stock exchange: the market for *securities* such as *stocks* and *shares*.

subsidy: a payment from the government designed to affect the demand, supply or price of a commodity or service.

subsistence sector: the farmers who produce primarily for the use of their families.

substitution effect: the effect of a change in the price of one commodity upon the demand for it arising from the change in the relative prices of commodities which can be used as a substitute for the first.

supply curve: a line on a graph showing a relationship between price and the quantity supplied at each price, with supply as the *dependent variable*.

supply price: the price required to maintain a given supply of a commodity, or of a resource in one particular use.

target workers: workers who aim at earning a particular sum of money in the shortest possible time, and who therefore have *backward-sloping supply curves* of effort.

terms of trade: the average price of a ton of imports divided by the average price of a ton of exports. Changes in these average prices are usually expressed as index numbers, and the terms of trade then become the ratio between two index numbers. A rise in the terms of trade implies that a country is worse off, since the price of imports, the things bought, rises relatively to the price of exports, the things sold.

time accounts: see *savings accounts*.

time-rates: wages paid for the time worked.

trade unions: societies formed by paid workers for their mutual benefit in bargaining with their employers over wages and conditions of work. Trade unions may include workers only in one occupation or craft; or workers of various types in one firm, the *company union*, or workers of many types in many industries, the *general* trade union.

traders' margin: the difference between the selling price and the buying price of the commodities traded.

transfer payments: payments such as gifts, pensions, etc., which are not connected with the production or sale of any commodity or service.

treasury bill: a short term loan to the government, usually for 90 days.

unit-elasticity: a demand or supply curve is said to have unit-elasticity when the percentage change in price equals the percentage change in demand or supply, so that the ratio of the two changes equals unity, and the total amount spent on the commodity remains unchanged.

utility: see *marginal utility.*

value added or *net output:* the value of the output of a firm or industry less the value of the purchased goods and services; value added therefore equals the payments made to the resources of land, labour, capital and management or enterprise.

value of money: the quantity of goods and services which can be bought by a unit of money at different times, usually measured by the inverse of the *cost of living index.*

variable, or *direct, costs:* costs which vary with the scale of output of a farm or firm.

velocity of circulation of money: the average number of times the units of money are used in the course of one year.

working capital: stocks of goods awaiting manufacture or sale, and the expenditure of a firm on variable costs during one cycle of production.

Index